617

Also by the author:

Non-Fiction
Cold Steel (Lakshmi Mittal and the Multi-Billion-Dollar Battle for a Global Empire)

Fiction
Cut and Run (writing as James Boyd)

Going to War with
Today's Dambusters

TIM BOUQUET

An Orion paperback

First published in Great Britain in 2012
by Orion
This paperback edition published in 2014
by Orion Books Ltd,
Orion House, 5 Upper St Martin's Lane,
London WC2H 9EA

An Hachette UK company

1 3 5 7 9 10 8 6 4 2

Copyright © Tim Bouquet 2012

Extract from *Meeting the Jet Man* by David Knowles (2008) has been
reprinted by kind permission of the author.

Every effort has been made to fulfil requirements with regard to
reproducing copyright material. The author and the publisher will
be glad to rectify any omissions at the earliest opportunity.

The views and opinions expressed in this book are those of the author
and contributors alone and should not be taken to represent those of
HMG, MOD, the RAF or any government agency.

As usual in all cases such as this the MOD cannot be held responsible
for the accuracy of the text and no statement tending to imply official
endorsement should be linked to it, nor should mention be made
that clearance has been sought and obtained.

ISBN 978-1-4091-2988-2

Typeset by Input Data Services Ltd, Bridgwater, Somerset

Printed and bound by CPI Group (UK) Ltd, Croydon, CR0 4YY

The Orion Publishing Group's policy is to use papers that
are natural, renewable and recyclable products and
made from wood grown in sustainable forests. The logging
and manufacturing processes are expected to conform to
the environmental regulations of the country of origin.

www.orionbooks.co.uk

To Ella and Milo
And for my father
Christopher Bouquet
(1925–2010)

Physically flying is strange. The world is frequently upside down, your body often weighs four or five times its normal weight – or less than nothing. Great distances are consumed in seconds. Into that environment warfare intrudes. Or at least a tiny upside-down frog's-eye glimpse of warfare intrudes. Overcoming disorientation, both spatial and situational, is at the heart of military flying.

David Knowles DFC (former 617 Tornado pilot and Squadron Leader)
Meeting the Jet Man **(Two Ravens Press, 2008)**

I am often asked if I was scared, exhilarated, excited, focused; yes, all of those and none of those. Your training is such that you are aware of those feelings but you bring them all in from the edges and have them under control so everything in the cockpit is pretty calm even if there are missiles going off all around you. If you are hyped up you won't operate and if you are too chilled you won't operate. It is exciting but it's not thrilling.

Group Captain S.P. 'Rocky' Rochelle OBE, DFC
Officer Commanding, 617 Squadron, 2006–2008

CONTENTS

PART 1
Back to the Future

1

FLY-PAST

The final autumn leaves were falling in the tree-lined streets of Woodhall Spa, an Edwardian village of imposing villas in the centre of Lincolnshire, as the 300-strong congregation clutching poppy wreaths filed out of St Peter's Church and formed up in a parade to honour the fallen. They marched at a sedate pace down The Broadway, flanked by an arcade of shops, estate agents and tearooms. Woodhall Spa, its healing waters a distant memory, was no different from any other community on Remembrance Sunday, except in one respect. Where most towns and villages have a single war memorial, Woodhall Spa has two.

The clue as to why was in the military uniforms marching behind the clergy and the Royal British Legion banners. Nearly all of them were of Royal Air Force blue. Alongside them silver-haired men of a certain age had decorated their civilian suits with DFCs and instinctively remembered how to march in time.

The Royal Air Force, particularly Bomber Command, is in Lincolnshire's DNA. During the Second World War there

3

were close to fifty airfields in this flattest of counties as the RAF and the US Air Group pounded German industry. Most of them have gone the way of history but from the air it is still possible to see the outlines of hangars and runways lurking like ghosts under cultivated fields and golf courses.

After a few minutes the parade stopped first at the traditional cross at the crossroads of the village, where community wreaths were laid. A few yards away in Royal Square there is an altogether more imposing structure. Twelve feet high, it is cast in the shape of a dam and is inscribed with 205 names on six slate plates which are set into its arches. The centre of the monument has been ruptured and the central slab representing the escaping water has carved into it a coat of arms depicting three lightning bolts, a smashed dam and an unforgiving motto: 'Après Moi Le Déluge'.

This is the monument to 617 Squadron, which on the night of 16 to 17 May 1943 took off from RAF Scampton near Lincoln, a few miles away, to carry out a daring night-time raid known at the time as Operation Chastise. Specially formed for a unique task, nineteen customised four-engine Avro Lancaster bombers, led by 617's first commanding officer, 24-year-old Wing Commander Guy Penrose Gibson, were to fly just 60 feet above marble black water at 190 knots (220 mph) to attack three massive dams which provided the water that powered Germany's heavy industry and main armaments factories in the Ruhr Valley.

Four hundred and fifty yards out from their targets they would launch a revolutionary back-spinning cylindrical bomb known as 'Upkeep', designed by inventor Barnes Wallis. It would bounce three times across the water like a skimming stone, clearing the torpedo netting. Then it would hit the dam wall and sink to 30 feet where it would explode, causing a massive shockwave that would breach the mighty structures, thereby unleashing millions of gallons of water.

Many, including Bomber Command's irascible chief Sir Arthur 'Bomber' Harris, who was wedded to the nightly blanket bombing of Nazi industry, were sceptical that this kind of precision targeting with an unproven weapon would ever work and they tried to stop it. Harris was 'prepared to bet my shirt' that Upkeep would be a costly disaster. 'Putting aside Lancasters and reducing our effort [was a] wild goose chase,' he warned Air Staff. But 617 Squadron, flying in three waves and hugging their bombs in the stripped-out bellies of specially adapted Lancasters, did launch their weird munitions, which duly bounced down on to the water. Spinning backwards at 500 rpm, they skimmed across the surface until they hit concrete, where they sank and blew a massive 60-yard fracture in the Möhne Dam, which was holding back some 330 million tons of water. They also breached the Eder Dam, sending forth a *Déluge* to further disable Germany's war machine. The third dam, the Sorpe, a huge structure made of earth and rock, suffered only minor damage.

The British press had a field day. The *Daily Telegraph* ran a triumphant three-deck headline on 18 May.

DEVASTATION SPREADS DOWN THE RUHR VALLEY.
BRIDGES AND POWER PLANTS ENGULFED.
BERLIN ADMITS HEAVY CASUALTIES.

'With one single blow the RAF has precipitated what may prove to be the greatest industrial disaster yet inflicted on Germany in this war,' the newspaper proclaimed, as the floods continued to spread fast for about fifty miles.

After a partial post-raid reconnaissance the Air Ministry

issued a statement. 'Railways and road bridges are broken down. Hydro-electrical power stations are destroyed or damaged; a railway marshalling yard is under water.'

Revisionist historians argue that more than 1200 civilians, and a number of prisoners of war, were killed and that German industry was back up and running in five months. This conveniently sidestepped the fact that it took huge amounts of cash, equipment and materials and 20,000 labourers to rebuild the country's biggest dams and destroyed factory plant, which Germany could not afford. This left gaps in Hitler's Atlantic Wall, under construction along the Normandy coast and through which the D-Day invasion would pour the following year. Revisionism also overlooks the shockwave that the Dams Raids caused to German confidence.

In Britain, Operation Chastise had the opposite effect on morale. The audacity of the 'Bouncing Bomb' and the adulation that pursued the airmen who had dropped it was sealed for ever. After the war, as Britain struggled with the economic cost of conflict, 617 Squadron was enshrined in a morale-boosting book and movie, *The Dam Busters*, which gave it the name by which it is known to this day: The Dambusters.

To the general public the Dambusters – who were recruited in such secrecy that initially none of them knew what they had been selected for, including Guy Gibson – are the most famous bomber squadron in the Royal Air Force. They are as synonymous with heroic aviation as the Spitfire is with the Battle of Britain. But in 1943 617 was simply known as 'the Suicide Squadron'. 'This squadron will either make history or be completely wiped out,' Gibson said with unemotional accuracy. Gibson, a small, driven man and the best bomber pilot of his generation, won a VC. Thirty-three others were awarded between them five Distinguished Service Orders ten Distinguished

Flying Crosses and four Bars, eleven Distinguished Flying Medals and one Bar and two Conspicuous Gallantry Medals.

But only eleven of the nineteen aircraft that left Lincolnshire on that historic night made it back. The Woodhall Spa monument carries the names of the 53 members of the 133 aircrew who set out on Operation Chastise and never returned from that against-all-odds mission, a casualty rate of nearly 40 per cent.

The Dambusters memorial is here because the Squadron subsequently flew out of RAF Woodhall Spa. They had their officers' mess in the requisitioned Petwood Hotel, an Elizabethanesque, half-timbered, oak-panelled pile built in 1905, which is set in 30 acres of woodland and rhododendron walks on the edge of the village.

The rest of the names on the monument are those Dambusters who lost their lives on 617's string of other bespoke wartime missions, which further cemented its growing reputation for precision bombing with pioneering weapons. Before D-Day, Dambuster sorties took out aircraft factories, viaducts, and the Paris marshalling yards at Juvisy and La Chapelle, to disrupt German transport and supplies bound for Normandy. The Dambusters moved on, flying missions to fool the Germans as to where D-Day was going to happen, destroying U-boat pens, V1 and V2 rocket launch sites.

Then notably, on 12 November 1944, 617 Squadron took part in the attack which sank the 42,000-ton German battleship *Tirpitz* in the Norwegian fjord of Tromsø, with another Barnes Wallis invention: a 12,000 lb 'earthquake bomb' known as 'Tallboy'.

Only three who flew on Operation Chastise are still alive – Les Munro, a pilot, who lives in New Zealand, Canadian gunner Fred 'Doc' Sutherland and Englishman George

'Johnny' Johnson, a bomb-aimer. Very few who flew on the other Second World War Dambusters missions are left either, but one of them, taking his place in front of the Woodhall Spa memorial on Remembrance Sunday 2010, was Tony Iveson, a kindly and astute 91-year-old, who had known Gibson and had piloted one of the Lancasters on the *Tirpitz* raid. Iveson was one of only two Battle of Britain fighter pilots to switch to bombers and he flew in some twenty-seven operations with 617. In 1945 he won a DFC for keeping his Lancaster airborne when it had been so badly shot-up by a German fighter over Bergen that three of his crew had baled out. Despite losing an engine and having a tail-plane shot to bits he managed, by 'jinking all over the sky', to land safely in Shetland.

When the 617 memorial was built after the war at Woodhall Spa it was Iveson – who took the controls of a Lancaster again in his ninetieth year – they asked to compile the list of names that appears on it. At every reunion Iveson looked for just one: that of his great friend Drew 'Duke' Wyness. Squadron Leader Wyness was on another low-level Dambusters raid to blow up the Kembs Barrage in Alsace in 1944 when he was shot down.

I saw Drew go into the Rhine. And from there I didn't know what had happened for years. We now know that Drew and his New Zealand wireless operator Bruce Hosie got into their dinghy but were caught by the Germans, taken to a village, interrogated, taken back to the Rhine and shot in the back of the head and chucked in the water. Their bodies were taken out of the water 50 miles downstream and buried side by side in a place called Toul, near Nancy, where they still lie. Extrovert, full of life, I often wondered if Drew knew instinctively that he was on borrowed time and had better enjoy it. I have visited his grave and his death touched me more than anything else.

As the Dambuster veterans paid their respects to the fallen a contemporary aviator's mind was equally focused on the lives of 136 people, most of them in their twenties, he would soon lead into the midst of a contemporary conflict.

Wing Commander Keith Taylor had taken over as Officer Commanding (OC) 617 Squadron just a few weeks before, following in the flight path of Guy Gibson, Lord Leonard Cheshire of Woodhall and other great pilots and navigators who have commanded the Dambusters. Like them Taylor was happier in a flying suit in a cockpit than he was trussed up in a dress uniform. Standing alongside him was one of his navigators, 29-year-old Flight Lieutenant Lucy Williams. Just two years on 617, Lucy was inspired by her squadron's history, answering the many requests for information that still come in about wartime exploits and all that had happened to the Dambusters since. In May of 2010 she had flown in a fly-past to commemorate the seventieth anniversary of the Allied operation to recapture the Norwegian town of Narvik and was also able to fly over the fjord where Tony Iveson and the rest of 617 helped sink the *Tirpitz*.

Keith Taylor didn't need to look at his watch to sense the time was close. A laid-back but meticulous man, he wanted everything to go just right on his first visit to the Memorial as 617's new boss. On the dot of 11 a.m. he heard a familiar sound: of air being torn and then ripped apart by power and speed. This year's fly-past, one of two that 617 Squadron performs at Woodhall Spa every year, was on the button. Not that he would have expected anything less. But still he relaxed with the visual confirmation of a single Tornado GR4 bomber from today's Dambusters that seemed to appear over the trees out of nowhere.

The jet's distinctive swing wings were swept back. Its twin

Rolls-Royce turbofan engines pumped out the thrust of thirty Grand Prix cars. The Tornado GR4, a two-seat, day-or-night, all-weather ground attack aircraft which can carry an array of laser-guided missiles and bunker-busting bombs, combines a certain grace and a guaranteed menace. It has an airspeed of over 1400 mph but the lone jet over Woodhall Spa was in relative cruise control as it swept in a wide arc just 500 feet above the monument, flying clean, its bomb pylons and weapons racks empty, as it paid tribute to the past. On the ground necks cricked, heads raised and hands twitched as the jet sped away. If this had not been a solemn occasion there would have been the kind of awed spontaneous applause that only aeroplanes can command.

The Tornado's sudden arrival and equally swift departure made the two-minute silence that followed even more poignant. And then, by the 617 memorial, there was the reading of the names of former wartime squadron members who had died in the past year. The final lines of the 'Ode of Remembrance' from Laurence Binyon's famous poem 'For the Fallen' hung on the breeze as 'The Last Post' was played. 'At the going down of the sun and in the morning; We will remember them.'

After the ceremony Keith Taylor mingled and chatted with Tony Iveson and the other veterans. He was aware that he was the new boy and he was struck by how all of them were special men who had seen more than they sometimes cared to remember. In spite of their years, and with unquenchable optimism, they had already booked their rooms at the Petwood Hotel for the annual Dams Reunion Dinner and Tornado fly-past to be held in May 2011. By that time he and 617 would be flying sorties 3500 miles to the east, out of the heat, dust and danger that is Kandahar Air Field, known to all who served there as KAF.

In just six months 617 would deploy to Afghanistan for the first time for a three-month tour supporting 3 Commando Brigade, which would be taking over leadership of Britain's Task Force Helmand in Helmand Province. They would also be working with the front-line troops of other countries that had joined the NATO-led International Security Assistance Force (ISAF) across a rugged and unforgiving country the size of France.

Seventy per cent of Taylor's young squadron had never deployed operationally anywhere before. On top of that they were coming to terms with the Strategic Defence and Security Review (SDSR) published the previous month and which had withdrawn the Harrier and the Nimrod. SDSR had also announced that two front-line Tornado squadrons would go, reducing the number from seven to five. However, it would not be announced until the following March (2011) which two they would be. The government had also vowed to cut RAF personnel by 5000 on its continuing mission to plug a £38 billion black hole in the defence budget. There were persistent rumours that 617's own home base at RAF Lossiemouth on the Moray Firth near Inverness would be closed down, with squadrons relocated to RAF Marham in Norfolk. Many of the Dambusters who had bought houses in nearby Elgin worried that they would be left with properties they couldn't sell.

However, pilots like Keith Taylor who lived to fly fast jets had opted to focus on the positive. 'I am confident that 617 Squadron will survive due to our lead Storm Shadow role,' he had said in the speech he had given the previous evening to the 617 Squadron Aircrew Association at its annual *Tirpitz* Reunion Dinner at the Petwood Hotel.

Storm Shadow was a 'bunker-busting' cruise missile first used in action by 617 to destroy Saddam Hussein's command-and-control centres during the invasion of Iraq in 2003.

'One of the main reasons the Tornado GR4 survived SDSR and the Harrier didn't was because of this capability,' Taylor said.

The new OC was also 'delighted to tell' his audience of old Dambusters that the Tornado Standards Unit's assessment visit to 617 in September had 'observed a broad spectrum of skill-sets and competencies and deemed the Squadron to be in good health. Squadron weaknesses: nil. Overall Assessment: High Average.'

Even so, as a veteran of seven operational tours over Iraq, Keith Taylor knew that however good the training – including a recent heavy weapons exercise at the Cold Lake Air Weapons Range in Alberta, Canada and continuing close air support exercises with the British army back in the UK – supporting troops in conflict on the ground in Afghanistan against the clock was altogether something else.

Come the New Year the Dambusters would ramp up training with a sole focus: taking over from 12 Squadron in April as the Tornado Force in Kandahar on Operation Herrick 14.

For 617 a high average was not going to be enough. Only high performance at all times would get the job done.

2

LIGHT THE FIRES

RAF Lossiemouth,
17 January 2011

There was sleet in the air and the wind driving in off the Moray Firth was so strong the long grass beside the main runway was bent double. Even the strutting gulls had retreated to the barrack roofs and shut down their noise. Out on the tarmac at 7 a.m. the temperature soared as orange-tinged white flames spat out from the back of a Tornado. The bomber waited, 27 tonnes fully-laden with weaponry and fuel, white strobe lights winking on its wings and rocking a little, like a sprinter going down into the blocks.

Cleared for take-off, the pilot pushed his throttle box levers forward as far as they would go to 'combat' position, soaking the twin engines with fuel to fire up the afterburners and produce enough forward thrust for take-off. The jet catapulted down the runway. The din it left behind was deep and sharp, painful enough to flip eardrums inside out and back again, and spewing out decibels that registered deep in the gut. The windows in nearby buildings rattled and hummed. Wagons circulating on the airfield's perimeter road were muted. Even the wind was silenced.

Five thousand feet down the runway the Tornado swooped off the long strip of black and rose up quickly, tucking away its landing gear at around 100 feet and then climbing rapidly up and away into a wide, watery Highland sky.

As it headed out west towards snow-topped mountains and the bombing range at RAF Tain on the Moray Firth another Tornado sped down the runway. And then another. Their engines burned like two round furnaces in the gloom, leaving ripped air in their wake.

In the high-arched Hardened Aircraft Shelters (HASs) – fast jet garages, which were built to withstand anything that the Soviet Union could throw at them in the Cold War years – the long noses of other Tornados could be seen. As grey as the day, their cockpit canopies were up, waiting for pilots and their navigators who bent into the wind and walked out towards them from the aircrew building. Engineers who had laboured during the night to get the Squadron's jets serviceable had made final checks and signed them fit for flying. The 'see-off' was supervised by technicians known as 'lineys'. Donning their ear-protectors and headphones, they strapped the crews into their cockpits before going through a series of final checks prior to take-off and then waved the jets out of the shelters for the taxi-out to yet more sorties in 617 Squadron's demanding flying programme.

Nearby, the sign outside a dark green single-storey flat-roofed Cold War building stood resolutely in the face of the wind and proclaimed in 617 Squadron's red letters on a black background: 'Welcome to The Dambusters'.

A trio of Barnes Wallis bombs that the Squadron had pioneered into service stood outside in a line like sentries. The rotund bouncing bomb was flanked by two others, standing on their noses: 'Tallboy', 21 feet and 5 tons, and its 26-foot, 10-ton cousin 'Grand Slam', which 617 had used in March 1945 to knock out the Bielefeld railway viaduct in North Rhine-Westphalia. Of more recent vintage in the Squadron's ballistic sculpture park was a Storm Shadow. This 16-foot-long, pre-programmed, 'fire and forget' air-to-surface cruise missile was first launched in April 2003 by 617's Tornados during the invasion of Iraq. According to one navigator the weapon was so new that the ink of the manufacturer's date stamp was still damp when it left the jet at more than 600 mph to destroy Saddam Hussein's command-and-control bunkers.

The aircrew base at Lossiemouth that housed 617 was much more flimsy and inside Keith Taylor's office there was a sense of flux. A broad-shouldered man of medium height, the new Boss scratched his full head of thick brown hair. He still had nowhere to store his bags and he could almost feel the imprint of his predecessor on his chair. But there was plenty of room for the Squadron's history. A large oil painting of Lancasters flying over the Möhne Dam hung on the wall behind his desk alongside a pen and ink portrait of Guy Gibson. A canvas of 617 Tornados in Operation Desert Storm dominated another wall. As the new Boss walked down the corridor to the crewroom to get a coffee he passed yet more portraits of squadron luminaries such as Leonard Cheshire VC, who had commanded 617 from November 1943 until July 1944.

One of the RAF's most highly decorated Second World War pilots, and its youngest group captain, Cheshire had also won the DSO and Two Bars and the DFC. 'The greatest bomber pilot of any air force in the world' said a caption. Cheshire – who was later awarded the Order of Merit and ennobled as Baron Cheshire of Woodhall, for his campaigning charity work and residential homes for the disabled – developed a white-knuckle low-level form of target marking. This involved flying Mustangs and Mosquitoes down to 300 feet to strike at and mark targets with flares so the main heavy bomber force above could accurately drop their bombs.

Another highly decorated low-level bomber pilot staring out from the Dambusters' walls at Keith Taylor was Harold 'Micky' Martin, an Australian who bombed the Möhne Dam, commanded 617 in 1943 and then became an air marshal and was knighted. Martin, who won the DSO and Bar, the DFC and Two Bars and the AFC (Air Force Cross), was described in his *Times* obituary as 'swashbuckling and brave, with scant respect for authority [but] knew that gallantry was of no avail without skill and tactical sense'. It was a sentiment Keith Taylor could identify with and recognised in some of his younger pilots but he agreed even more with Martin's 'insistence upon rigorous flying standards [which] enabled many young pilots to stay alive who might otherwise have died'. It was something to instil into his untested pilots and navigators before they deployed.

The 617 crewroom walls were covered in yet more photographs of a treasured history when the wearing of wide moustaches over super-confident forget-tomorrow grins seemed to be compulsory for aircrew. A heavy section of armour and decking from the *Tirpitz* – donated by 'your friends in Norway' – was mounted on a wall. Pride of place was taken by a display cabinet containing Guy Gibson's cap, photograph and a facsimile of his logbook, permanently left open at May 1943. On the left-hand page in a confident but matter-of-fact script he had written, 'Led attack on Möhne and Eder Dams. Successful'. On the right-hand page his entry in capitals for 25 May read simply: 'AWARDED VC'. Displayed nearby was the script of the famous film of Paul Brickhill's book *The Dam Busters*. Such was the enduring power of the raid and the men who flew on it that the movie was going to be remade by *Lord of the Rings* director Peter Jackson, with a script by Stephen Fry.

'All the wartime Dambuster leaders were men of intense ability and exceptional airmanship combined with what was called press-on spirit,' says Robert Owen, who is the 617 Squadron Aircrew Association historian. 'They were people who rose to a challenge and they had the experience and the ability that once given a problem they would find a solution to it.'

There is no escape from the Squadron's history of pressing on for today's 617 pilots, navigators and ground crew. It is ever-present in the series of 'firsts' racked up by their illustrious predecessors. The Squadron's Vulcan B2s were the first to be equipped in 1963 with the Blue Steel nuclear missile. In 1977 it was the first non-American squadron to enter the US Bombing Competition. The Dambusters won it three years running. Huge leather scrapbooks in the crewroom reveal that a new world record for a flight between Britain and Australia was set by 617 in a Vulcan B Mk 1 on 21 June 1961, completing 11,500 miles in 20 hours and 3 minutes. The following year a 617 crew of five took off from RAF Scampton in a Mk 2 Vulcan to set a round-the-world record.

'Those were the days,' Keith Taylor nodded, with a characteristic big grin. But it faded quickly because he knew that these days the RAF was going be reduced to fewer front-line fast jet squadrons in total than it had once had stationed in former West Germany alone. Home and away they were being asked to tackle an ever-increasing workload.

'For my guys to have all this history around them is great and I hope it is inspirational,' Taylor said, 'but they're so busy they don't have time to either wallow in it or be intimidated by it. They have more pressing business.'

*

At the beginning of 2011 that pressing business was to train relentlessly until the beginning of April, when the Squadron would arrive in Kandahar to provide close air support (CAS) to troops on the ground in Afghanistan on a three-month detachment. Day and night the pilots and navigators of 617 would be spending hours airborne and in the simulator on training sorties that would be recorded on video and then analysed and assessed second-by-second back on the ground. Nothing could or would be left to chance. Coalition forces in direct contact with the enemy and who needed a fast jet to get them out of a hole had to have one in minutes.

One hundred of the Squadron's engineers, who worked in a block 150 metres from the aircrew building and would deploy with them to Kandahar, were just as crucial to the lives of the troops on the ground. Without them jets would not fly and meet a 24-hour, seven-days-a-week flying programme. They would be going through a pre-deployment work-up programme to hone all the skills needed to keep jets flying in exactly the climatic conditions that jets don't like.

On the ground and in the air the next three months would be the technical rehearsal for all aspects of counter-insurgency (COIN): low-flying shows of force to spook and drive the enemy out from the shields of civilian communities, strafing and bombing of proven targets, convoy protection and perhaps most importantly the life-and-death search for improvised explosive devices (IEDs), the insurgents' increasingly sophisticated and destructive weapon of choice, using spy-in-the-sky cameras to bring back day-by-day intelligence of the battle space for analysis back at Kandahar.

By the first week of April, when the first of the Dambusters headed for Kandahar, Keith Taylor would have to have moulded his Squadron to provide every facet of air power, or as current RAF branding liked to put it, to be 'agile, adaptable, capable'.

Another jet rattled the crewroom skylights and there seemed to be an added eagerness about Keith Taylor's work as he headed off for the daily early-morning met, intelligence and tasking briefing. The Dambusters were the only front-line fast jet squadron never to have joined the rolling Tornado deployment in Kandahar, where squadrons changed every three months. For 617, with a history of firsts, this had been hard to take, much to the amusement of the other squadrons, who guarded their history just as proudly. The 'Suicide Squadron' had been dubbed the 'Stay at Home Squadron', the 'Bumdusters'. That was not the original plan when it was announced that Tornados would take over from Harriers in Kandahar in the spring of 2009. First to deploy should have been 12 Squadron, with 617 replacing it. But thanks to the delay in building the ramp at KAF to accommodate Tornados the takeover did not happen until the summer, which meant that although 12 still went in first 617 Squadron was bumped to the back of the queue. Now it was 2011 and some squadrons had deployed to Afghanistan twice. If Keith Taylor could not be first he was adamant that his squadron, the RAF's youngest, would be the best. They would fly more hours, achieve more tasks and have fewer mechanical breakdowns.

The Dambusters' new boss also had a personal reason for wanting to succeed; one that long predated his immediate professional pride. A talented and highly experienced pilot with more than 3,000 flying hours, Keith Taylor had spent years waiting for a front-line squadron command and had almost given up hope of ever getting one.

*

19

The son of a Metropolitan Police officer, Keith's interest in aircraft stemmed from his grandfather, who had been an RAF fitter in the Second World War, but his passion for flying was kindled when he was ten years old and his Scottish parents took a lodger at their home in Croydon. His name was John Allison. A wing commander from RAF Coningsby, down the road from Woodhall Spa, Allison had been posted for two years' desk duty to the Ministry of Defence in Whitehall. One weekend he took the Taylor family flying down at Redhill.

'It was a five-seat single-engine piston aeroplane called a Jodel. That was pretty exciting,' recalled Keith, who has a nice line in understatement. 'That was it for me. Maybe I could get a job as a pilot.'

In his career John Allison flew the Lightning, Phantom and Tornado F3 before becoming an Air Chief Marshal, serving as Commander-in-Chief of Strike Command, responsible for the RAF's entire front line. He would retire from the Air Force with a knighthood in 1999.

Keith Taylor's parents managed to educate him privately at Dulwich College in south-east London, because his older brother already had an assisted place at the school. There Keith joined the Air Cadets and won a Sixth Form RAF Scholarship, which got him thirty hours flying at Dundee Flight Club. By the age of 17 Keith had his pilot's licence – a full year before he passed his driving test. At Bath University, where he studied mechanical engineering, he joined his university air squadron: a traditional and still well-trodden route into the RAF. Straight after graduating he joined the RAF, starting his initial officer training at RAF Cranwell in Lincolnshire in 1989 as Cadet 122 IOT.

Very early on in his basic training he knew he wanted to fly fast jets. Piloting the heavy metal of transport and tankers

– and being referred to by all fast jet pilots as a 'trucky' – had about as much allure to him as driving a transit van. After working up through the grades of training aircraft he moved in 1991, aged 23, to RAF Valley in Anglesey for advanced fast jet training, where he was taught to fly the twin-seat Hawk – the jet used by the Red Arrows. He was already in a minority. Only one in forty fast jet hopefuls ever makes it to Valley, which is known as 'the pilot factory'. Unknown to Keith a particular senior officer had asked to come to Valley and present him with his wings. It was John Allison, who was by then an Air Vice-Marshal.

The next four years were increasingly hard graft as Flying Officer Taylor learned, with an instructor in the back seat, how to fly the red and white Hawk, wearing a fast jet pilot's helmet and oxygen mask, darting low-level at 420 knots (480 mph) through the valleys of Snowdonia and all the other key skills of the fast jet pilot, such as instrument flying, navigation, high-level formations and vertical climbing. They were relentless, exciting, exhausting days.

'When you fly the Hawk you step up a gear,' he said. 'In fact, many gears.'

Keith qualified to fly fast jets, but that was only half the package. Next up was tactical weapons training at RAF Chivenor in Devon.

'That's when you learn how to *fight* with an aeroplane rather than just flying it.'

He began to stock his skills armoury: mastering the gun sight and weapons systems, how to tail-chase another aircraft, keeping it in firing range, and strafing and bombing. Next came the air defence phase. In lay speak this is raw-handling: quick-fire offensive and defensive manoeuvres as another jet tries to 'shoot' you out of the sky.

Ground attack training culminated in around fifteen simulated attack profiles, or SAPs, where each time he had to complete a fully integrated mission based on targets and intelligence scenarios provided by the instructors. Finally he had to wrap all his new skills up into an Operations Phase: a mini-war involving evasion at low-level, air-to-air combat and targeting bombs and bullets. Always ahead of the game whether flying vertically, upside down or caressing the ground until it threatened to swallow him up, Flying Officer Keith Taylor had learned Micky Martin's lesson that 'gallantry was of no avail without skill and tactical sense'.

The kind of split-second decision-making and judgement that a Tornado pilot needed was a long way from the First World War pilots who used to practise their aerial combat manoeuvres on the ground on bicycles.

'We tried that once at Valley,' Keith said with a knock-off smile. 'It didn't go too well. We were all pretty drunk. Quite a few injuries.'

The motto of 151(R) Squadron which then conducted tactical weapons training is 'Fidelity unto Duty'. The duty was very demanding. Of the eleven who started on Keith's course he was the only one to finish it. 'Everything is easy when everything is working to plan,' he said, 'but when bad weather intervenes or things just don't go your way then you have to re-plan and come up with something different. That's going to be the story when we get to Afghanistan. We will be tasked to get airborne and then suddenly the pre-arranged sortie we have prepared for over several hours will be scrapped because something more urgent will need doing. In seconds you could go from flying armed over-watch on a routine convoy in Helmand to being asked to fly hundreds of miles north to drop a bomb or strafe insurgents. Some people don't have the mental flexibility to be able to do that. You can have all the technical flying skills but the key to being a good fast jet pilot is flexibility and rapid, reasoned decision-making.'

And a large dash of press-on spirit.

Flight Lieutenant Taylor then moved on to conversion training for Tornados, first at RAF Cottesmore in Rutland and then at RAF Honington in Suffolk. Today the Valley set are turned into Tornado pilots by the Operational Conversion Unit (OCU) run by 15(R) Squadron at RAF Lossiemouth.

Posted to RAF Brüggen in West Germany on 31 Squadron for three Cold War years, Keith met his future wife Lizee, who was teaching in one of the service schools, and together they went back to Anglesey where Keith spent four years as a fast jet instructor from 1995. He enjoyed his time there and his daughters Lucy, now 15 years old, and Hannah, now 13, were born in Bangor Hospital. But the pilot factory was beginning to get repetitive. He yearned to return to front-line squadron life. In 1999 he got his wish and was posted to 12 Squadron at Lossiemouth.

Like all pilots he realised that to gain promotion he would at some point have to leave the cockpit and fly a desk. Now a squadron leader, Taylor was posted to RAF No.1 Group Air Command, part of the then Strike Command at High Wycombe, to supervise all aspects of Tornado training, but then he was released back to 12 Squadron.

'My boss said that he wanted to break me out of the training mould and so as a flight commander he put me in charge of the day-to-day running of the squadron's flying programme, which was great and out of that I was promoted to wing commander.'

He notched up seven operational tours over Iraq with 12 and 31 Squadrons, flying out of Saudi Arabia, Kuwait and Qatar, policing the southern no-fly zone to prevent Saddam Hussein's jets bombing or dropping chemicals on the Kurds and flying patrols on Operation Southern Watch over Iraq's Shi'a population in the south. But always the desk beckoned, first at Shrivenham, near Swindon, where he did an MA in Defence Studies, and then back to High Wycombe supervising all the desk officers who look after the career management of junior officer pilots, navigators and non-commissioned aircrew.

In charge of the careers of others, Keith began to feel that his own was stagnating. He desperately wanted to be back in the cockpit as officer commanding a front-line squadron. OC opportunities came at 15, 12 and 14 Squadrons at Lossiemouth and XIII Squadron at RAF Marham. Every time he was encouraged to go before the appointments board but each time he narrowly missed out.

'I admit I was quite depressed. Because I was close to the RAF appointments process I knew I had been well in the running.'

Then in 2009 he was asked if he would put his name forward to take over 208(R) Squadron at RAF Valley. It was a good posting, but it was back to training. With the RAF shrinking and career opportunities with it 'to turn down the chance could have been a bad career move but I also knew that some fast jet squadrons were due to come up'. Keith asked to delay the board for 208 Squadron until after the front-line slots were decided. His request was refused. *If things just don't go your way then you have to re-plan and come up with something different.*

He now took a courageous decision. 'I asked to have my name withdrawn from the 208 job. I then waited and hoped.'

The next board came along for command of five front-line fast jet squadrons: 2, 9 and 31 at Marham and 617 at Lossiemouth. 'The Dambusters was the jewel in the crown for me. I'd have been very happy to go anywhere but to have one's name on the same squadron board as Guy Gibson and Leonard Cheshire would be a tremendous honour.'

If Keith Taylor sometimes doubted that he would ever get a squadron to command, his switched-on wife Lizee never wavered.

'Keith is a very positive person until it comes to his own potential achievements but I always believed in my heart of hearts that he would get a squadron; and I always said to him "It's going to be 617". He just laughed it off; told me not to be silly.'

But this time his luck stuck. Keith Taylor did pass the board. He not only won command of a squadron: he had got OC 617. Finally, he could put the triangular badge of a Tornado in outline and the legend '617 Sqn Dambusters' in vivid red reversed out of black on the left shoulder of his flying suit.

At the start of 2011 as Keith walked, mug in hand, down the corridor from the crewroom to his office, just a few months into his post as officer commanding the RAF's most famous bomber squadron, the name of 'Wg Cdr Keith Taylor' was already there in gold script on the dark brown officers commanding board, underneath those of Guy Gibson, Leonard Cheshire and Micky Martin.

'I don't put myself in their class,' he said, pausing to look at the board, but quietly he was thrilled. 'There are also many other names on there who may not mean much outside the RAF but they mean a great deal to me.'

His wife Lizee recalls: 'When Keith did get 617, just as I always predicted he would, he looked at me quizzically, smiled and said: "Are you a witch?" But all the signs were there,' she insists. 'Look, even his mobile phone number, which he got back in 1996, ends in 617.'

3

FLY, FIGHT, DO ADMIN

Keith Taylor had inherited a high-performing and committed squadron, but its operational experience was limited. The vast majority of them had never deployed operationally before. Many were on their very first tour of duty on a fast jet squadron and in a few months they would be flying in a warzone. They were excited to try out their skills for real. Professional enthusiasm was to be encouraged but it also had to be tempered with some realism. As part of the NATO-led International Security Assistance Force (ISAF) deploying alongside 3 Commando Brigade, which was taking over from 16 Air Assault Brigade at the helm of Task Force Helmand, the Dambusters were not going to be fighting a conventional Iraq-style state-on-state war in which they might expect to drop bombs every sortie. The Dambusters' job was to provide close air support (CAS) to troops on the ground from all coalition nations – and of course, the Afghans themselves – as well as 3 Commando Brigade, who were now on a mission to win hearts and minds in the fractured and tribal society that was Afghanistan. Surveillance, intelligence and where necessary a threatening presence would be as much a part of the Dambusters' armoury as precision weapons strikes.

Four years before, Afghanistan had been very kinetic but

in 2011 the focus was on counter-insurgency (COIN) and the challenge was providing the security that would allow Afghanistan to take charge of its own destiny, free from interference and intimidation by the Taliban and other insurgent groups. The buzzword was 'Transition' and everybody was using it.

It sounded very logical and desirable when the politicians and the strategists trotted out the hearts-and-minds mantra but in the real world of war there were grey areas of when to drop bombs and when not to. The political and strategic drive was all about when not to.

The softer focus had begun with the doctrine of 'Courageous Restraint' introduced by General Stanley McChrystal, the US commander in Afghanistan and commander of the ISAF forces in 2009 and 2010. To cut down the number of civilian casualties in Afghanistan more restrictive rules of engagement (ROE) had been brought in.

Barack Obama's surge of 30,000 additional troops in November 2009 brought the total number of American servicemen and women to nearly 100,000. In total ISAF troops numbered 131,000 from forty-eight nations, with Britain the next biggest contributor after the United States with 9500 conventional forces. June 2010 was the bloodiest since ISAF soldiers had entered Afghanistan in 2001, but this could be explained in part by the fact that there were now more troops on the ground taking the fight to the insurgents. Twenty British troops had lost their lives in that month, the second-highest losses ever in Afghanistan. The number who lost limbs to bomb blasts, or what the Ministry of Defence describes as 'traumatic or surgical amputation', in 2010 was up by nearly 40 per cent on 2009, although these figures had fallen sharply by the end of 2011.

It was widely reported in the media that critics in the military, especially those taking the big hits on the ground, complained that they were unable to use all the tools at their disposal. When Obama replaced McChrystal with General David Petraeus in June 2010, Petraeus reviewed the courageous restraint doctrine but now at the start of 2011 the policy had been reaffirmed. Nevertheless, the 'surge' appeared to be working and tangible progress was being made.

Keith Taylor acknowledged that for stability to be lasting in Afghanistan a political settlement was essential. Equally he had under his command a group of highly motivated aircrew who had been trained and trained to drop precision bombs and who were ready to produce those skills in a war.

Taylor's biggest challenge was managing that offensive spirit within the current military imperative, which was to employ the psychological threat and presence of air power rather than the delivery of that threat. Striking at the enemy remained a major option but, equally, civilian casualties were to be kept at zero. There would be times where stepping back would be the most effective weapon.

Luckily, in his four flight commanders, known as the 'Execs', the new Boss had a lot of operational experience in Iraq and from Afghanistan to call on. The Execs were responsible for training and supervision, weapons capability and operational support, and generally moulding a group of young and mostly inexperienced flight lieutenants and flying officers ready for the Boss to take to Afghanistan.

Chief of the Execs was Squadron Leader Chris Ball. Chris Ball was 617 Squadron's second-in-command, aka 2iC, aka 'Chief of Staff', aka all-round popular and respected guy by both aircrew and the squadron's engineers, not a band of men and women who were easily impressed. You could tell when Chris Ball, his nickname 'Ballsy' emblazoned on his overalls, was in a room. Suddenly the pace picked up. Putting in some energetic work on his computer and itching to get back into flying mode, Ballsy signed every email, 'Fly. Fight. Do Admin'. A signal to others and a reminder to himself of where his priorities lay.

Chris Ball was one of many on 617 who had just had his hair cropped back to the scalp.

'It's nothing to do with deploying to Afghanistan and going "warlike",' he said, 'it's admitting defeat to the baldness.' He rubbed his palm over the chisel of black stubble shaped by his fast receding hairline.

One of the few current Dambusters who had experienced air warfare in Afghanistan, 36-year-old Chris Ball knew the younger members of the squadron were now thinking increasingly about dropping weapons for real.

'It's not something they are talking about a lot,' he said, 'but as the time gets closer they know they will be flying with the capability to take lives.'

Firing live weapons on training runs to Garvie Island, the uninhabited lump of wave-lashed rock off the northern coast of Scotland a few miles east of Cape Wrath – one of the only military bombing ranges in Europe where live 1000 lb bombs can be dropped – ensured technical flying expertise and accuracy of delivery, but no training could ever fully prepare for the human target.

Occasionally they would ask him what it was like when a weapon left the jet, knowing that somebody was going to die as a result in a matter of minutes.

'I think about it, I do think about it,' Ballsy reflected. 'Guilty is the wrong word; but killing somebody is obviously not guilt free. I think about it but I don't regret. If you are removing genuinely bad guys from the battle space who are trying to kill our troops and if you are doing it professionally and to the rules of engagement, it is a good job done well.'

A working class boy from Standish near Wigan – 'my dad's a mechanic, my granddad's a pig farmer, so pretty average background' – Ballsy and the RAF met up in 1996.

'I thought it would be cool to be a pilot. I guess I'm a product of the *Top Gun* era.'

He flew 'three excellent years' with 13 Squadron, based at Marham, which included Operation Southern Watch, enforcing the Iraqi no-fly zone, and the Second Gulf War in 2003. He remembered vividly the first time he was shot at.

'We had done all these briefings about Triple A [anti-aircraft artillery] but on one sortie my flight leader had a reconnaissance pod so he was taking pictures and my job was to stick on his wing; the extra set of eyes looking out. I saw these clouds, about three of them, white clouds with black in the middle. I thought, *those are weird-looking clouds,* and then three more appeared and they were all about the same height as us and it finally twigged we were being shot at. You always expect there to be a loud bang and a flash but of course there isn't; so the next time I saw it I was a bit quicker to twig and we ducked and weaved out of there a lot faster. I kicked myself for being so slow.'

The word slow did not stick to Chris Ball. As soon as he got back from the Gulf War he married his Norwegian wife, Silja, and for two years was an instructor with 15 Squadron, the Tornado Operational Conversion Unit (OCU) at RAF Lossiemouth. Being an instructor meant he would see more of his wife and his new daughter Ester than if he had been on a front-line squadron and at this point he felt operationally sated.

But then fate stepped in. The weapons instructor's course he was hoping to start was cancelled. There would be at least a six-month wait for the next.

'I was told there were some exchange jobs coming up in the States. A pilot exchange had always been on my wish list.' He spent the next three years as a flight commander with 336th Fighter Squadron, known as the 'Rocketeers', part of 4th Fighter Wing, one of America's most legendary fighter wings. Based at Seymour Johnson Air Force Base in North Carolina, 4th Fighter Wing has its roots in the RAF Eagle Squadrons which were formed in the Second World War for volunteer American pilots, before the United States entered the war.

Flying his first sortie in the twin-finned F15E Strike Eagle, Ballsy knew that *Top Gun* had won out over career advice. The 1650 mph, sleek-nosed Strike Eagle was a jet that was easy to love.

'A European jet like the Tornado you climb into; there's a lot of metal obscuring the view,' he said. 'The Strike Eagle you just strap it on to your back and go flying. It's 50 per cent bigger than a Tornado, like flying a tennis court, and comes with all the toys for air-to-air combat and air-to-ground deep strike,' he said, reeling them off. 'Great airframe, great air-to-ground avionics, multiple computer screens, electronic moving maps to navigate, nice big bubble canopy, great visibility. When you're leading a four-ship (four jets in formation) you just feel like you own the world.'

Ballsy was commanding twenty American airmen. 'There was no resentment. They were very professional, very good operators, seven-days-a-week guys, but there were some differences from the RAF'. During an exercise at Nellis Air Force Base near Las Vegas the Rocketeers were granted a Sunday at-ease Fun Day. 'I suggested to the guys we play some golf to chill out and I'd book three tees,' Ballsy recalled. 'Eleven hands went up. Then another flight commander asked for a show of hands for a church run. Thirty-five went up for that.'

Towards the end of 2007 4th Fighter Wing was posted to Afghanistan. For four and a half months Ballsy was flying out of Bagram airfield north of Kabul, way up near the Hindu Kush mountain range.

'It was a great opportunity. The airfield was 5000 feet up with a 17,000-feet mountain right in front of you. When we arrived it was 40 degrees C and we didn't see a cloud for two months then it dropped to minus 15 and there was snow everywhere.'

The flying programme was tough. At one point he flew ten days straight. 'There were a lot of kinetic drops back then.'

Back to the States and the Deep South began to lose its fascination, especially for Silja. 'She struggled a bit culturally living out there. There wasn't a lot to do. We are a very well-travelled European family. My brother is married to a Spanish girl, Silja's sister is married to a Frenchman and her brother is getting married to a Polish girl but in North Carolina we were an hour and a quarter from Raleigh the state capital. You'd have an hour's drive in any direction just to get out of the swamp.'

Ballsy returned to the RAF. 'But we did come back with a souvenir,' he smiled. 'We had our son, August, while we were out there; our own little American that we brought home.'

A posting to Scotland with 617 was just about ideal, especially when he discovered that he was to be one of four Dambuster aircrew who would fly alongside 12 Squadron in 2009 when it replaced the Harriers – the first Tornado squadron to deploy to Kandahar. It was the best way to gain experience of operating the GR4 in Afghanistan for when 617 took over from 12.

'The jet was very different to the F15 but the airspace was

the same. Kandahar also smelt just the same as Bagram: dust and aviation fuel. We got a couple of months in but in the end the deployment schedule changed and we didn't take over from 12 Squadron.'

Now finally the Dambusters' first full squadron deployment to Afghanistan was looming. It was also likely to be Ballsy's last operational flying tour, given the shrinking of the RAF.

As the days ticked by, as they would increasingly quickly as Kandahar beckoned, Chris Ball reckoned that first and foremost 617's aircrew had to be strong-willed individuals and also great team players. But they were also as he knew creatures of habit who compartmentalised their lives.

'Compartmentalisation of information, processes and drills is essential to operate in a jet but you tend to take it into the rest of your life as well,' he admitted. 'When I am at work I very rarely phone my wife because I am at work then; the two don't kind of mix. So you are drawing a divide, compartmentalising functions and the way you do things.'

Ballsy had many compartments, all of them crammed full of action. Compartments for running, boxing, skiing, and partying. But even though the pace was beginning to hot up in 617's pre-deployment training Ballsy made sure he kept one compartment free every week: to take Ester, now six, to her piano lessons.

'I saw this great video on YouTube called *The Failing Aviator* where a US Air Force psychologist does a briefing on the psychology of pilots and describes a typical aircrew day. "You are extremely predictable and you must be in control. You get up and you shave in exactly the same number of strokes in exactly the same way day after day after day." I thought, "That's exactly me. He's hit it bang on the button."'

*

Squadron Leader Ball was not the only one who liked to be in control. In the fast jet profession, where not to be in control in the air for a single second could lead to ultimate wipe-out, it was not surprising that pilots especially, and also navigators, liked to keep tabs on everything from the ground up.

'There's more to being a fast jet pilot than light the fires, kick the tyres,' Squadron Leader Ian 'Rocksy' Sharrocks smiled. Open-faced, straight-backed and blessed with a neat turn of phrase, Rocksy was 617's OC Weapons and another important member of the Execs. Hailing from Coventry and now 36 years old, he had started his military life as a midshipman flying helicopters for the Royal Navy off HMS *Invincible* on surface sweeps, seeking out fast boat bombers like those that had attacked the American destroyer USS *Cole* in 2000. Also off *Invincible* he had flown 'some interesting people' low over the rooftops of Kosovo and dodged telegraph poles along the main street of Albania's capital, Tirana. 'That was probably the zenith of the Brit carrier,' Rocksy reflected. As an ex-Naval man he did not immediately understand why it had been announced that carriers were being sent to the scrapyards before replacements had been built.

It was watching Sea Harriers taking off from *Invincible*'s flight deck and going on ops that made Sharrocks realise, 'I want to be doing *that*.' He switched from rotary to fast jets and flew with 9 Squadron. His very first 'Shock and Awe' mission, which kicked off the invasion of Iraq in 2003, was an attack on the Iraqi Republican Guard barracks in the southern approaches to Baghdad, with surgically accurate Paveway laser-guided smart bombs.

'It was a dream ticket, a proper night mission with a big batch of aircraft, night vision goggs turning everything green. There was lots of flak and a lot of missiles coming up but they all missed. Everything was working 100 per cent and with intense clarity. You could hear all the radio calls. We didn't miss anything. When an attack goes well it feels like everything is in slow motion. We dropped the bombs, seconds later we knew we had hit the target and then when the attack was over we broke left, the burners came in and the speed kicked back in on the run home to Ali Al Salem Air Base in Kuwait and the real world.'

Sharrocks, who relaxed by reading James Bond and the Flashman novels, had joined 617 in June 2010 and even though he was now a flight commander he still had to put up with fast jet banter towards helicopter pilots. Only the best pilots went direct to fast jet, they said, while those who went rotary flew egg whisks in formation.

'We'd tell them, "You jet jockeys may well fly very fast but when you bang out [eject] it will be your rotary mate coming in to pick you up."'

Rocksy was particularly pleased that the Dambusters were going to deploy to Afghanistan with 3 Commando Brigade. He had spent three years seconded to the Royal Marines, first as an air adviser and then working on the British withdrawal from Basra with Major-General Andy Salmon, who was Multi-National Division-Southeast Commander and later went on to become Commandant General Royal Marines.

'There is absolutely no cap badge snobbery with the marines,' said Sharrocks. 'As far as they are concerned you can either do your job or you can't. They are incredibly hard-working, incredibly focused and a brilliant bunch of guys. They know how to play too.'

Sharrocks ended up organising the security for Iraq's provisional elections in 2009. 'A big task but absolutely fantastic. I spent a huge amount hands-on on the streets of Basra, talking to people in the teashops, working with the politicians and seeing the mix of players in an emerging democracy, from the intelligent guys who could see how it would shape their country, the idealists wanting to do their bit, the cynics who said it would never work and the criminals who never wanted it to work and lose their grip on power.'

Helping put the country back together having flown twenty-four combat sorties there achieved a kind of symmetry for Sharrocks.

One of his jobs now was to be 617's liaison man with 3 Commando Brigade and in September 2010 he had been invited by its boss, Brigadier Ed Davis, to an Operation Herrick 14 Study Week at Stonehouse Barracks in Plymouth. The Brigade comprised 4800 fighting men. Its spine was three battalion-sized Commandos: 40 Commando, based in Taunton, 42 Commando in Plymouth and 45 Commando in Arbroath. A core component of Britain's Joint Rapid Reaction Force and on permanent readiness to deploy anywhere across the globe, the Brigade also included an assault squadron, an information exploitation group, a logistic regiment and attached army units and RAF air advisers.

Once again Sharrocks was impressed by the way the marines went about their business.

'Way ahead of stepping out the door for a six-month tour they sit down and say right let's apply some intellectual rigour to the problem and find out what is really going on.'

Brigadier Davis and all his key officers and company commanders were joined by a team of speakers to brief them on Afghanistan. Academics explained the complex and often tortured history of the country, going back to Alexander the Great. That it had been a nation often in name only that had refused to succumb to the interventions of foreign imperial powers, including Britain. A mujahideen fighter who had fought against and defeated the Soviets gave them an insight into the mind-set and durability of the Afghan fighter. Diplomats who had served in Kabul brought in their contemporary perspective of the complex Afghan political landscape. There were talks on the ethnic breakdown of Afghanistan, the tribes, their cultures, languages, customs and the dos and don'ts of dealing with village elders at *Shura* meetings, all very important to building relationships on the ground.

From here the study week shifted focus quickly from Afghanistan to central Helmand, digging deep into the fine detail of what lay ahead. A lieutenant-colonel from 16 Air Assault Brigade, from which 3 Commando Brigade would be taking over command of Task Force Helmand, explained the current state of play.

'It was a focus on who is the enemy; what is the enemy; and who is *not* the enemy,' Sharrocks said. 'For me it was really interesting because the more you understand about Afghanistan the more chance you have got of making a decision correctly in the air about whether you should be dropping a bomb or not.'

It was clear to Sharrocks that Brigadier Davis was not out to change the world. He wanted to go in with a strong hand on the thread of continuity and keep the mission going in the right direction; which was to win hearts and minds through providing security for communities and to mentor the Afghan National Army (ANA), preparing them for taking full security responsibility at the end of ISAF's combat mission in 2014. 'He wasn't going in as the man with the new plan. It was very reassuring.'

Davis then spent some time at RAF Marham, the UK's other major Tornado base and the centre of GR4 engineering, where all major servicing takes place and the jets are stripped right down and put back together again. Sharrocks had shown Davis round the hangars and engineering bays and had explained what the aircraft could do for troops on the ground. The Brigadier didn't need a PowerPoint presentation on the bombs 617 had and what they could do. The marines had that stuff in spades. Sharrocks emphasised the flexible support from the air that the Dambusters could provide Brigadier Ed's troops on the ground.

He told Davis: 'We can sit at 20,000 feet and see what you can't. Who is doing what in a compound, where improvised explosive devices [IEDs] have been buried and ambushes laid. We can tell you where the bad guys are and deliver a weapon precisely against them.'

In Afghanistan the Tornado Force was equipped with three main weapons. The Dual Mode Seeker (DMS) Brimstone missile was for surgical strikes, designed to attack and destroy armoured targets but in Afghanistan for taking out fast-moving targets such as individual insurgents on motorbikes or IED emplacers. Paveway IV was a 500 lb laser/GPS-guided precision bomb that would destroy buildings. Tornado's 27 mm Mauser cannon could strafe targets. Like Brimstone and Paveway, the cannon would be unleashed with unfailing accuracy from long range.

However, in a war where increasingly intelligence was as important as strike power, the Dambusters would also be armed with two surveillance pods. The LITENING III would not only be used for targeting weapons but it would also feed live video images of insurgents to troops on the ground. From medium or high altitudes the Reconnaissance Airborne Pod TORnado (RAPTOR), one of the most advanced reconnaissance sensors in the world, harvested pinpoint-detail still images. It could peek unseen inside high-walled compounds that might contain IED factories or weapons dumps. It could detect changing patterns of behaviour in towns and villages indicating where IEDs might have been buried, such as locals taking a new route to avoid a footpath or disturbances in road surfaces or near culverts.

'For your ground commanders it's a major combat advantage over the Taliban,' Sharrocks told Davis. 'And if your guys are out doing some framework patrolling way out from their FOBs [forward operating bases] and they start taking incoming or an IED goes off we can get there very quickly.'

Sharrocks hoped that when Brigadier Ed was standing around his 'bird table' (military meetings conducted standing up are reckoned to be more time-efficient than those conducted sitting down) planning his ops, or more importantly when his company commanders were, they would be remembering that air provided that extra dimension to back up a guns battery or a mortar troop.

Another key member of Keith Taylor's Execs was Tony 'Griff' Griffiths. Like Rocksy, Griff seemed to have been to the same severe barber as Ballsy. Squadron Leader Griffiths was the Dambusters' Warlord. Keith Taylor would lead 617 in Afghanistan but it was Griffiths' job to devise the Battle Plan that would lead up to and deliver the Squadron's deployment in theatre. He had been hard at it for months, working with key players in all parts of the Squadron and talking to the Warlord of 12 Squadron, currently the Tornado Force in Kandahar.

Griffiths was a contemplative man who did not suffer fools or endure bullshit. He was setting the targets and operational benchmarks that 617 would have to meet. He would also take action when they were not. He was the logistics supremo and trouble-shooter. He was the man who would be all over the deployment, knowing every single aspect of the Squadron's performance in Afghanistan, and all this on top of his own full flying programme.

For Griffiths, Afghanistan would be no time-and-motion desk job. He was the link between aircrew and ground crew, the Boss's ears and eyes and also his shield, allowing Taylor to concentrate on his management responsibilities to his twin masters on Operation Herrick – the American-led Combined Air Operations Centre (CAOC) based in Qatar, which ran all air space in Afghanistan, and RAF Air Command back home in High Wycombe.

'I have given Griff the job of Warlord not only because I know he can do it but I also want to give him the opportunity to shine and stamp his credentials for promotion,' Taylor said. 'Like the other Execs there is not much that Griff doesn't know about 617. As the newcomer I rely on that.'

Tony Griffiths may have been outwardly quieter than some on 617 but he had a quick sense of humour and the kind of grown-up grip on reality that only being the father of four children, all under seven, can give you. He came from Christchurch in Dorset and had joined the RAF relatively late in 1998, opting for navigator. Following a degree at Nottingham he spent two years on a soccer scholarship in Niagara, on the Canadian border.

'I was good enough to be semi-pro but never good enough for professional. After two fantastic years in America I thought it was time I settled to something.'

Something more settled had included six operational tours in Iraq flying back-seat in Tornados. Griff had been on 617 just over four years, first as a flight lieutenant and qualified weapons instructor (QWI). QWIs (pronounced *queue-why*) ensured that aircrew had a thorough competence with and understanding of weapons, their delivery techniques and sighting calculations. He was then promoted to squadron leader and flight commander, responsible for operations support.

Griffiths had passed his aptitude tests at Cranwell with higher marks than most pilots but he accepted that as a character he was more suited to being in the back seat.

'Pilots tend to be more extrovert than navigators, although we have one or two on the squadron who'd run them a close second! I know that I have made a better navigator than I would a pilot.'

Perhaps navigators were more thoughtful and intelligent? Griff paused and smiled.

'As the only navigator among the Execs, I'll give you the diplomatic answer,' he said, raising an eyebrow. 'Pilots are chosen initially to fly single-seat aircraft and if you are on your own you have to sort things out yourself. If you are a navigator you are always going to have to work with someone else.'

There was always good-natured banter between pilots and navigators. Pilots wound up navs by calling them failed pilots or referring to the back seat of the jet as 'the office' and its occupant as 'the secretary'. In a two-crew jet the navigators or weapon systems operators (WSOps) as they were now known (or 'WISOs' in contemporary RAF parlance) were responsible not only for navigating but also for capturing targets and programming bombs and missiles with their destination coordinates, talking to troops on the ground and passing on details of enemy positions – as well as operating the jet's RAPTOR surveillance and LITENING targeting pods and the onboard computer systems. They also took an equal role in planning sorties. Compared to that, navigators said, pilots were just fast jet jockeys who flew the plane and pressed the pickle button (trigger) once a bomb was ready to go.

Ultimately though it was the pilot who was the captain of the ship, as pilots traditionally referred to their jets, even if the navigator was senior in rank and experience. Two jets flying a sortie together, as they would in Afghanistan, were always known as a two-ship, with the senior aircraft the 'pair's lead' and the second jet the wingman. As to be expected, 617's pilots and WSOps would wind up singleton crews from other squadrons by insisting that two heads in the cockpit were better than one, especially when there was a decision to be made between dropping and not dropping a bomb.

'Everybody knows those ships would not be up there, if you don't mind me mixing *your* metaphors, if it wasn't for the engineers,' said a 'blue suiter' – the RAF number two uniform worn by non-aircrew – walking into the Exec's office.

Sporting a tan that was not the product of a damp and dismal Scottish summer and described by a colleague as 'mad as a box of frogs', Squadron Leader Stuart Clarke was 617's Senior Engineering Officer (SEngO).

'I am responsible to the Boss for the generation of sufficient assets to achieve his flying programme,' he said brightly.

It was as complex a job as it was simply put. Clarke ran two shifts of engineers totalling 130. Each one was supervised by a Junior Engineering Officer (JEngO) and a flight sergeant and comprised aircraft and engine mechanics, electricians, avionics technicians, the armourers – who loaded the gun, put on the bombs and pods and serviced the ejection seats – the survival equipment fitters, responsible for all aircrew kit, and the line controllers, who did final checks before seeing off the jets from their shelters on the ramp and out on to the taxiway.

Chris Ball may have been right hand to the Boss, Ian Sharrocks the crucial contact with 3 Commando Brigade and Tony Griffiths the all-important Warlord, but without a top-class SEngO Keith Taylor could come unstuck, especially in Afghanistan, where he had to provide a round-the-clock flying programme in a climate and in temperatures – even at night – that could wreak havoc with fast jets and their engines.

It was a position that Taylor needed to fill shortly after arriving at 617.

'The SEngO is as pivotal to the performance of the ground crew as the Warlord is to the aircrew,' he said.

The SEngO was the only engineer to sit physically in the aircrew building. It was a relic of them-and-us Air Force history that the aircrew and the engineers on nearly all squadrons occupied different buildings when logic said they should all be under the same roof like a Grand Prix team.

Then Taylor got a tip-off. 'An RAF friend in Saudi Arabia who was working with Stu Clarke told me that if I ever got the chance I should grab him. I did get the chance; so I've grabbed him!'

Stu Clarke – who had rarely been known not to smile and with a constant stream of jokes, puns and double entendres – had joined 617 in December 2010 after spending five years working with the Royal Saudi Air Force, the last two and a half in Riyadh, upgrading its version of the Tornado. Now 39 years old, and happy to rib his wife Debbie that she was about to hit 40, Stu Clarke had begun life in the RAF as an airman.

'I went for General Technician Ground Support Equipment, looking after power rigs, hoists, hydraulic rigs, generators. I picked the trade with the longest sounding title! After eight years somebody pointed out that I looked ridiculous in overalls, didn't get greasy enough and should consider a commission.'

Studying engineering at night classes, he eventually made it through officer aircrew selection at Cranwell and crossed what was then a big class divide from the shop floor to the Officers' Mess. He had by then worked as a JEngO on a tanker squadron and as an avionics specialist on Merlin helicopters, and he had done a stint at the Defence Procurement Agency, but he wanted to get back to working on aircraft. With typical aplomb he talked his way out of it and got himself 'loaned out' to the Saudis.

When Keith Taylor came calling, Clarke 'jumped at the chance' to join 617. 'Well, it's top team isn't it?' Apart from his all-round engineering knowledge and recent Tornado experience, Keith Taylor was attracted to Clarke because he had also been on operations in support of the no-fly zones policed by 617 and other Tornado squadrons between the two Gulf Wars. Even more important, Taylor's friend in Saudi, a fellow wing commander, had said that Clarke's man-management skills were second to none.

'I don't claim to be the best engineer,' the SEngO told the Boss shortly after joining the Dambusters, 'but I know a hundred on this squadron who are and it's my job to get the best out of them.'

The final player in Keith Taylor's core team was also an engineer but unlike Stu Clarke, who shared an office with Chris Ball, he lived in the bustle of the engineering block located 150 metres away across the airfield. His name was Stewart Thomson, the Squadron Warrant Officer, aka 'Mr T' if you were the SEngO.

'We call him Chainsaw,' one of the armourers whispered as the Warrant walked past. 'Well, that's *one* of the things we call him.'

Warrant Officer Thomson, the equivalent of a regimental sergeant major, was resolutely old school. In his office there was a place for everything and everything was in its place, gazed over by a portrait of Guy Gibson bearing the legend 'Hero'. Warrant Officer Thomson was bull-necked, a proud man and master at having the last word. You knew instantly you were in trouble with the Warrant if he addressed you as: '*Fellah!*'

There was something of the forceful Sir Alex Ferguson style of management to Warrant Officer Thomson.

'It's my job to run the engineering side of this squadron. I only answer to the two people, the Boss and SEngO.'

Every day Mr T could be seen marching around 617's hangars, pacing around inside, staring, glaring, looking for any piece of equipment that was not in its rightful place, any engineering process not being followed correctly. Cutting corners was a personal affront to the Warrant and spelt danger to aeroplanes and those who flew them.

'Managers on other squadrons drive around the base,' Thomson said disdainfully, his broad Scottish accent rippling deeply from the back of his throat. 'Me? I walk. That's the only way to see what's really going on.' Every week he paced out miles.

Afghanistan was to be Thomson's eighteenth and final operational deployment, including fourteen detachments on Operation Telic in Iraq. He had joined the Air Force in 1976 and would retire thirty-six years later just shy of his fifty-fifth birthday and a few weeks after 617's return from Herrick. Thomson had worked his way up the ranks on Buccaneers, Jaguars and the Tornado, where his level of knowledge was second to none.

Apart from seeing to it that 617 met all its challenges in Afghanistan the Warrant had an overriding aim: 'to hand over to my successor the best-performing Tornado squadron in the RAF. Best in terms of flying hours. Best in reliability and maintenance. Every month we achieve 105 per cent of our flying target, this month we have hit 120 per cent. That's down to my guys over here. But we're not the best yet overall. 31 Squadron is a little bit ahead. For now!' When jets were not fixed fast enough, following the Warrant down the engineering wing, a warren of rooms, in search of culprits was like trailing the wake of a storm. But anybody who dismissed his 'Get a grip!' attitude as irascibility, as some did, would have been wide of the mark.

'Pride in what you do is fundamental to what we do here, because we work massively on trust,' Thomson said. 'The aircrew trust us to do our jobs properly. I tell the young guys, if you haven't got that pride to do your job to the highest capability then I have a major issue with that.'

The Warrant was a disciple of the 6 P's: Prior Planning Prevents Piss Poor Performance.

Stew Thomson was as keen on this deployment as he had been on his first. In some ways more so, because now, promoted to warrant officer in 2010, he was in charge. And it also had a lot to do with this being his last operational hurrah.

'Do I live my job?' He flashed a smile, eyes twinkling behind his glasses. 'Absolutely! Do I enjoy coming to work every day? Absolutely! Do I enjoy going on holiday?' A slight pause. 'Yes; but I have to work at it.'

Some of Thomson's colleagues wondered how Mrs Thomson, Irene, a primary school head teacher in Perth – whom he had started dating back in Dundee, when he was 13 years old and she was 15 – would cope with Mr T at home all the time when his Dambuster days were over.

'Talk to me about Tornados,' the Warrant said, steering

the conversation back to the known, the tried and the trusted. 'I've been on the jet since '86 and it is a hell of a lot more capable now than it was then. It is a massively capable aircraft. I love them because I've been on them so long. I really love the aircraft.'

4

TORNADO FORCE

The object of the Warrant Officer's unquestioning love was a trusty product of the Cold War, that had since seen action in Kosovo, both Gulf Wars and now Afghanistan. Since the First Gulf War the Tornado had been on operational service somewhere every single day. An august volume produced by the Air Staff at the Ministry of Defence entitled *British Air and Space Power Doctrine* states that

the employment of military force has traditionally been conceived in terms of the functions *find, fix, strike* and *exploit*. In the Cold War, *strike* took precedence, as finding the enemy's large, conventional fielded forces would have been a relatively easy task. In contrast, the emphasis in contemporary operations is on the *find* function.

Fix and *find* are the bookends which encapsulate the story of the Tornado, a 54-foot-long weapons platform which, by the time the Dambusters were to fly it out of Kandahar Airfield, would have flown close to a million hours on a journey of reinvention: from the strategy and technology of the Cold War via Kosovo and Iraq to fighting counter-insurgency over the mountains, deserts and villages of Afghanistan.

The Panavia Tornado is a Multi-Role Combat Aircraft

(MRCA) developed jointly by the UK, West Germany and Italy. Crewed by a pilot and a navigator it was designed to fly very fast and very low, at 100 feet off the ground, in all weathers, day or night, to penetrate Soviet air defences and strike military installations with nuclear weapons. Its distinctive swing wings enabled it to perform efficiently at low and high speeds. When its wings were swept back to form a 28-foot-wide delta it maximised performance, with its twin Rolls-Royce engines each supplying 16,000 lb of thrust and propelling it at low level at greater than the speed of sound. Up higher it could achieve speeds of up to Mach 1.3 (around 1000 mph. Fully loaded with weapons and seven tonnes of fuel, its top operational speed in Afghanistan would be lower. The first prototype flew in 1974 and the RAF, which had long been looking for a replacement for the Avro Vulcan and the Blackburn Buccaneer strike aircraft, took delivery of the Tornado's first incarnation, the GR1, in 1981.

Eleven years later Keith Taylor flew the GR1 for the first time on a four-month course at the Tri-National Tornado Training Establishment (TTTE) at RAF Cottesmore in Rutland, which had been set up to train pilots and navigators from the Luftwaffe, the RAF and the Italian Air Force (AMI).

To Taylor the new supersonic jet seemed incredibly advanced. 'The Hawk didn't have a moving map display or any cockpit map displays so having that in the Tornado was great. It was also much bigger than the Hawk and much more powerful although not as nimble. I remember feeling that this is now a proper war machine.'

Indeed the Tornado's 'armament suite' carried 19,842 lb of ordnance including Sidewinder missiles, nuclear bombs and anti-radiation missiles.

'We flew them there with no pylons, no stores and no

nothing,' Taylor explained. 'But it was still pretty good to fly.'

Disbanded in 1981, 617 Squadron had been re-formed to operate the RAF's new combat aircraft and on the afternoon of 16 May 1983 a score of Dambuster veterans assembled at HAS 44, RAF Marham, where 617 was then based, to celebrate the fortieth anniversary of the Dams Raids. Not only did they watch their history in the shape of a Lancaster flying overhead but also the future as four Tornados zipped by low and fast, simulating an airfield attack, followed by a formation fly-past. As a newspaper reported enthusiastically:

Today the Tornado could carry out such an attack at up to five times the speed of [a Lancaster] and under precise computer control, without the pilot touching anything. A single £13 million Tornado has the destructive power of a squadron of Lancasters.

Among the veterans who sat in the Tornado cockpit were former Dambuster commanding officers Sir Leonard Cheshire, with 103 missions and the youngest and most decorated group captain of his day, and Air Marshal Sir Harold 'Micky' Martin, who had flown in the First Wave against the Möhne Dam. Tony Iveson was also there. He said that sitting in a Tornado cockpit was as bewildering as sitting in a spacecraft.

'With all its ranks of dials, its screens and its switches it was so different from the planes I had flown that beyond it having a stick nothing made sense, although it didn't stop me asking if I could take it for a turn around the airfield.'

That evening the veterans and guests sat down in the RAF Marham Officers' Mess to a Fortieth Dams Anniversary Dinner, to the accompaniment of fine vintages and music by the Royal Air Force Salon Orchestra. Martin and Cheshire had earned their place in history as well as their dinner. The

Tornado had yet to win its place in the RAF's hall of fame.

With the fall of the Berlin Wall and the collapse of the Soviet Bloc the nature of air warfare changed. The notion of sixteen-ship formations of Tornados all at low level penetrating a layered Soviet anti-aircraft defence system as part of a big NATO push – and if that all went horribly wrong then strapping on a nuclear bomb, going back and lobbing it at a pre-selected target – now seemed as dated as the layered 'gaggle' formations of Lancaster bombers that pounded German cities in the Second World War.

The Tornado's combat debut was in the First Gulf War when it was among the first strike aircraft in action from January 1991. Forty-eight GR1s flying in two-ship and four-ship formations from bases at Muharraq in Bahrain and Tabuk and Dhahran in Saudi Arabia carried out 1500 low-level, high-risk attacks before and during Operation Desert Storm, dropping 1000 lb bombs on air defences and bridges and JP233s, which delivered a cluster of small bombs that disabled runways. The Tornado's brief extended to surveillance, patrolling the no-fly zones in Iraq after the First Gulf War – missions flown by Keith Taylor and others currently serving on 617 – and then service in 1999 in Kosovo.

The comprehensively upgraded GR4 entered service in 1998. The airframe was the same but it was packed inside with the latest kit including a forward-looking infrared (FLIR), a wide-angle head-up display (HUD), improved cockpit displays, enhanced computer software, new avionics and weapons systems, night vision goggles (NVG) and GPS.

In 2003 it was rearmed with a new air-to-surface missile. Sixteen feet long with an in-flight nine-foot wingspan and weighing 2800 lb it could be launched up to 155 miles from a target. It homed in at 600 mph, guided by GPS on a terrain-hugging trajectory to avoid enemy radar and air defences. On final approach it shed its nose cone to reveal a high-resolution imaging infrared camera that could see the target and compare it to the pre-programmed coordinates and image stored in its software. Highly accurate, the 'fire and forget' missile was designed to hit and destroy well-defended strategic targets such as bridges and command-and-control bunkers. When it achieved impact an initial penetrating charge would breach the outer layers of its objective and once it was inside the target the main warhead would detonate.

The new bunker-busting cruise missile was called Storm Shadow. It was a weapon that would have impressed Barnes Wallis and so it was fitting that the first squadron to use it operationally was 617.

It was on 21 March 2003, three days after the invasion of Iraq and the beginning of the Second Gulf War, that Wing Commander Andy 'Turkster' Turk, who went on to become OC of 9 Squadron, but then a flight lieutenant navigator on 617, and his pilot, Squadron Leader David 'Noddy' Knowles, who was four years with the Dambusters, flew on the first-ever Storm Shadow mission into Baghdad from Ali Al Salem Air Base in northern Kuwait, 23 miles from the Iraq border.

'For three weeks the missiles had been arriving at night on C17s,' Turk recalls. 'You could tell from the date stamps on the missiles how new they were.'

That first Storm Shadow mission was a night sortie.

'On our night vision goggles even at 20,000 feet we could see coalition vehicles crossing the border and there were lots of explosions on the ground, artillery fire, tank battles, RPG firings. There were probably eight or nine explosive events every second.'

As the aircraft progressed north towards Baghdad, Turk saw

one big flash on the ground but thought nothing of it. 'But then a bright dot came out of that explosion and followed us.'

Knowles banked quickly right. It was a moonlit night and the dot adjusted its flight to follow them. Knowles turned the jet to the left. The dot did the same and it was getting bigger. Turk likened it to being on the fast lane of a motorway and 'having a car coming towards you from the left lane on a collision course if it didn't move relative to you. Collision was inevitable.' But this was no bad driver, this was a SAM-2.

'Missile launch! Missile launch!'

Describing the next few seconds as 'making snap decisions on the verge of a massive cock-up', Knowles jettisoned his under-wing fuel tanks to make his aircraft lighter so he could manoeuvre it a lot harder to try and shake off the SAM. As they got nearer to Baghdad the sky became overcast and cloudy. Here was his chance. He banked left, punched out metal chaff to try and throw the radar-guided missile off track and then dropped the Tornado straight down into the cloud.

'They were moments of sheer bloody terror but equally we were mad keen to get the job done,' says Knowles, who is now a publisher, poet and crofter on the Isle of Lewis.

Minutes later Knowles and Turk's wingman reported seeing an explosion where they had been a few seconds earlier.

'He said the flash had lit up our belly,' says Turk, 'but I couldn't see it; we were upside down.'

They had shaken off the missile but then Knowles saw his fuel gauge. 'Oh, Jesus Christ, have we got enough to get to the target and home?'

Turk did the calculations. They could complete the sortie, he said, as long as they picked up a tanker on the way back and there should be plenty of those given that the invasion was in full swing. Climbing higher to find thinner air and eke out their fuel, they continued on to complete their mission. In the midst of what quickly became known as 'Shock and Awe' Knowles remembers 'Baghdad being illuminated like a giant firework display. Captivating and chilling.'

Now desperately low on fuel, Knowles and Turk turned for home but they were unable to find a tanker that was free immediately, due to the amount of Baghdad-bound air traffic. They could not afford to sit in a queue at the flying fuel station.

They might just have enough fuel to make it back to Kuwait but they were right at the limits of the aircraft. If something went wrong, even a minor fuel leak, they would be forced to eject over Iraq and lose the jet. Their other option was to try and get clearance to land at another airport just a few miles over the Iraqi border, which was under US control.

Knowles made the approach to the airfield – all lights were out. There was a patch of darkness within an empty desert where they hoped the airfield would be. Turk called the control tower.

'Mayday. Request permission to land. We are on Emergency Fuel.'

Silence. Nobody was expecting a British jet to land.

'Mayday, British Tornado inbound on Emergency Fuel.'

Their remaining tanks running to empty, Knowles and Turk finally got clearance to land. They parked up in pitch-black, lights out right at the end of the strip and hoped they could scrounge a tank of gas. They took refuge in the cab of the fire truck that had come out to meet them. In a bizarre juxtaposition of often clashing realities that are the jigsaw of war, the fire chief turned out to come from Montana. Having no idea where the British aviators had flown in from, he gabbled excitedly about having just come from watching the bombing of Baghdad live on CNN.

'Those poor bastards won't know what's hit 'em.'

As Knowles was to write in a poem he called 'Post Modern Warfare', at that moment he felt he had delivered a warhead not to unseat a dictator but to Disneyland.

Shock and Awesome, live on CNN.
I really should have seen it.

Over the next five weeks Turk and Knowles dropped more Storm Shadows and other weapons and both won the DFC, joining the Dambusters' roll of honour. The Squadron had established a new marquee weapon for the Tornado and the RAF. Three days after that first sortie Labour Defence Secretary Geoff Hoon was in no doubt: 'It makes a significant difference to our options.'

As Keith Taylor was later to tell the 617 Aircrew Association it was the ability to deliver Storm Shadow that was one of the many factors which weighed in favour of the Tornado in the defence cuts that saw the end of the Harrier, which could not deploy the weapon.

However, there was currently no requirement to use Storm Shadow in Afghanistan where in 2009 the Tornado Force took over Britain's close air support role from the Harrier at Kandahar Airfield.

'There was a huge sensitivity because the Harrier had been very successful,' says Alistair Monkman, who was OC 617 Squadron from 2003 to 2005 before overseeing the arrival of the Tornado Force into Kandahar during his tenure as the Station Commander at RAF Lossiemouth from 2007 to 2009 and then latterly overseeing NATO Air Power as the Director of Air Operations ISAF Joint Command in Kabul during 2010.

'Let's not forget how attritional and complex the conflict in Afghanistan was in 2006 and 2007,' Al Monkman says. 'For five years the Harrier Force did incredibly well, but it was a small force, two or three squadrons rotating through there constantly. No force can take that pressure forever. The Tornado Force was bigger. And when 12 Squadron took over in Afghanistan, surprisingly, some of the strongest praise for the Tornado came from Harrier pilots.'

Monkman is the only Dambuster to have won a DFC for leading a bombing raid over Belgrade, flying the then futuristic F-117 Nighthawk stealth bomber as an exchange pilot with 9th Fighter Squadron US Air Force.

The Nighthawk was retired in 2008, but the Tornado just kept on going. 'I loved flying the Tornado,' says Monkman. 'It was reliable, easy to fly and resilient. Because you had two engines and double hydraulics you could suck up a bit of damage if somebody was trying to shoot you down and still keep going. It was never going to win a dressage competition but it has always been capable of turning its hand to most things and delivering.'

Now Afghanistan was to be another of those things Tornado was turning its hand to, but that did not endear it much to the British public. The problem has always been that in the public's eyes the Harrier is to the Tornado what the Spitfire was to the Hurricane – winning more affection and instant recognition following its service in the Falklands War and for just being a great bit of groundbreaking British engineering. Not only had the Harrier done a great strike job, it could take off vertically and tip its nose to spectators at air shows. And it was much prettier than the Tornado. But both share the honours in Britain's post-war conflicts where air power has played a significant role. Equally, people forget that it was the Hurricane every bit as much as the more illustrious Spitfire that saved Britain in 1940.

'There was lots of banter between Tornado and Harrier squadrons, but ultimately a shared respect based on professional understanding,' says Al Monkman, who retired in 2011 as an air commodore and can now relax in his garden near Elgin as today's Dambusters fly training sorties in their Tornados overhead.

'Since 2003 and the Second Gulf War when the Harriers played a wonderful role, they and Tornados became joined at the hip. And you now see that there is no "them" and "us" in the Typhoon force where you find former Harrier and Tornado pilots flying together. There is an operational maturity to the modern RAF, born out of over 20 years of constant operations, which means that we are now much less tribal. We define ourselves by the nature of the wars we fight rather than by squadron apartheid or aircraft type.'

However much the electronics, sensors, weapons systems, software and navigational aids had been upgraded on the Tornado it still remained a thirty-year-old airframe designed to fly fast and low through damp and chunky air across the cold plains of Eastern Europe. It was now being asked to fly out of Kandahar Airfield – more than 3000 feet above sea level with runway temperatures of 50 degrees Celsius (120 degrees Fahrenheit) and more – climbing to Himalayan heights and above where the air was so thin it could put maximum strain on engines. For pilots and engineers alike the challenges of simply keeping the fleet airborne were daunting, let alone the round-the-clock pressure of prosecuting a war.

5

THE WARLORD'S BATTLE PLAN

Operation Herrick Work-up Briefing,
RAF Lossiemouth, 17 January 2011, 8 a.m.

'I cannot emphasise enough how important today is,' Squadron Leader Tony Griffiths told the aircrew at the start of 617's work-up to Afghanistan. 'We have ten weeks to get to perfection. Ten weeks to get your shit in one sock. I don't want anybody getting on that plane at Brize [RAF Brize Norton] with any doubts about what we are going to do in Afghanistan and how we are going to do it.'

The aircrew expression 'get your shit in one sock' means variously get yourself organised, pull yourself together, get things squared away – and its origins are best glossed over.

'At the moment we are running our own script,' Griffiths told them, 'but once we are in theatre the Taliban, Al-Qaida, whoever, gets a vote on the way things go.'

Working together was a key theme in the briefing room on a cold January morning as Griffiths issued his Herrick Battle Plan.

'It details the administration, planning, training and execution required to ensure that the detachment is a success.'

The Squadron's deployment to Kandahar would comprise 136 people: 26 aircrew, 100 engineers, and the remainder made up of operations and intelligence staff, survival equipment fitters, and the Ground Liaison Officer (GLO), Captain John 'Jock' Adams, of 1st Regiment Royal Horse Artillery, who would be the Squadron's daily link with 3 Commando Brigade and other ISAF army units. One hundred and thirty-six people to keep eight Tornados, equipped with the latest weapons and self-protection equipment, in the air at Kandahar Airfield, providing close air support to troops on the ground 24/7.

The Battle Plan was an exhausting schedule. Over the next ten weeks everybody would fly numerous sorties covering thirty different objectives focused on the Tornado's weapons package, which they would 'deploy' in a range of scenarios they were likely to face in theatre; from armed over-watch of convoys to shows of force, strafing and bombing. Everybody would also fly four Herrick-specific simulator sorties, including a night sortie. Two crews at a time would visit the Sim with one crew 'flying' and being scrutinised by the other and then they would swap places. A total of twenty-two hours' simulated Herrick sorties were in addition to the routine Sim sorties they would still fly.

Every time they went to the simulator they would be presented with a scenario. Once they were strapped into the cockpit and 'airborne' the Sim operators, most of them former Tornado aircrew, would programme in hazards and threats, mechanical and human, to see how they would react. There would be weapons malfunctions, equipment failure, near collisions and dust storms that reduced visibility to zero. And when they had got them acquainted with taking off and landing at Kandahar Airfield (KAF) they would then have the KAF runway go black with a crashed plane, diverting them, short of fuel, to Camp Bastion – Britain's gateway to and operational hub in Helmand – or Bagram, the big US base north of Kabul. And just to get them acclimatised they turned the heat up in the cockpit. Every minute would be monitored and analysed, Griffiths told them. The Sim operators had a long menu of hazards from which they chose with relish.

'All weapon-related events must be debriefed by a qualified weapons instructor [QWI],' Griffiths emphasised. 'Merely completing the objective is not enough to be ticked off.'

The Battle Plan included every aspect of the Squadron's deployment: flight safety in theatre, refuelling from tankers, targeting directives, Afghanistan air threat assessments. All training would be geared to honing routine close air support (CAS) sorties and ground close air support (GCAS), where jets were kept cocked in ready state with all systems go and crews standing by to get airborne to go to a troops-in-contact (TIC) alert within minutes.

There was also an extensive reading list of nearly thirty mandatory titles including Op Herrick handbooks and covering the three weapons systems carried in Afghanistan by Tornados, tactical directives, how to file a mission report, rules of engagement (ROE), theatre targeting processes and much, much more. There were then a similar number of recommended titles on air space planning, counter-insurgency and air power atmospherics. To make sure that these were being read and understood the aircrew would be set a ten-page quiz to be completed, once in slow-time and then again against the clock, just prior to deployment.

On the personal welfare side there was a programme of families liaison to fix for while 617 was away, along with the kitting schedule, passports, Afghan driving licences, travel orders, fitness tests, ID cards and a course of injections to get them to theatre. Everybody would be issued with phone cards that entitled them to thirty minutes of free calls a week on a secure line, which they could top up at their own expense. It was a strict British military rule that no personal mobiles would be allowed in theatre. They were insecure, a known security risk.

Finally there was some other necessary paperwork which nobody wanted to dwell on but everybody had to complete: next-of-kin forms and wills. Some were already writing letters to be read if the worst happened and recording story tapes for their children to listen to while they were away.

'Various individuals have been given specific tasks to ensure that the Squadron is ready to deploy,' Squadron Leader Griffiths told the aircrew.

The engineers too would be doing their detailed work-up, guided, assessed and measured by the enthusiastic SEngO Clarke and beady-eyed Warrant Officer Thomson, both working closely with the Warlord as they would in theatre.

'However, it is everyone's responsibility to ensure that they are fully prepared,' Griffiths said. Heavy emphasis on *everyone's*.

The Warlord gazed around the room, his dark eyes taking everybody in at a single sweep. The aircrew were sitting six rows deep surrounded by yet more memorabilia of the sorties that had made the Squadron's history and their heritage. They were soon to add their own. Griffiths saw a mix of emotions laid out in front of him, from the steady appreciation of the realism of the task ahead from those who had gone on operations before to excitement and nervousness in equal measure from the vast majority who had not.

To the rookies Afghanistan had seemed a long way away in every sense before Christmas. Now they sensed time was picking up speed.

The Dambusters could only be declared fit to deploy once they had met all targets demanded by the Battle Plan, collectively and individually. And on top of everything else there would be a period of pre-deployment training focusing on battlefield casualty drills, emergency rescues and firearms training. Anybody failing any part of it would undergo further training until they achieved the required standard.

'Everybody happy?' Griffiths asked, the way that military people do.

A collective 'happy' murmured back. A nod of the head here, a shrug and a smile there.

'Happy days,' Griffiths smiled. 'Let's get on with it.'

As the aircrew filed out of the briefing room, heading for the planning room to prepare for the day's flying programme, Wing Commander Taylor knew that in Tony Griffiths he had made the right choice of Warlord. Griff was thorough, firm and had a total belief that every member of 617 would be hitting every single target set because if nothing else he would see to it that they did.

Over the next ten weeks any Lossiemouth burglars would be well advised to steer clear of 617's sock drawers.

A windowless, bomb-proof Pilot Briefing Facilities (PBF) building attached to the aircrew block housed 617's planning and debriefing rooms. With its waist-high tables covered in maps and charts, and cabinets of mission-planning documents, the planning room would have passed for a scene from Len Deighton's Second World War novel *Bomber*, were it not for the computer screens over which pilots and navigators were hunched, perched on high stools and preparing their sorties. There was much scribbling in notepads, hitting the print key and visits to the photocopier. A counter set into a large hatch between the planning room and the neighbouring ops room was the authoriser's desk. The authoriser was always a senior officer qualified to give final sanction to a sortie before the crews walked to their jets. A wall of screens in the ops room kept crews up to date on weather and airfield conditions and air traffic. Black phones and red phones rang in and were dialled out incessantly.

A three-hour sortie amounted to a lot more than the three hours spent in the air. It would start with a weather and intelligence brief followed by a mission brief then one or two hours planning the route, the flight profile – the step-by-step summary of how every phase of the sortie would be flown with height, fuel and in-flight refuelling requirements – and the weaponry required to complete its objectives. There would then be an out-brief with the authoriser who would double-check details and ensure that each crew or pair of crews – most sorties were being flown as a two-ship formation as they would be in Afghanistan – had not miscalculated or missed anything important. Post-sortie there would be an in-brief with the authoriser followed by an hour-long mission debrief of and by the crews involved and then a detailed analysis of the cockpit video taken of the sortie by a QWI. All in all a three-hour sortie could require four to five hours of planning, briefing and debriefing. Everybody from the Boss to the most junior flying officer went through the same process irrespective of rank or experience.

For the younger members of 617 who had little experience to fall back on, the planning was mentally tiring. The engineers said that you could always spot aircrew because they went around as though their hair was on fire, but it was most probably that their brains had been ignited by procedures, best practice and protocols. When the aircrew were in the planning room their body language said: Do Not Disturb.

*

Flying Officer Alasdair Spence, a laid-back 26-year-old Scot, had only joined 617 in September 2010 and was the youngest of the pilots. Talented and committed to making a career in the RAF, he was having a sortie video examined by one of the QWIs, Flight Lieutenant Conan Mullineux, an experienced navigator who had served in Afghanistan before with another squadron. Bespectacled and studious and ten years in the RAF, Conan looked more like a country padre than a barbarian as he went through a sortie that Spence had flown with the Warlord, simulating a series of attacks over Scotland of the kind they could be delivering in Afghanistan.

It had involved 'destroying' an 'IED factory' with a Paveway IV, taking out an insurgent's car with a Brimstone, providing armed over-watch on a convoy, carrying out surveillance on another suspicious vehicle and then real-life strafing on the range at Tain on the way home.

The Herrick ops book, containing all the different profiles for firing weapons at a variety of targets in Afghanistan such as compounds, buildings, vehicles and insurgent fighters on motorbikes, was a constant companion for Al Spence and the junior aircrew. By the time he deployed he would know them all without having to refer to a book.

Spence ran the video, taken through the LITENING pod, which showed the crew's-eye view of coming in to a simulated 'release' of a Brimstone missile on the 'terrorist' car.

Griffiths' voice came clear through the crackling soundtrack. 'Target captured. Waiting . . . .' 'Can you pause it there?' Conan asked. Spence froze the action, expecting to be pulled up for doing something not quite by the ops book. Conan had watched hundreds of cockpit videos and was a perfectionist.

He admitted that QWIs became very wedded to systems and processes.

'There will be pilots who in the heat of the moment will hear the words "target captured" and will pickle the missile off too far out. That was close to faultless.'

Spence breathed more easily.

'Run the tape on,' Conan said. 'What I am looking for is a nice calm attack, ordered chatter in the cockpit and crews who listen to each other.'

He did find fault with some of Al Spence's work but the young flying officer and his experienced navigator seemed to think the faults were minor and to an outsider would seem esoteric. But then to an outsider a QWI debrief sounded for the most part like Demotic script. Roughly translated it meant establish that your target really is a threat, capture it and programme the bomb accurately, take your time and shoot straight.

On 27 January 2011 Squadron Leader Sharrocks and Wing Commander Taylor were greeted by waves of Chinooks, Apaches and Sea Kings dropping combat troops on to Salisbury Plain. The major exercise was the backdrop for a media day at Copehill Down, an MoD urban warfare and close-quarters battle training village, where Brigadier Ed Davis unveiled the new formation of Task Force Helmand that would be taking over from 16 Air Assault Brigade in early April. Totalling some 6500 men and women from across the armed forces, the bulk would be from 3 Commando Brigade – including 42 and 45 Commando – making it the first brigade to deploy to Afghanistan four times. It would be supported by units of 7 Armoured Brigade, elements of several Royal Artillery regiments, the Mercian Regiment, The Rifles, the Royal Ghurkha Rifles, the Royal Regiment of Scotland and others drawn from logistics, signals, the Royal Military Police, the Royal Electrical and Mechanical Engineers and the Royal Navy.

The Task Force would meet force with force but this deployment was not about firefights, the Brigadier stressed. The days of purely kinetic operations were past, he said.

'This is about the people of central Helmand. It's about dealing with the cause of the insurgency, which is the disenfranchised and vulnerable population, not focusing on the symptom, which is the insurgent fighter. We will be working very closely with [the Afghans] as we prepare to hand over responsibility for the security of Afghanistan to its own government.'

Fixed-wing air advisers would be a vital component at Brigade Headquarters in Lashkar Gah. They would be in daily contact with 617 and once in theatre Squadron Leader Griffiths and Captain Jock Adams would pay an early visit to Lash. Adams had been with 617 for six years and was the Squadron's Ground Liaison Officer (GLO), Keith Taylor's adviser on operations that the Squadron might be asked to support on the ground prior to any missions. It was Adams' responsibility to ensure that the Squadron had as much information as possible about what they would be likely to see from overhead. He would brief the crews at the start of every shift and mission. Adams would not only be a vital link with 3 Commando Brigade but also with all other GLOs based in Kandahar.

Back at Lossiemouth the pace of pre-deployment training was picking up and so were expectations.

'Busy keeps me happy,' said Flight Lieutenant Lucy Williams, 29, emerging exhausted from a couple of hours in the simulator – where aircrew seemed to be arriving by conveyor belt – after taking off from a virtual Kandahar Airfield and flying day and night sorties around Afghanistan. Williams, born in Namibia, brought up in Portugal and Wales, was one of five female navigators currently on 617.

'I was only the third girl on the squadron, but we have now gone through novelty value and withstood the banter. Now it's all down to who you are.'

The first-ever female pilot to fly fast jets operationally in the RAF was Dambuster Jo Salter back in 1995, who patrolled the no-fly zones in Iraq. Tall and slim, Lucy was diligent, confident and popular, not afraid to express her concerns at meeting the challenges that lay ahead. Bravado was a rare currency on 617. Her brown hair scraped back from her freckled face and secured behind her head, Lucy clutched her helmet with the kind of long delicate fingers you'd expect to see wrapped around a violin.

'I don't think anybody from outside realises the planning that goes into dropping bombs or how nerve-wracking it can be.'

Lucy had dropped live weapons on exercise in Canada and on Garvie Island, but now the challenge of dropping them and not killing innocent people was becoming more real by the day.

'In the air you just do your job – yesterday the QWIs told us that by the time we get out to Kandahar it has to be second nature and that's why we train as hard as we do.'

Friends back home did not always understand the mounting pressure that the Squadron was under as departure day neared. It helped that Lucy's boyfriend, Steve 'Westlife' Westley, a flight lieutenant pilot who was training to be a weapons instructor at Lossiemouth, had been on 617 until the previous October and had also flown in Afghanistan with 12 Squadron.

'It's not that he briefs me on what to expect because he knows there's no substitute for first-hand experience, but he knows the signs, the pressures, of somebody who is working up to deploy. He knows when to say the right thing, and when to say nothing.'

Afghanistan was something Lucy chose not to discuss with her parents. 'They are proud of me and happy that I am doing a job I really want to do but my mother especially prefers not to talk about it. I think if I had chosen another career they would have been happier. It's a good job they live in Denver,' she said, 'because they won't have to face any headlines about British deaths in the newspapers there.'

Twenty-nine-year-old Flight Lieutenant Gary Montgomery had joined 617 eighteen months before. Monty was a pilot who would be happy flying all day every day; further, faster and lower than anybody else. With a face that could have graced a Roman coin, Monty's wry sense of humour masked an ambitious nature. He had read aeronautical engineering at Queen's Belfast. He remembered vividly the moment he wanted not just to be a fast jet pilot but a Tornado pilot.

'I was eight years old and watching footage from the First Gulf War of Tornado GR1s flying low over the desert and it totally amazed me. I'd never seen anything like that before. I've been fascinated by the aircraft ever since.'

By the time he was 22 years old Monty was sitting in a Tornado out on the runway at Lossiemouth, about to fly his first sortie.

'You're sitting with the engines set at max dry and then you plug in the re-heat for take-off. Feeling that huge power generation and vibration go through the aircraft and right into the small of your back was incredible. Every time I do it I still get a thrill.'

Monty was also passionate about military history, and Dambuster history in particular, and he and Lucy Williams answered the many requests for information that 617 received.

'The Dams Raid was the standout mission of taking it to the enemy,' Monty said, 'and to be part of one of the most famous bomber squadrons in the world is something special.'

Taking it to the enemy in Afghanistan was just as likely to involve aerial intelligence gathering as bombing runs. Like the rest of the junior aircrew Monty was happy to be protecting coalition troops.

'A successful deployment isn't always the same as an exciting one,' he smiled, as if quoting from a briefing. However, he was not alone in wanting to employ all his skills. 'I've trained seven years now to do a job, and reconnaissance is part of the job, but the most difficult thing we do is deploy weapons and in Afghanistan there are some weapons profiles that will test our training to the utmost. It would be good to get the chance to do that in a high-pressure environment and do it successfully.'

Like all the pilots and navigators Monty was aware of the dangers and challenges of military flying but how could you be scared strapped tight inside millions of quids'-worth of missile-launching, computerised, pumped-up weapons platform? But there was more to it than high-tech chutzpah. Years and years of exacting daily training meant that in place of fear and apprehension stood calm and reason. An awareness of fear, risk and danger was embedded into their DNA, but none of those got you airborne. These were individuals doing an extraordinary, demanding, split-second job by making it seem at times ordinary. High or low, they flew in perfect balance between their skills, experience and a 360-degree awareness of the potentially perilous situations they would confront. Only those who flew fast jets could really understand that absolute and systematic focus displayed in the eyes of a fast jet bomber pilot strapped into the cockpit and about to fly a sortie.

*

Twenty-six-year-old Flight Lieutenant Poppy Cormack-Loyd ('With one "l".') headed up and spoke for the junior aircrew, flight lieutenants and below. The junior members of 617 Squadron were a pretty varied bunch socially. Very few came from RAF backgrounds although early exposure to fast jets was a common thread. Poppy was from Oxford, beautifully spoken with blonde hair swept back and a helium giggle that could be heard from some distance. She had joined her school cadet force at the age of 14 and on a Combined Cadet Force (CCF) camp at Lossiemouth two years later she realised that, 'I really like the jets, the lifestyle. I'm not a desk person. From a nav's point of view you are always busy in the back of a jet. It's very varied.'

She was worried that there had still been no announcement on which Tornado squadrons were going to be axed, although she knew that if 617 went she would be reassigned to another squadron.

'If we don't get to deploy I will be absolutely gutted,' she said.

There was always a lot of banter between junior squadron members. Flight lieutenant navigators Caroline Day and Jon Overton – who were due to get married weeks after the deployment ended – and Timmy Colebrooke had all come from Tornado F3 squadrons. The F3 was the air defence version of the GR4, protecting airspace over the UK and the Falklands.

'Because we don't get operational medals they call us peace chests or war dodgers,' said Timmy, who moved everywhere at incendiary speed as though his hair was on fire. 'Even when I get a medal for Afghanistan, to these guys I will always be an F3 pumper.'

The 617 junior squadron members also organised social events and jolly raids on other squadrons' buildings, which they would drape in Dambuster colours. In 2009 they 'requisitioned' the Lossiemouth Officers' Mess, jamming red and black balloons in the double glazing and covering the floor to ceiling windows by the front doors with lightning bolt banners. Elsewhere on the base they plastered the guardroom gate with stickers bearing the letters AJ-G, the fuselage number of Guy Gibson's dam-busting Lancaster 'George'. Neighbouring squadrons would exact revenge. They always did.

'We went a bit turbo that year,' admitted Lucy Williams. 'We weren't flying as much then as we are now.'

They had also burned a few pianos, another RAF tradition.

'When "dining in" new members of the squadron, we'll burn a piano,' Lucy said. 'If somebody dies we'll definitely burn a piano.'

When a Tornado from RAF Leuchars in Fife, then Britain's most northerly defence station, crashed into a hillside in Argyll in 2009, Lucy and other aircrew friends burned a piano at the funeral of the pilot. His mother played it as it went up in flames.

Nobody is completely agreed on the origins of piano burning, although it is said to have started in the Second World War, when a fighter pilot who used to play the piano every night in the mess bar was killed in action. His Squadron buddies decided that in honour of his memory nobody should ever play that piano again, so they set fire to it.

'We only buy rubbishy old £20 pianos that nobody wants,' Lucy added. Predictably, the practice is welcomed by local second-hand dealers stuck with pianos they can't sell and frowned upon by the higher echelons of the Air Force and also Tim Colebrooke's father-in-law, who had banned him from burning one when he married his daughter Diana, an RAF doctor. It had been painted white and covered in glitter by Caroline Day.

Not to be outdone, Colebrooke had introduced 617's newest tradition, the Arrogance Rug.

'The Arrogance Rug aka the Fighting Rug, is black and red and covered in our Squadron battle honours,' said Colebrooke, who was keeper of the rug and not averse to a prank or two.

He had come across one when he was on his F3 squadron.

'When we want to wind up other squadrons we take it into the Officers' Mess and lay it on the floor. It runs the length of the bar, minus a metre, and only 617 officers and their guests are allowed to stand on it, taking up bar real estate.'

He paused to smile at the memory of epic fights for the rug.

'Predictably other squadrons will then try and push us off, nick it and burn it.' (Especially when all concerned have 'got a shed on', RAF slang for being 'extremely inebriated'.) 'Every time it survives we add another battle honour.'

But 617 is not the only squadron with bizarre trophy objects. For instance, 12 Squadron, from whom 617 was taking over in Kandahar, have a stuffed fox they call Fox2, its code word for firing an air-to-air missile. The squadron's badge is a fox's mask and echoes the days when it was the only squadron equipped with the Fairey Fox. For twenty-five years 14 Squadron had had an honorary squadron leader called Eric, a bad-tempered 15-foot Burmese python. Eric had even been known to take to the air.

'It was the junior crews' responsibility to look after Eric,' Colebrooke said. 'I don't think many crews have been through 14 without a snake bite.'

In just a few weeks 12 Squadron's fox would be replaced by 617's Arrogance Rug.

'The rug is just a bit of fun, like Mess rugby, and generates a bit of *esprit de corps* in the force, which is good,' Timmy said.

Then he added: 'Sadly, there are no bars in Afghanistan, well not as we know them. But we're taking it anyway.'

Perhaps the keenest Dambuster was not a Dambuster at all; not a British one anyway. Thirty-two-year-old Lieutenant Josh Thompson from Granger, Northern Indiana, a small town two hours' drive from Chicago, was a US Navy pilot with Strike Fighter Squadron 195 who for the last three years had flown an F/A-18C Hornet off US nuclear-powered super-carriers *Kitty Hawk* and *George Washington* – part of Carrier Wing 5 based in Atsugi, Japan – on reconnaissance and interdiction missions all over the Far East.

He had been inspired to fly by the events of 9/11.

'It made me want to do something to support US military forces and their allies.'

Josh was on a two-year pilot exchange with 617. Apart from wanting to fly with a front-line squadron in a war zone and experience 'another great jet' he had a particular reason for wanting to be with the Dambusters.

'In the Korean War my squadron were flying AD1 Skyraiders and there was a heavily defended dam, Hwacheon, in the north which they were having trouble successfully striking. They had numerous strikes going against it and no success and so they decided to think outside the box. They didn't come up with a bouncing bomb but they decided to try something that had not been tried before. They strapped torpedoes to the wings and dropped them into the water in front of the dam.'

Hwacheon Dam was destroyed on 2 May 1951 and Squadron VFA-195, previously nicknamed 'The Tigers', has been known in America ever since as the Dambusters.

Josh Thompson was the world's first double Dambuster and he was going about his work with real press-on spirit.

'This job is so fun,' he said, 'I'm learning so much. I can't believe I am flying a multimillion-dollar British airplane for a living right now.'

It wasn't only his laid-back honeyed accent that made Josh easy to spot, or his courtesy and old-fashioned manners, or his clean-cut movie-star looks. At six feet two he was easily the tallest pilot on the squadron.

'I put the cockpit seat all the way down to the floor, bend my head when the canopy goes down and I make it but not by a lot.'

Emblazoned on his flight suit was his US Navy nickname, 'Stalk'.

'When you join a front-line squadron you grab a nickname pretty quick. I was a tall skinny guy, so it was beanstalk, and that became "stalk" pretty soon.'

Stalk stuck. Flying the Hornet it was also his call-sign. Now at the controls of a Tornado the nickname had been given a new earthier meaning by his colleagues on 617.

'I like to talk a lot, in the crewroom and in the air,' he explained. 'Maybe I get that from my dad, who is a DJ on an AM station called News Talk Radio. Anyway, because I talk a lot the guys tell me that Stalk now stands for shit talk.'

This was Josh's first taste of British banter. It was a sign that already he belonged and that his skin was sufficiently thick. Stalk couldn't wait to get to Kandahar and support fellow Americans on the ground.

As well as preparing for and flying the kind of profiles they would be asked to do in theatre, Josh and the rest of the squadron were now starting their pre-deployment training: a series of lectures, firearms practice on the ranges, intelligence briefings and battlefield casualty drills. The aircrew had three days taken out of their flying schedule. The engineers, however, were required to do five days' training as statistically they were more likely to be involved when Kandahar Airfield was attacked with rockets and mortars.

In the last few months a Taliban suicide squad had attacked KAF armed with bombs and rockets and had come within inches of the outer security fence. All six had been killed. As recently as 19 January a 22-year-old soldier with the US 101st Airborne had been killed by a rocket that made it into the base. Six days later more rockets plunged into KAF launched from about four miles away.

All such incidents were a feature of the daily briefings, a vivid reminder to all that even though the majority of the Squadron were not on the front line they were still in a warzone where people got killed and injured.

For the aircrew one of the most important briefings was on rules of engagement (ROE) which governed when they could deploy weapons. This was given by an RAF lawyer – another unseen cog in the war effort.

6

WAR WEEK

On 1 March the MoD put out a press statement that brought to an end speculation about which Tornado squadrons would be going as demanded by the Strategic Defence and Security Review the previous December. Its message was stark.

The Royal Air Force's Number 13 and 14 Tornado squadrons are to be disbanded and formally stood down on 1 June 2011. These squadrons have been selected by the Air Force Board Standing Committee, taking into account operational commitments and the relative seniority of the squadron at each base.

The RAF had been reduced to five front-line Tornado squadrons with a total fleet of 138 GR4 aircraft, less than the number that used to be based in Germany alone.

With the Dambusters on the verge of deploying it was always unlikely that it would be for the chop, but even so the sense of relief among its members was palpable.

Poppy Cormack-Loyd was thrilled. 'Yes! We're going!' However, her fiancé, Flight Lieutenant Richard Leask, to whom she was to be married on return from Afghanistan, was a pilot on 14 Squadron. She could not help but wonder what the future would hold for those on 14, even though the MoD had pledged that there would be no automatic redundancies 'in the short term' and that aircrew and engineers from 13 Squadron at Marham and 14 at Lossiemouth would be absorbed into other squadrons, including 617.

There was to be no reprieve for 14's Eric the Burmese python. He would lose his honorary commission and was to be 'rehomed' with his squadron flying suit, service history and memorabilia to the Amazonia Centre in Motherwell.

The biggest sigh of relief at 617's reprieve could have been heard in the Boss's office.

'Everyone is relieved, none more so than me,' Keith Taylor said. The Squadron still didn't know if Lossiemouth would still be there when they returned. That decision, originally due the previous December, had been delayed.

The aircrew now knew who they were being paired with to fly in theatre. Normally everybody flew with everybody else but in theatre settled partnerships were proven to work best. In Guy Gibson's day a squadron's worth of aircrew would assemble in a hangar and be told to sort the crewing out themselves. Today it was more scientific with the Warlord, the Boss and the Execs trying to match experience with inexperience wherever possible and sounding out pilots and navigators for their preferences. When the list was issued the aircrew clamoured for a copy, like pupils getting their A-level results.

'Have I lucked in?' Lucy Williams grinned. She would be flying with Flight Lieutenant Joe Hourston. Thirty-two years old, Hourston was from the Black Isle and had been on the Dambusters eighteen months. He had been recognised as a talented pilot when training at RAF Valley and as cream of the crop selected to stay on as an instructor, which was known as a 'creamy tour'.

Joe had been Lucy's first choice. 'We are friends out of work anyway. We get each other. Joe is quite calm, I'm reasonably calm; less calm than Joe!'

Monty would be flying with the Warlord and Timmy Colebrooke had drawn the Boss.

'No pressure there then,' he grinned.

Over the weekend of 12 and 13 March a large team from the Joint Force Air Component Headquarters (JFACHQ) at High Wycombe arrived at RAF Lossiemouth. They set up camp in one of 617's briefing rooms, covered it in maps and task sheets and declared it out of bounds to the Squadron.

Monday 14 March was the start of War Week and from 617's HQ the JFACHQ team would stage a series of exercises and incidents to test how ready the Dambusters were to go to war in Afghanistan. The Squadron would carry on with its normal work-up training and would have no idea what was going to hit them next.

'Herrick is a very dynamic environment and we are going to mirror that in ground and aircrew training,' promised Squadron Leader Simon Reade. 'On ops everybody focuses on the high-end bits like getting jets in the air and dropping bombs, but the majority of hazards are likely to happen at Kandahar Airfield.'

To most of the Dambusters Kandahar now seemed within touching distance. Departure could be counted in days. Injections were well under way, wills had been signed and next-of-kin forms completed. But something more visible was about to happen that would signal to their families and friends that the detachment in Afghanistan was here for real.

On the Monday afternoon Squadron Leader Ball drove

from 617's base across the airfield to a warehouse building. At the entrance he was handed a deep wheeled bin with the capacity of a small bath. He pushed it inside. There were aisles of six-foot-high steel shelves stacked with helmets, flight suits, trousers, tunics, boots, socks, long-johns and flying gloves. This was the Operational Kitting Store and today was the deadline for getting kitted out for theatre.

Down at the end of one aisle Poppy Cormack-Loyd had already mounded up her bin and she seemed to be having trouble negotiating it to the check-out.

'I've got a lot of this stuff from other tours,' Ballsy said, piling in desert boots and T-shirts but refusing a pair of £90 wrap-round blast-proof eyeshield glasses that came with lenses in three different colourways. 'On second thoughts,' he said and tossed a pair into the bin. High-factor sun cream and sweat scarves followed, topped off with a helmet and weighty body armour.

By the time Ballsy got to the check-out Poppy had filled two bins and was going to bring her car closer to load the new gear.

'If we were deploying into an Afghan winter, you'd need twice as much gear to keep warm and dry,' Ballsy said, offering to give her a hand.

As bags of new kit arrived in houses all over Lossiemouth that evening it wasn't just the amount of it or that it included body armour that suddenly reinforced to 617 families that the Squadron's deployment was imminent. It was its colour. Gone were the familiar green flight suits and green and brown camouflage. In their place were desert hues of salmon, sand and darker brown. From the next morning until the day they returned from theatre the Dambusters would be dressed for Afghanistan. Dressed for operations. Dambuster wives, husbands and partners with small children did their best to banish inevitable thoughts as they watched their toddlers rushing about excitedly in a newly issued helmet and staggering under the weight of body armour.

Next morning there was something different about the planning room. The aircrew were all prone on the floor in their helmets and body armour. The siren had gone off; a rocket attack was imminent. In one of the indirect fire (IDF) briefings a matter-of-fact sergeant from the RAF Regiment Force Protection Team – which provided security around Bastion airfield – had emphasised the importance of hitting the deck whatever they were doing when the siren went.

'There was a Canadian woman playing basketball at KAF who chose to ignore it,' he warned. 'The rockets came in and she lost an arm.'

A member of Simon Reade's team now appeared, picking his way through the legs and arms, making sure that nobody moved until two minutes had passed and the all-clear had sounded. In the engineers' block it was the same story.

War Week had begun but even so it was still business as usual. Out in the aircraft shelters engineers and aircrew were practising ground close air support (GCAS) see-offs daily. GCAS aircrews would walk out to their jets fully kitted, start the engines, check all systems with the line crew and then shut them down, leaving them 'cocked' and ready to go. They would then either be held on standby in the crewroom or be sitting by the jet ready to be airborne within minutes of receiving a TIC alert. It was a sharp ask but it had to be seamless.

And during War Week the attacks, the air raid warnings and the explosions kept on coming. Suddenly the smooth planning and flying of sorties was being disrupted.

'We want people to feel a little bit on edge,' said Squadron

Leader Tony Griffiths. 'We want them feeling a little bit uncomfortable, because it's training for the next stage and intensity before we go to ops. In theatre we won't have three or four weeks to learn about our environment. There could be an IDF attack the first time they walk to an aircraft.'

For Griffiths it was equally important that War Week did not jeopardise getting aircraft into the air safely. He went to talk to the SEngO.

'Are we putting enough pressure on the Squadron?' he asked Clarke. 'Are people reacting correctly?'

'No worries so far,' SEngO told him. 'On the engineering side the guys are getting up to speed; we're not missing any taskings.'

Rocksy Sharrocks was head-down hard at work one afternoon in his office and didn't hear the small explosion set off by the War Week team, but he sure as hell heard the screams that followed it. He looked out of the window and saw a cloud of black smoke above the grass and underneath it was a writhing body covered in blood. He was missing part of a leg. Sharrocks grabbed his medical pack and rushed out of the aircrew building. The man was screaming. His leg was covered in blood. When Rocksy knelt down beside the man he realised that he really was missing half of his right leg. Instinctively he did as he had been trained and grabbed a tourniquet and fixed it as tight as he could around the man's bleeding stump and then wrapped a field dressing around the wound. He shouted to somebody to call the airfield ambulance.

'We have one times T1 casualty.' T1 was the severest injury category. 'We need an emergency response team as soon as possible.'

While he waited Rocksy did his best to calm the man and make him comfortable, checking his pulse and breathing rates and looking for any other injuries. Suddenly there was a loud bang and the sound of crunching metal, followed by an explosion. Rocksy looked across the tarmac. A car had just crashed into the engineers' block, hit by a rocket.

This might be a training exercise and Rocksy might just have mimed giving his casualty morphine while being filmed by the War Week team but it was creepily realistic. The organisers had hired amputees from a company called Amputees in Action, many of whom had lost limbs in Iraq and Afghanistan. They not only contributed to the training of troops about to deploy by posing as 'victims' but they also assessed how their 'wounds', from breaks to burns and particularly realistic abdominal and chest trauma, were treated in that vital golden hour when the initial treatment of traumatic injury and blood loss made the difference between life and death. It was a bizarre by-product of continuing conflict that these real victims of war also chose to work on films such as *Saving Private Ryan* or the *Band of Brothers* TV series.

As the 'victim' Rocksy had treated was lifted into the back of a military ambulance the Dambusters' corner of the Lossiemouth airfield seemed to be covered in injured bodies. The air was rank with the sour smell of spent explosive charges. At the other corner of the aircrew building, a moaning man playing the part of somebody who had become disorientated and traumatised by a bomb attack was sitting on the ground rocking back and forth, his face blackened. Two aircrew walked past and ignored him as if he wasn't there.

'What the fuck . . .?' Rocksy yelled at them.

Washing the 'blood' from his hands Squadron Leader Sharrocks vowed: *I am going to put 'Walk on By' on their iPods and make them listen to it until their ears bleed.*

*

One of the many visitors to Lossie during War Week was Captain Mathew Hills of 45 Commando (pronounced *four-five*) based at Condor Barracks in Arbroath. He had come to brief 617 on 45's operational role on the ground when they took over from 16 Air Assault Brigade in Nad-e Ali South on 4 April and how the Squadron could best support them.

Four-five would be based at FOB Shawqat, one of the largest areas of operation (AO) just west of 3 Commando Brigade's HQ at Lashkar Gah. In yet another example of Afghanistan's history repeating itself FOB Shawqat, a creation of white tents and steel shipping containers, had been built at the suggestion of local elders inside an old mud and brick British fort called Farangi, which translated as the 'Foreigners' Castle'. Farangi had been built in the Second Afghan War around 1880, part of 'The Great Game' played by the British and Russians as they vied for empire in central Asia. The fort was not as secure as it had been in those days. In 1997 the Taliban had destroyed its three main gates, eight towers and sections of the 15-foot-high walls. Even so, it was still an imposing sight.

This would be the fourth time 45 had deployed to Afghanistan. They first went in 2001 immediately after 9/11, to the north, then to Helmand in 2006, working right across the province. In 2008 they focused on Sangin as part of Northern Battle Group on Operation Herrick 9. Sangin, a town of 14,000 in Helmand, had been nicknamed Mordor by British troops after the Black Land in Tolkien's *Lord of the Rings*. Its tight alleys were a stronghold of insurgents and drug traffickers. When 45's Whiskey Company arrived in Sangin by Chinook they came under indirect fire within hours and it stayed that way. 'Sangin was a tough urban environment to work in, IEDs, small-arms fire,' Hills told 617's aircrew, who were crammed into three rows in an airless briefing room.

'This time we will be operating differently to how we were operating two and a half years ago. In contrast, Nad-e Ali is probably one of the most advanced districts in terms of transfer to the Afghan security services so the main aim of our tour this year is to start putting into place the conditions for that transfer.'

The process was known as 'Transition' and was seen as key to success in Afghanistan. Four-five's main effort now was enabling rather than leading the Afghan National Army (ANA) and the Afghan National Police (ANP) and training them up for success and ultimately operational independence. In the past large patrols of UK company-sized groups of eighty men with a small Afghan element attached were the norm.

'Now you are going to see smaller patrols of sixteen men with a similar-sized Afghan element,' Hills said. 'Every patrol will be planned and partnered alongside the Afghans, with by the end of 2011 the Afghans taking control of the planning and execution in districts that have transitioned. They'll take the key decisions.'

'How ready are they for that transfer?' Wing Commander Taylor asked.

'It varies from district to district,' Hills admitted. 'Nad-e Ali is said to be one of the closest to transfer, following Lashkar Gah, but even within that district there are areas where the ANA is more capable than others.' Hills recognised that there were cultural differences, of the military kind, that could always make transfer challenging.

'They plan differently to us,' he said. 'Their working day is different, their work ethic is different. I think we have enough experience as a Commando group to address those problems. We'll have a good working relationship with the ANA and the ANP.'

At the same time, the inquest was about to get underway into five soldiers and military police who had been killed in Helmand as a result of gunshot wounds they had sustained in an attack by a rogue Afghan police officer. Six other soldiers and two Afghan policemen were wounded in the massacre.

Captain Hills was eager to stress that the Tornado was a crucial element of close air support to marines on the ground. 'It's the ISTAR [Intelligence, Surveillance, Target Acquisition and Reconnaissance] effect; the ability to find the enemy and strike him from the air or the ground is key. With RAPTOR you have the ability to see and collect imagery before a mission which means we can plan more effectively, and during a mission you can feed live footage from a LITENING pod down to our JTAC [Joint Terminal Attack Controller] on the ground and increase our situational awareness.'

Hills concluded: 'There are, however, certain areas on the fringes of the AO where the insurgent is active and the ground is still contested so I'd expect to see Tornados engaging targets in those areas perhaps a handful of times during the tour but I wouldn't expect to see fast air weapons being used in Nad-e Ali DC.'

The big push 3 Commando Brigade was planning was called Operation Omid Haft (Operation Hope Seven) and the link between the Tornados and the marines in forward positions on the ground would be the Joint Terminal Attack Controllers (JTACs), also known as Forward Air Controllers (FACs).

Embedded with patrols and convoys or at forward operating bases (FOBs), the JTACs played a central role in the battle space. They were the ones who would call for fast jets whenever they needed eyes in the sky, ensuring a proportional response to any threat. Live video captured by Tornado navigators on their LITENING targeting pods would be downloaded simultaneously to the JTAC, who would view it on a ROVER or Video Scout laptop and then discuss next steps with his ground commander and the aircrew, especially the rules of engagement under which weapons were to be deployed.

The JTAC would advise his ground commander on the airspace and the air assets within it and know the strengths and weaknesses of fixed-wing, rotary and unmanned aerial vehicles (UAVs), aviation weapons capabilities and the use and timely submission of joint tactical air strike requests (JTARs).

As 617's jets took off over the next few days they would be working with JTACs who were located all over Scotland as part of War Week, calling in their Tornados to a variety of scenarios. For added War Week realism aircrew from 201 Squadron were running a Combined Air Operations Centre (CAOC), replicating that at Al-Udeid Air Base in Qatar, which controls all air tasking and air assets in Afghanistan.

In theatre the Dambusters would not just be responding to Royal Marines JTACs but also those from Italy, Norway, Estonia, Canada, the United States and other countries. The roles and training of JTACs, a term coined by the United States in 2003, had only been standardised and agreed in September 2010 in a Memorandum of Agreement between the Deputy Commander US Joint Forces Command and the defence, naval, marine corps and armed forces representatives of twelve countries, including the RAF's Deputy Commander-in-Chief Operations, Air Command. Less than a month away from theatre it was vital that 617 learned the JTAC processes and language first-hand.

Two JTACs were not shivering out in the Highlands waiting for the comforting sight and sound of a fast jet streaking low over the heather. Both from 3 Commando Brigade, they

'The Boss'. A veteran himself, Wing Commander Keith Taylor with his first squadron command was taking a group of largely untested aircrew to war.

After their daily 'Gentlemen's Breakfast', Squadron Leader Stuart Clark (*left*), 617's Senior Engineering Officer (SEngO), Sergeant Al Sharp and Warrant Officer Stew Thomson can return to base having identified any engineering problems.

A typical honeycomb of high-walled, impenetrable compounds in Helmand Province. Every day the Tornados of 617 would photograph and film them, eavesdropping and forewarning troops on the ground of ambushes and IEDs.

(*above*) A Tornado swoops down over a barren Helmand landscape of dusty hues only broken by a few slithers of green vegetation.

(*below*) Flight Lieutenant Al Spence eases his Tornado's refuelling probe, to the right of his cockpit, into the metal refuelling basket of a Boom Drogue Adaptor (BDA) dangling from an American fuel tanker 16,000 feet over Afghanistan. Known to all as the 'Iron Maiden', the BDA is much more challenging to access than the nozzle-end refuelling hoses used on other tankers and is only used in daylight.

(*left*) No place like home; the signpost tree at the Boardwalk, Kandahar Air Field. With a population of 35,000 KAF is the biggest NATO base in the world.

A Tornado takes-off from Kandahar Air Field. With 400 aircraft and 5,300 military flights every week, KAF is the world's busiest single-runway airport.

Flight Lieutenant Joe Hourston flaps behind the AIRCM, the beady-eyed airborne infrared countermeasure that warns of incoming heat-seeking missiles and pumps out multi-spectral flares to draw them away from the jet.

At the end of their detachment, the aircrew pose on the Kandahar flight line over the Squadron insignia painted by the engineers.

Relaxed towards the end of the squadron's tour, Wing Commander Taylor takes flight. Taylor's management style was laid-back and to quietly lead his young aircrew by example from the front. However, nothing missed his gaze.

Squadron Leader Tony 'Griff' Griffiths (*left*), a navigator on his seventh operational tour and the squadron's 'Warlord', with his pilot Flight Lieutenant Ollie Moncrieff, on his first ops tour. Wherever possible, experienced hands flew with the rookies.

(*below*) Flight Lieutenant Alex 'Hutch' Hutchison focuses in the final minutes before the taxi to the runway. Every sortie is as much about mental strength as physical challenge.

Flight Lieutenant Joe Hourston has a *Top Gun* moment.

(*below*) Squadron Leader 'Kiwi' Spencer (*left*) and Squadron Leader 'Griff' Griffiths shoulder arms.

(*below*) A Canadian Chinook over KAF. Aircraft artwork in war zones is a tradition going back to the Second World War, notably the Memphis Belle.

(left) Flight Lieutenant Gary 'Monty' Montgomery (left) and his navigator, Flight Lieutenant Timmy Colebrooke, walk to their jet for a sortie carrying their mission boxes. Over their flying suits they wear green anti-G trousers stuffed into which are their mission documents and flight procedures. GR4 crew regularly pull more G than the Space Shuttle on re-entry.

(right) Flight Lieutenant Poppy Cormack-Loyd.

First-day smiles for navigator Flight Lieutenant Poppy Cormack-Loyd and Flight Lieutenant Ollie Moncrieff taking time out from their Reception, Staging and Onward Integration (RSOI) programme at Camp Bastion, the British hub and point of entry to Afghanistan, before deploying on to Kandahar.

above) In the navigator's back seat Poppy Cormack-Loyd goes through her pre-sortie instrument checks. The largest screen is a full colour digital moving map and radar display known as TARDIS. The small screens are used for forward-looking infrared and weapons targeting.

below) Never one to shun a photograph, Squadron Leader Stuart Clarke, 617's Senior Engineering Officer (SEngO), poses with a charity mascot.

Distinctive Bell Boeing V-22 Ospreys, an American tiltrotor aircraft that takes off like a helicopter and once airborne can rotate its engines to fly as a turboprop aeroplane.

Flight Lieutenants Lucy Williams and Joe Hourston astride a Tornado's under-wing fuel tanks. During air-to-air refuelling, six tonnes of fuel can be delivered in ten minutes.

had driven up from Poole to fly in the back seat of a Tornado and see their world from the sky down. As they went to kit up Squadron Leader Sharrocks was keen to show them the Tornado.

'We're going to take them flying so they understand what we are all about and experience what the jet can do. Get them to think about the 3D war and what air brings to the party. You don't always need to use mortars or light guns; use a precision guided weapon from the air instead. In theatre there will be no disconnect between them doing the patrolling on the ground and Biggles in the air.'

At the end of War Week Keith Taylor met with his senior team.

'We've got people pretty much where we want them to be without pushing them over the edge,' the Warlord reported. 'It's the balance between feeling confident and slightly uncomfortable. We've emphasised that they are not going to get out to KAF and have three or four weeks to learn about their environment. They could step off the plane straight into an IDF attack.'

A few of the younger aircrew still had to pass elements of their level 1 skills assessment to qualify them for deployment to a warzone.

'We aren't quite there but we are not far off,' Taylor said. 'It's more a confidence thing for some of the younger guys and we are going to have to manage that in theatre. However, we could deploy today, we really could.'

An advance party of six aircrew led by Chris Ball would leave at the beginning of April for Kandahar to fly missions with 12 Squadron. A second advance party including Squadron Leader Griffiths, but consisting mainly of engineers, would depart RAF Brize Norton on 5 April, to shadow 12 Squadron's engineers.

Keith Taylor hoped that when the remainder of 617 arrived in theatre five days later they would not be flying straight into what he called 'complex action. For most of them this is a big step into the unknown so a chance to get used to operating in the air space is what I am hoping for before anything major happens.'

With just weeks to go he was optimistic. It was reported that the poppy harvest was later than normal due to a poor winter and the guns-for-hire '$10-a-day Taliban' – the farmers that the insurgent commanders relied on to plant IEDs and ambush patrols – would still be out in their fields when 617 touched down in Kandahar.

Closer to home Keith Taylor had just had some bad news. There was one member of the Squadron who would not be touching down in Kandahar. During War Week Taylor had heard that Josh Thompson would not be flying with the Dambusters in Afghanistan for operational reasons.

On the evening of Saturday 18 March and going into 19 March Tornados from 9 Squadron, commanded by former Dambuster Wing Commander Andy Turk, took off from RAF Marham and flew two of the longest missions since the Falklands War; an eight-hour, 3000-mile round-trip to fire Storm Shadow missiles against the military infrastructure of Colonel Muammar Gaddafi's forces. Operation Unified Protector, an international military intervention backed by United Nations Resolution 1973, to enforce a no-fly zone to stop Gaddafi's jets from strafing and bombing anti-regime rebels, was under way.

The Libyan uprising was the latest popular revolt against a

dictatorship in what was now being called the Arab Spring and which had so far toppled the regime in Tunisia and President Hosni Mubarak in Egypt. On 20 March the MoD announced that Tornado and Typhoon aircraft would be deployed to Gioia del Colle Air Base in southern Italy to fly further kinetic missions against Gaddafi's airfields and command-and-control buildings.

Some of the aircrew of 617 shortly to be heading for a counter-insurgency war in Afghanistan could not help but wonder if they had bought a ticket to the wrong gig.

PART 2
Theatre of War

7

MISSION CONTROL

Monday 4 April 2011 was Keith Taylor's seventeenth wedding anniversary but there would be no celebrations that day. He kissed Lizee and his daughters Lucy and Hannah at his parents' house just south of Edinburgh, where they had all spent the weekend, and drove a hire car down to Oxfordshire to catch a flight from RAF Brize Norton the next day. On the evening of 5 April his plane touched down on the runway of a Middle East staging post.

Located in the desert 21 miles west of the Qatari capital Doha, Al-Udeid wears its billion-dollar price tag with pride these days. Its vast aircraft ramp has accommodation for more than 100 aircraft, far more than the dozen or so fighters that the Qatari Air Force owns. However, until 2002, when the then US Vice-President Dick Cheney paid an official visit in support of Operation Enduring Freedom, the post-9/11 invasion of Afghanistan, Al-Udeid was referred to only by a handpainted sign at the front gate that said, 'army camp'.

Al-Udeid is the home of the Combined Air Operations Centre (CAOC). The CAOC (pronounced *kay-ock*) runs the allied air space over all Afghanistan – and nineteen other countries from the horn of Africa right across the Indian Ocean. It was built at a cost of $60 million, 'creating the most advanced operations centre in history', says its website. 'The CAOC plans, monitors and directs sortie execution, close air support/ precision air strike; intelligence, surveillance, reconnaissance, airlift, air refuelling, aerial evaluation, air drop, and countless other mission critical operations.'

The CAOC directs and monitors the use of air power through the daily air tasking orders (ATOs) which it issues to ISAF air force squadrons and the fleets of refuelling tankers flying in Afghanistan. It also requires other aircraft to be on standby at all times to provide precision air strikes and close air support to troops in contact (TIC) with insurgents. Simply, the CAOC provides the command and control of Air Power in the battle space.

Half of the CAOC's massive hangar of a building is taken up with a maze of offices. The other half is a cavernous open space just like Cape Canaveral with hundreds of people, thousands of computer screens and dozens of servers connected by more than 67 miles of high-capacity and fibre optic cable. Vast projection screens displayed situational information from across Afghanistan.

In the centre of the shop floor there is an elevated section from where the US military who run the CAOC preside. Encircling them are different operational sections representing all the coalition nations and aircraft types involved in the Afghan campaign.

Taylor headed for an intense half-day of pre-deployment briefings. He made his way to Britain's 'watch-keeper', a flight lieutenant who monitors and moves all the UK's air assets in Afghanistan and would be the man on the other end of the real-time communications feed via which the CAOC would be communicating minute by minute with 617.

Keith Taylor then met the Chief of Staff Operations (COS

OPS) in 83 Expeditionary Air Group (83 EAG). He is the UK's Red Card Holder at the CAOC. He was the man who could overrule a JTAC or an aircrew if he felt they were about to use disproportionate or illegal force in supporting troops on the ground which could result in civilian casualties (CIVCAS). The briefing reinforced that preventing civilian casualties at all times, and winning hearts and minds, was at the forefront of a military strategy geared towards ensuring that the Afghan National Security Forces (ANSF) had the capability to protect their own national security.

'The Tornados are a highly valued asset in theatre,' COS OPS told Taylor. 'You will always be matched to the highest priority so if that is British, American, French or Italian then that is where you will be going.' Following another meeting with the air component commander – responsible for the hardware side of all UK air assets in theatre – Keith was sole passenger in a Hawker Siddeley 125 business jet used for VIP transport. Sitting beside the pilot he was definitely getting the rock star treatment. As it left the runway Keith Taylor reflected that it was almost exactly five months since he had stood in front of the Dambusters memorial at Woodhall Spa.

A few hours later on the evening of 6 April he was standing for the first time on Afghan soil at Camp Bastion, the UK's major transit hub into Afghanistan. The rock star treatment had come to an abrupt and surreal end. Taylor sat in the pitch-black with his bags and had no idea where to go. There was no sign of the second advance party from 617. The Boss sat with his luggage on a hard bench in an arrivals area too basic to be called a terminal and waited.

Four hours later he was relieved to at last see some familiar faces as Tony Griffiths, SEngO Stu Clarke, Warrant Officer

Thomson, GLO Jock Adams and twenty-one Dambusters engineers came in off a long journey from the UK.

Before they could follow Chris Ball's first advance aircrew party to Kandahar they would have to complete one last bit of pre-deployment training, a Reception, Staging and Onward Integration (RSOI) programme. All new arrivals, regardless of rank, had to do RSOI to acclimatise to the heat and prepare them for going out into theatre. The tutors all had front-line experience which they passed on to those who had just arrived. Those going out beyond the wire would do an eight-day training package. Aircrew and those only working on a base would be through RSOI in two days. The programme included treatment of battlefield injuries, and counter-IED and weapons skills training. Some sessions took place in mock-ups of an Afghan village and a forward operating base.

Home to 17,000 British service personnel and civilian contractors, and with an airport as busy as Gatwick, Camp Bastion sits in the middle of a flat desert in Helmand Province. It is often engulfed in a white dust haze when it is impossible to see the horizon, mountains, trees or landmarks of any sort. Without the war there would be no reason for its being here. Even if the British have found wells and are bottling Bastion Water it is never going to match that well-known French brand. To a new arrival Bastion can seem claustrophobic and disorientating. Walled and ditched and laid out on a grid of straight tented 'streets', Camp Bastion is like a Roman outpost on Mars.

The RSOI lectures and demonstrations were a valuable introduction but Keith Taylor was itching to get to Kandahar and start work.

8

WELCOME TO KANDAHAR

6 April 2011

A big bold sign on the wall of the single-storey terminal said: 'Welcome to Kandahar Airfield'. Above it on the yellow masonry were painted the flags of the thirteen nations based there. It was late at night when Chris Ball and the 617 aircrew advance party arrived. Landing at night in Afghanistan minimised the risk of rocket attack, but the desire for safety increased the surreal nature of touching down in a very strange place and not knowing where you were in relation to anywhere else. If you were ground crew it would stay that way for the whole deployment. The only way to see Afghanistan and get real bearings on a country of shifting deserts, huge mountains and a patchwork civilisation strung along its few rivers and man-made waterways was from a cockpit.

The Dambusters filed into the interior of the KAF terminal, a series of arched cellar-like spaces. Every inch had been colonised by the bags, boots and guns of bored gum-chewing soldiers, mostly Americans, waiting to fly out. There was an immediate contrast between 617's fresh, expectant faces and these tanned and dusty troops on notice to depart or to deploy to other unfinished business. In a war that was as much about

97

the waiting as the waging, they grabbed what sleep they could or were plugging into iPods and a cultural bubble that was any place else but there.

If Afghanistan is the 'theatre' of war, Kandahar Airfield, known to all as KAF, is the stage door and the props department for the NATO-led fifty-nation International Security Assistance Force (ISAF) that is charged with bringing security and stability to a country that for hundreds of years has known little of either.

Intent on finding their bags, the 617 party could be forgiven for not noticing the blackened terminal ceilings and bullet-pocked plaster. But these were the significant blemishes of Afghanistan's recent violent history. Now known as the military arrivals and departures terminal, older hands called this building the 'Taliban's Last Stand'. It was in these low-vaulted spaces in November 2001 that Taliban fighters and their Al-Qaida allies made their final fight against the US 15th and 26th Marine Expeditionary Unit, after a massive American and British bombing campaign. A bombing campaign that launched Operation Enduring Freedom, the American response to Al-Qaida's 9/11 attacks on the World Trade Center and the Pentagon.

It was at Tarnak Farm on the edge of Kandahar Airfield – a collection of some eighty sheds, huts and offices, now largely reduced to shell and rubble and used by the ISAF as a gunnery and training range – that Osama bin Laden plotted those attacks and others. In 1998 Al-Qaida had truck-bombed US embassies in Nairobi and Tanzania, killing 223 and injuring more than 4000. In 2000 the suicide boat that rammed the United States Navy destroyer USS *Cole* as she refuelled in the Yemeni port of Aden killed seventeen American sailors and injured thirty-nine more.

Bin Laden's Afghan host was the Taliban. In 1996 it had seized the power vacuum created by the withdrawal of Soviet occupying forces and the vicious civil war that followed. It had governed Afghanistan with a zealous mix of terror and brutality, closing girls' schools, banning music, dancing and sport and turning football stadiums over to public executions.

It was also the ideal home for Al-Qaida, which had been told it was no longer welcome in its former home of Sudan. As Al-Qaida stepped up its terror campaign, the Taliban defied UN sanctions and refused to turn in for trial Osama bin Laden and the other Al-Qaida leaders who were running terrorist training camps in Afghanistan. The Taliban leaders were told repeatedly that all they had to do was surrender bin Laden and close down the training camps and Afghanistan would not be invaded.

There was no chance of the Taliban ever betraying their guest. Not only would such an action go against the Pashtunwali code of *melmastia* (hospitality), where the guest is to be respected and protected, but bin Laden, who had declared war on Jews and Christians, was also bankrolling the Taliban, led by his friend Mullah Omar.

And then came 9/11, dubbed by Al-Qaida 'The Manhattan Raid'. Bruce Riedel, a CIA officer for 30 years and now a Senior Fellow at the Brookings Institution, has said that 'it was bin Laden's dream that 9/11 would prompt the United States to invade Afghanistan', where they could be engaged in protracted guerrilla war. 'His son has told us that it was his father's dream.' A month after almost 3000 people had lost their lives in the 9/11 attacks, bin Laden had his wish. President George W. Bush ordered his armed forces to launch 'sustained, comprehensive and relentless operations' against the Al-Qaida training camps in Afghanistan, many of which were near

Kandahar City. With a population of 1.2 million, Kandahar, Afghanistan's second-largest city, just ten miles north east of Kandahar Airfield, was the spiritual home of the Taliban.

'The United States of America is an enemy of those who aid terrorists and the barbaric criminals who profane a great religion by committing murder in its name,' Bush declared, speaking from the Treaty Room of the White House. The 'War on Terror' was declared. By 7 December 2001 the Northern Alliance warlords had taken Kabul. The Taliban had retreated south to Kandahar City. From there they were driven back to the airfield and squeezed into the building where the Dambusters had just checked in, and were defeated. Fifteen days later Pashtun politician Hamid Karzai was sworn in as head of an interim power-sharing government and the process began that would lead to his becoming president.

The bullet holes of that 'victory', still visible in the walls of the terminal building at KAF, were now a decade old but as Sherard Cowper-Coles, Britain's ambassador to Afghanistan from 2007 to 2010, has said: 'The Taliban were not defeated, but simply driven from power. The floodwaters had been pushed back, but they had not been drained.' In 2003 allied eyes, particularly American and British, strayed to another war in Iraq and the Taliban began to filter back into the south of Afghanistan.

In 2011 the relentless quest for a peaceful 'solution' to Afghanistan had reached its tenth year. The costs of the largest logistics operation since the Second World War were phenomenal. According to the House of Commons Foreign Affairs Committee the UK alone spent £3.8 billion on operations in Afghanistan in 2009–10 and this was expected to rise to £4.5 billion in 2010–11 but this was dwarfed by US spending.

America's original military footprint of 2500 troops had

mushroomed to almost fifty times that size. The decade since 9/11 was also characterised by the constant and epic motion of human and mechanical military assets across a large, tough-in-every-sense country as the ISAF forces tried to win the kind of economic, governmental and military stabilisation that it and President Hāmid Karzai said was essential to make peace possible.

A decade after it had been 'overthrown' at Kandahar Airfield the Taliban were still running drugs and levying taxes on the villages to fund its war effort and punishing those who collaborated with the 'invaders'. Militarily it was out to show the Afghan people that the Karzai government would be incapable of protecting them once its ISAF allies started withdrawing its combat troops in 2014. Taliban suicide and other attacks were taking place almost daily – not just on the coalition forces but especially on local figureheads and institutions co-operating with the government. Attacks that belied the pressure the insurgents were under and were designed to undermine the credibility of a transition that was now under way to hand over security to the Afghan National Army (ANA) and the Afghan National Police (ANP).

Just weeks before 617's arrival, the Taliban had attacked the ANP Headquarters in Kandahar City with a car bomb, rocket-propelled grenades (RPGs), machine guns and suicide bombs. Fifteen policemen and four others were killed and dozens injured.

Stepping out into the night to find the transport that would take them to their accommodation, the Dambusters were greeted by the usual crush of people and trucks that is typical of any Asian airport, but nobody was selling souvenirs. The temperature had dropped to a manageable 22 degrees Celsius. After all the briefings and a rigorous training programme they

101

were as professionally prepared as it was possible to be, but apart from Chris Ball none of them had any real idea of the world they had just flown into.

Kandahar Airfield sits on an ancient dry lake 3330 feet above sea level, surrounded by jagged brown peaks. The nearest was Three Mile Mountain, beyond which lay Kandahar City. Large and sprawling KAF looked like a vast film set. *The Longest Day*, *The Dirty Dozen*, *Apocalypse Now*, *Band of Brothers*; every war movie you could think of had been rolled into one reel-to-real epic.

Even though the departure of ISAF combat troops was to start in 2014 KAF just kept on growing. It was the biggest NATO base in the world and now covered an area the size of a large county town. It had a population of 35,000, 18,000 of them American, living in tented encampments or in prefab bunk houses laid out in neat rows. When Chris Ball had been there in 2009 KAF was mostly under canvas but now a growing number of buildings were made of concrete and brick, reinforcing an impression of permanence.

KAF was also cut into neighbourhoods, each one colonised by nationality, so there was a Canadian, an American and an Australian quarter. The British area that Ballsy and the others checked into in the early hours was known as Cambridge Lines. This would be the home for the entire Squadron during its deployment and was currently occupied by 12 Squadron.

Built on a grid system it comprised row upon row of identical single-storey dormitory blocks with ridged pitched roofs which were almost the same colour as the dusty shale on which they sat. Each block house was split into twelve rooms, four to a room in bunks, with a single 'suite' of showers and toilets shared by all. A clunking air-con unit stuck out of the window of every room. The occupants of some blocks had made decking out of old pallets on which they had set up deckchairs and sunbeds. At one of the blocks to be home to 617 an old cable reel had been salvaged to serve as a table and the decking was edged with a makeshift paling fence. There was even a kelim on the floor. But the effect was more sharecropper than holiday camp.

Nearby there were rows of stiflingly hot prefab boxes topped with mushroom radar dishes. These contained phone-booths with secure lines to call the UK or computers with Internet access. Cambridge Lines also boasted a NAAFI store selling comfort food and all the supermarket essentials you would find back home alongside factor 50 sun cream and diarrhoea remedies. Across the way a coffee bar and café beamed endless sport and rock videos. And between the two was a gathering place where those off duty sat on pub benches smoking and drinking. On Saturday evenings some of the civilian girls working at KAF got dressed up almost as if they had been on a beach resort holiday in Turkey or Greece. At KAF though, the nightlife was severely limited to soft drinks, coffee, cigarettes and sandflies.

Next day the 617 advance aircrew clambered back on board a minibus to ride over to the Tornado ramp at the other end of the airfield. As the temperature rose they soon realised that the only natural colours at KAF were shades of brown and light grey under a sheer blue sky and scorching sun. There were some trees but their green leaves were filmed with white dust making them look bleached and tired.

Convoys of sand-coloured, supersized, heavily-armoured US combat and transport vehicles with darkened slit windows and gun turrets rumbled slowly on huge tyres through ad hoc streets, some metalled and others of compacted shale. Other troops rode around the airfield in battered Japanese pick-ups, Land Rovers, elderly buses and trucks in an endless 20 mph procession – a speed limit that was enforced by traffic police and governed by traffic lights and speed bumps – that stirred up clouds of fine abrasive dust that got everywhere, even places one would not want to go with a dual-cyclone vacuum cleaner.

Roads and living compounds were hemmed in with towering, muscular reinforced concrete blast walls and wire mesh and hessian Hesco bastions, filled with rubble and stacked two high, the ubiquitous building block of military fortification that had spread across Afghanistan. These divided KAF into a patchwork of sectors and compartments – each with its rectangular reinforced concrete blast shelters – to contain the effects of mortar and rocket attacks. Heavy looms of black power cable festooned and draped the rooflines, threatening to snap the wooden poles that bore the load. Every surface, flat roof, every spare foot of space was covered in white satellite dishes, red and white radio pylons, oil drums, pallets of bottled water and powerful portable arc-light stands that buzzed and blitzed out white light at night.

And all the while there was the constant hum from thousands of generators that played against the shrill power of fast jets streaking off the runway. Swarms of helicopters speeding low over KAF, US marine legs dangling out of their open doors, cast shadows like black metal insects.

On the ground troops roved in gaggles around the narrow streets. The contrasting camouflage patterns of American, Canadian, Australian, British, French, Estonian, Belgian, Italian, Turkish and Bulgarian troops merged into a mobile military mosaic. Not forgetting the fighting forces of many other smaller ISAF nations including Albania, Georgia, Latvia, Tonga, the Former Republic of Macedonia and nine soldiers from the Grand Duchy of Luxembourg.

Then there was a substantial supporting army of thousands of civilian security contractors, cooks, canteen workers, carpenters, cleaners, drivers, builders, computer doctors, communications consultants, fuel station operatives and others who underpinned the logistic enterprise and the daily grind. Many of them were from developing countries such as Bangladesh, Sri Lanka and Nepal come to ply their trades in a climatically inhospitable place where the temperature soared past 42 degrees Celsius in the summer and scorching winds whipped up fog-like dust-storms that turned day into night. Everybody developed short, abrasive coughs. In winter it fell to five below zero. The rains came and the dust turned to mud.

And through it all, in all weathers and at all hours of the day and the night, groups of joggers, mostly American, padded around dustbowl streets that had self-consciously reassuring names like All American Blvd.

Compared to the front line, KAF was paradise.

KAF was no longer a camp like Bastion. It was an international town fast-tracking its way to becoming a garrison city. All languages were spoken but the war from missiles to lunch menus was always fought in English.

The aircraft ramps were forever being extended. Another helicopter pad was almost complete. Yet more watchtowers appeared along its security perimeter overnight, peering down on Sniper Alley. There were now thirty-six of them girdling the base. They were reminiscent of those that used to dot the landscape of Northern Ireland and were a statement of security for those inside KAF and of renewed intent to those looking to attack this alien high-tech stockade, which seemed to have landed like a UFO in the middle of a barely changing agricultural landscape.

The wave upon wave of steel, ramped earth bunds, concrete, concertina razor wire and anti-vehicle bollards stood in stark contrast to the seemingly tranquil wheat fields and mud-brick compounds, beyond which the inhabitants of KAF could see but where they would never walk. It was from these rustic acres the previous August that a six-man Taliban suicide squad armed with bombs and rockets had tried unsuccessfully to breach the wire on a tractor. KAF was surrounded by a substantial Ground Defence Area to protect incoming and departing air traffic, which was patrolled by ISAF troops armed with early-warning devices and enough weaponry to eliminate the threat of attack as far as possible. But even so some rockets still managed to make it inside the base every month.

The 617 advance party drove past hundreds of ISO steel shipping containers stacked two high, another signature KAF 'sight'. Blue, red and yellow, these were the only colours to be had on the airfield. Emptied and unwanted they had been formed into further defensive walls. Some had had holes jagged into them by insurgent rockets. The container mountain was added to daily by the highly decorated 'jingly' Pakistani and Afghan trucks that shipped in the water, food, fuel, medical supplies, vehicles, and everything else that could not be sourced locally, to sustain those at KAF who every month consumed some 1400 tonnes of food and more than 30 million gallons of water.

The four main supply lines were long and could be dangerous – some ran through Pakistan and others through central Asia. In 2010, 136 NATO tankers were destroyed in 56 insurgent attacks in Baluchistan, Pakistan's largest province – mainly by ambushes and IEDs – resulting in the deaths of 34 drivers.

On the southern edge of the main runway, which was like a frenetic catwalk of aviation hardware, the Dambusters drove past a curved building with nine fan-shaped roofs. This was the terminal of Kandahar International Airport. It was originally constructed by the Americans in the late Fifties as a refuelling stop for piston-driven aircraft. The advent of the jet rendered it largely forgotten until December 1999, when Indian Airlines Flight 814 was hijacked and forced to land on the airfield. The terminal had been badly damaged during the Soviet occupation and then by the Taliban, but it had been somewhat restored since.

With a lick of paint it would have looked like something plucked out of the 1950s Florida Keys. Instead it was drab and mostly deserted beyond being home to a few elderly civilian aircraft belonging to airlines no one had heard of, flying to places nobody wanted to go.

Fifteen minutes after leaving Cambridge Lines the 617 advance party pulled into a large compound of single-storey buildings at the north of the airfield, opposite a cement and concrete works that was churning out reinforced blast walls around the clock. The temperature and the dust were already at their worst. An RAF Ensign hung limply in the stiff dry heat from a flagstaff at the compound gate. The Dambusters had arrived at the headquarters of 904 Expeditionary Air Wing (EAW). Its job was to provide logistical and technical support – from water, food and accommodation to fuel, oils and lubricants, weapons and parts – and overall command for the RAF assets based at Kandahar, including the Tornado and Hercules fleets.

Outside 904's main wing there stood a line of large replicas of the badges of the Tornado squadrons that had served at Kandahar since 2009. This was to be the Dambusters' home for the next three months.

Those on 617 with an interest in history, of which there were many, were intrigued to discover that the RAF's involvement in Afghanistan was nothing new. In the Third Anglo-Afghan War – which lasted for three months in 1919 and was about reaffirming the border between Afghanistan, then an emirate, and a British India that was suspicious of Russia's intentions in the region – the newly-formed Royal Air Force bombed Kabul. A raid on the royal palace undermined Afghan morale and brought the king to an armistice. Such was the potential of air power that the British also used fighters and light bombers to carry out aggressive punitive raids against rebellious tribes in what was then the North West Frontier of India, now Pakistan. It was called Imperial Air Policing and it continued right up to the Partition of India and Pakistan in 1947.

As 617's advance party of pilots and navigators flinched at the heat, coughed back dust and prepared to fly familiarisation missions with 12 Squadron, their brief did not include the words aggressive or punitive.

9

NAILING THE ENEMY

8 April 2011

In every Tornado Force handover at KAF the advance aircrew party from the arriving squadron would fly their first sorties with those they were replacing. So the newly arrived 617 pilots would fly with navigators from 12 Squadron, and 617 navigators would back-seat with pilots from 12. This was the tried and tested way for new-in-theatre crew to get to know the airspace and the battlespace quickly from those who were fully up to speed. They could then pass on their newly acquired operational expertise to the rest of the Squadron when it arrived.

Every day in theatre, 617 would be expected to fly a number of close air support (CAS) sorties, responding to the daily air tasking orders (ATOs) issued by the CAOC at Al-Udeid. The Dawn Patrol would be followed by the Champagne Wave, late morning and into the afternoon, and then the Night Watch. In addition the Squadron would have to provide two jets, cocked and ready to go, for ground close air support (GCAS) every day, to go to the aid of troops in contact. Sorties could last for a number of hours with air-to-air refuelling. The strain on the engineers to have eight jets available in any 24-hour period would be immense.

As somebody about to fly his third operational tour in Afghanistan it was fitting that Squadron Leader Chris Ball was to be the first Dambuster to fly a mission on Herrick 14. Sporting the shadow of a 'lucky' Zapata-style moustache, he stepped into the kitting room and strapped his anti-G trousers over his flying suit. G is a unit measuring the inertial stress on a body undergoing rapid acceleration or, as Robert K. Wilcox put it in his book *Black Aces High*, 'One G can feel like 180 pounds on the body; six Gs, like a crushing half ton.' GR4 pilots would regularly pull around 4Gs at 500 knots (575 mph). The Space Shuttle crew during launch and re-entry would pull 3Gs. Not really trousers at all, and sometimes called 'speed jeans', anti-G trousers were to a novice a bewildering puzzle of flaps, straps and Velcro fastenings, attached to a long flexible tube which would be connected to the jet once in the cockpit. Wrapped around Chris Ball's legs they would inflate with air fed from a G-sensitive valve in the aircraft and squeeze them tight during high acceleration. This would prevent his blood draining from his head to his feet. Blood pooling in the lower parts of the body would starve his brain and cause temporary hypoxia leading to a 'greyout' where his vision would dim, followed by tunnel vision, blackout, G-induced loss of consciousness (G-LOC) and finally, if the G-forces were not reduced, death.

Kitting up alongside Ballsy was 12 Squadron navigator Squadron Leader Carl 'Wiz' Wilson, who was equally experienced. Even though they were the senior of the two crews flying this two-ship sortie it was another rule that Ball would be wingman and not lead the pair (pair's lead) on his first outing. Leading the mission was Flight Lieutenant Guy Lefroy of 12 Squadron with 617 navigator Flight Lieutenant Jane Pickersgill in his back seat. Once 12 had handed over to 617 Ball and Pickersgill would then pair up as a crew.

Twenty-six-year-old Pickersgill, who had joined the Air Force in 2005, was one of the strongest characters among the junior aircrew. A forthright Mancunian who had studied law at Durham, she said: 'I like to think I stand my ground in the cockpit. You must be professional and prove yourself in the same way as any junior guy on the squadron will have to prove themselves. As long as you get a reputation for being able to do the job I don't think it really matters what sex you are.' She was now about to do that job and was visibly excited.

With the pockets of their anti-G trousers bulging with mission documents, wearing high-collared life vests, and Sig Sauer 9 mm pistols tucked into their shoulder holsters, Ball and Wilson and Lefroy and Pickersgill looked bulky and wide-legged as they walked down a long, low corridor, helmets in one hand and clutching their mission boxes, containing video cassettes and sortie software to be plugged into the jet, in the other.

They took a right doorway into the engineers' room. At Kandahar the aircrew and the engineers were all in the same building. The two crews made their way through a world of technical wallcharts and whiteboards divided up into the different engineering trade areas by desks, filing cabinets and computer screens. They stopped at a chest-high counter where they pored over a big thick ledger of different coloured forms that detailed their jet's maintenance and service history, and recorded its previous sorties and any snags that needed fixing but were not flight critical.

Known as the 'Aircraft 700', the ledger also detailed the weapons the Tornado was carrying for this upcoming mission, the number of rounds in the jet's gun, the surveillance and targeting pods on the aircraft and its take-off fuel load.

Satisfied that the aircraft was fit to fly, they signed the 700, 'taking ownership' of their Tornado from the engineers, then left the building by a rear door. Their boots hit the thick, black rubberised walkway that had been laid over the dust and shale to prevent them walking foreign object debris (FOD) on to the ramp, which could be sucked up into the air intakes of a Tornado's jet engine and cripple it.

Sixty metres further on they walked through a big steel gate in the high Hesco-bastion wall that protected the ramp. Eight large canvas versions of the HAS, known as Rapid Erect Shelters (RES), stood over the Tornados like a line of vast bonnets, shielding them from the sun and the heat as the engineers and armourers went about their work.

Already the heat was up in the high thirties and climbing. The burning rays bouncing off the swept-clean concrete cranked it up another ten degrees.

'Here we go,' said Wilson as they reached their jet.

'Super,' said Ballsy, using a favourite Ballsy word. He was up for it. Felt perky. The work-up training at Lossiemouth had been as testing as it had been thorough, but however good the flying in cockpit and simulator, nothing was quite the same as putting all that knowledge and all those flying hours into a live operation. Also, he had not sat in a cockpit for a week; this was a very long time for a fast jet pilot to be earth-bound. A squadron flying programme was relentless and addictive. The fix needed to be frequent. When you hit the right tempo life was great.

Chris Ball slipped on his soft black leather flying gloves. The pre-mission brief was fresh in his ears. Their task was to fly 264 miles northwest of Kabul to Bal Chiragh district, Faryab province, just 30 miles from the border with Turkmenistan, and provide support and armed over-watch to a Norwegian patrol that was clearing insurgents out of valleys. Over the last week it had been repeatedly targeted by 'shoot-and-scoot' small-arms fire.

It was airspace Chris Ball had flown in his Strike Eagle with the Rocketeers and he was keen to get back. And with the RAF shrinking in size the way it was he knew that the odds of him getting another operational flying tour were getting longer. He was also keenly aware that he was only going to get to fly half of 617's detachment, because he had been posted to a desk-bound ground tour at Air Command, High Wycombe – ironically being given the job of allocating young flying officers and flight lieutenants to fast jet cockpits.

He climbed the steel boarding steps to the cockpit of the jet, stepped in, slid down and was strapped in tight and connected into the aircraft's communications and life support systems by one of the lineys. He put his helmet and oxygen mask on and was soon into his stride with the lead liney over the intercom as they went through the final checks prior to the see-off.

Fifteen minutes after the canopy went down over his head and with a final thumbs up to the ground crew Ballsy moved his jet out into the punishing glare, pulled down his sun visor and followed the lead jet down the flight line of towering reinforced concrete blast walls, which protected the Tornado ramp, and out on to the taxiway.

As they waited their turn in a string of aircraft of every type and nationality to go to the head of the runway Ballsy realised that the airfield was even busier than it had been on his last visit to Kandahar. The right-hand side was a vast park and ride for transport planes. Hercules, C17 Globemasters and Russian Antonovs sat in neat dark rows like big steel whales. Their rear doors were opened aloft and their ramps were down, as forklifts unloaded and loaded pallets piled with kitbags and sacks and sturdy crates containing engines, spare parts, ammunition and the nuts and bolts and grease of war. More bombs for the Brits at KAF had come down on the 'bang run' from Bastion. Troops and civilians were ferried out to the airfield in elderly Afghan buses with dusty curtains to board the Hercules 'thumper flight' to Bastion and then on up to Kabul.

Although the front-line fighting was being done on the ground there was no doubting the role that air power still played in transporting, supporting and protecting ISAF and Afghan Army troops and removing insurgents from the battle space. That is why Kandahar Airfield had become the world's busiest single-runway airport with 400 aircraft and more than 5300 military flights a week landing on and leaving its 10,000-foot runway.

There were sixty different types of aircraft based at KAF and around the clock at any one moment the taxiway was a plane spotter's paradise as French Mirages, Belgian F-16s, American F-18 Hornets and A-10C Thunderbolts, British Tornados and high-flying RAF Sentinel surveillance planes waited in line for air traffic control to slot them into the gaps of a similar cast coming in to land. And then there were the insect-like remotely-controlled unmanned aerial vehicles (UAVs) – American Predators and British RAF Reapers that were flown via satellite by the drone pilots of 39 Squadron.

It was not something that appealed to a fast jet pilot like Chris Ball. He trusted his abilities to 'put a warhead on the forehead' with as much precision as the remote-control jockeys.

Sealed and detached inside his cockpit he observed this relentless activity in mute as he edged closer down the taxiway to take-off. Apache helicopter gunships sped across the airfield and out beyond the wire while on the runway the noise and dust built in layers with every fixed-wing take-off into the cloudless blue sky of southern Afghanistan.

In minutes Ballsy would be joining the world's biggest military air show. He made a final check that his flaps were in the right place, that everything was ready for the take-off roll. The lead Tornado shot off down the runway. Ballsy switched to the control tower frequency and moved his Tornado into position.

'Ready for take-off,' he said.

Thirty seconds later, as the lead Tornado left the ground, the control tower came to him. A reassuring American voice: 'Runway full-length clear for take-off.'

'Roger. Take-off.'

His afterburners flame-grilling the engines, Chris Ball hammered his Tornado down 10,000 feet of tarmac. At around 177 knots he pulled his stick back. Ten knots later, at just over 215 mph, he was airborne. Pulling into a steep climb he tucked his wheels neatly into their wells.

The first sortie flown by a Dambuster on Herrick 14 was successfully away.

Although he had left a scene of hyperactivity behind him on the ground, Squadron Leader Ball now faced the challenge of the choreographed maelstrom that was Afghan airspace.

The airspace over Afghanistan is stacked high with aircraft: rotary, fixed-wing, fast jet, transport, manned and unmanned. In areas like Helmand and Bagram, where the fighting and troop movements on the ground are traditionally the most intense, air traffic can resemble half a dozen M25s stacked one above the other. But the traffic does not move in a circular motion and leaving one height for another, or moving to adjoining major 'roads', requires precision timing by air traffic controllers and pilots, because there are no fixed exit junctions either laterally or vertically.

To ensure that ISAF troops on the ground are supported from the air as effectively as possible and that insurgents are targeted accurately, the coalition has divided Afghanistan's map into a navigational grid known as Kill Boxes. A three-dimensional area used to facilitate the integration of joint fires, the Kill Box area reference system works by ensuring that attack helicopters and fast jets can be routed to troops on the ground as quickly as possible. It also enables the various air traffic agencies that control different parts of the airspace to clear an area of unnecessary traffic when air assets are supporting troops in contact with insurgents by declaring a restricted operating zone (ROZ). If rockets or mortars are being fired navigational areas will be sealed off to avoid hitting friendly aircraft.

At any one time it is possible that over a single area air traffic controllers would be working with two Tornados, four American A-10s, two Belgian F-16s, a couple of French Mirages, an unmanned RAF Reaper and an RAF Sentinel plane all stacked one above the other at various altitudes. At all times there are scores of jets racing to the refuelling tankers, which fly in large fixed ovals like American IndyCar tracks. These are known as 'towlines' and are as busy as motorway service stations with thirsty aircraft arriving at ten-minute intervals to load on tonnes of gas while flying 20 to 30 feet behind tankers at 280 knots (322 mph).

The language of war becomes even more vivid with a cast of JTACs and their call-signs. It was these that the Dambusters flying in Ballsy's slipstream would have to deal with when flying around Afghanistan. They would be 617's principal point of contact with the battle space.

Such is the competing traffic over Afghanistan, and ever-changing troop demands on the ground, that transiting from one Kill Box to another or from one altitude to another was never as straightforward as transiting from A to B. It might only take minutes to get from A to B, but for fast jet pilots and their navigators it was a high-precision, high-tension commute to work.

Now he was into an airspace described with some understatement by Rocksy Sharrocks as 'very, very busy and very complicated', Squadron Leader Chris Ball realised he had lost sight of his lead aircraft. The radio traffic moved around as fast as the assets in the sky; all talking at once on every frequency in every accent known to man. *Holy shit! I've been airborne less than a minute and this is not going well.* Ball was *only* half a minute behind the lead Tornado, but that was still two miles away and with the sun dazzling high in the sky a Tornado was a difficult dot to see. The Tornado does not have a data link to lock on to the lead jet and he had also missed a couple of radio calls confirming its position. This was not super at all. His navigator came to his aid.

'Ballsy, no worries,' Wilson said. 'It's like this the first time for everyone.'

It didn't stop Ballsy, with all his experience of flying fast jets in Afghanistan, feeling embarrassed. 'For the first five minutes I was a clatter of bits.'

He was not alone. Sitting in the back seat of the lead jet navigator Jane Pickersgill, strong character notwithstanding, spent the first ten minutes of the sortie 'feeling like I was clinging on to the tail fin, just making sure that every switch was in an eye-pleasing fashion. The radios were really, really busy.'

Back in Scotland if you were holding Scottish Military on one radio and a chat frequency on the other, negotiating airspace was easy. Pickersgill knew which air traffic agency she had to contact to clear their route up to Kabul and beyond, but she didn't know how it would work in practice.

'Don't worry about it,' Lefroy reassured her. 'In two trips it will be easy.'

Five minutes into the sortie Ball caught up with Pickersgill's jet. At 350 knots (400 mph) he swung his wings back to 45 degrees. Cruising at 18,000 feet the terrain beneath him had changed from desert to high hills. Ahead lay the snow-capped mountains that marked the start of the great Hindu Kush, the 500-mile mountain range stretching from central Afghanistan to Pakistan, reaching more than 25,000 feet at its highest point. As the altitude increased the air thinned, making the Tornado's engines work harder. The radio traffic had quietened right down but as the distance from air traffic control centres stretched out behind them communications signals began to drift in and out and the Tornados had to radio-relay messages via a tanker. At 3.15, one hour and fifteen minutes after leaving Kandahar, both Tornados had reached their destination Kill Box.

It was Pickersgill who first established contact with the Norwegian JTAC with Telemark Battalion, a motorised infantry unit. Telemark was based in Maymana, the capital of Faryab province, which straddles Highway A7. A7 loops and winds from Mazar-e-Sharif in the east to Herat in the west, where it joins Highway 1 to form a ring road encircling the country, first built by the Soviet Union in the 1960s.

Ensuring security along the ring road and the communities alongside it was a crucial strategic challenge for ISAF and as part of that endeavour Telemark Battalion was working with the Afghan National Army to drive insurgents out of a narrow steep valley in Bal Chiragh district. Although ethnically diverse, Faryab is the only one of Afghanistan's thirty-four provinces to have a majority Uzbek population. It is a poor state reliant on agriculture, fruit growing and livestock, where politics has often been a power contest between rival warlords, resulting in violent clashes between their militias.

The ensuing lack of security had allowed the Taliban back into most districts of Faryab from which they had been driven following their fall from power. Now they were killing village elders and pro-government politicians who resisted their tax collecting, as well as Norwegian and Lithuanian soldiers. They were also trying to wrest the opium and heroin smuggling routes from the warlords.

Just four days before this combined 617 and 12 Squadron sortie two American soldiers had been shot dead by a 'rogue' Afghan border policeman they had been training in a base in Faryab.

More than five thousand feet above sea level, Bal Chiragh district is a mixture of mountains and hilly grasslands. The Norwegian patrol of fifteen men and vehicles had been trying to get to a forward operating base (FOB) when it had come under more small-arms fire.

'Please look at the caves along the valley for hotspots,' the Telemark JTAC asked Jane Pickersgill. As they flew a route at 16,000 feet over the south side of the valley she looked through her LITENING targeting pod but all she spotted was a man moving a flock of sheep. The Tornado carried on with its sweep.

Chris Ball was flying over-watch on the north side. Beneath him on the valley floor was the familiar Afghan dense honey-comb of houses and barns hidden behind high mud-walled and gated compounds. It was only possible to see inside them from the air, which is why eyes in the sky were so important to troops on the ground.

Just after 4 p.m. Wilson spotted a man on his own walking along a high ridge. Every so often he paused to look down into the valley. He had no animals and he wasn't on a footpath to anywhere. Then he stopped and pulled something out from his pocket.

'Looks like he's talking on a mobile phone,' Wilson said and passed the coordinates for the man's position, generated by the targeting pod, to the JTAC on a secure frequency.

'He's setting up some guys along the valley to attack us,' the JTAC told Wilson. 'Small arms and mortars. There could be as many as seven of them.'

An intelligence picture was building fast. The man up on the ridge was an insurgent commander.

'We've got him on our optics,' the JTAC told the jet. 'We think he's carrying a long-barrelled weapon.'

Ball and Wilson followed the man along the ridge with their pod. Even though he was wearing baggy dark clothes they could now see the gun. Whatever it was, it was no farmer's rifle.

It was 4.10 p.m. Whether they went forward or back the Norwegians were trapped in a valley with no cover.

The JTAC called Chris Ball's Tornado: 'We'd like to strike this guy. What do you recommend?'

'We recommend Brimstone,' Ball said.

A Paveway IV would have done the job just as well because the man was all on his own up a mountain so there was no danger of collateral damage, but Ball still wanted the pinpoint precision that the Brimstone offered.

Just under six feet long, the supersonic Brimstone entered service with RAF Tornados at the end of 2005 and was originally used in Iraq to take out tanks and self-propelled guns such as howitzers with its tandem high-explosive warhead. The front charge would explode the armour and clear a path for the main charge to penetrate it with a high-explosive anti-tank jet dart. Early in 2009 it was introduced to Afghanistan in an upgraded Dual Mode Seeker version, specifically designed to hit smaller targets like insurgents on foot, on motorbikes or in pick-up trucks. It could also destroy a Taliban gunman or IED emplacer lurking in a compound, but leave the compound completely intact. At £175,000 a pop it was the perfect counter-insurgency weapon.

'Are we going laser or dual?' Wilson asked.

At the flick of a button the Brimstone could either be guided by a laser fired on to the target by the pod or a combination of laser and radar. For a fast-moving target, like a vehicle travelling at 40 mph, or in bad weather and at night when visibility was poor, the Brimstone would be told to go dual. It would leave the jet locked on to a laser beam but homing in on the target it would switch to its millimetric wave radar seeker, allowing even greater accuracy, unaffected by battlefield smoke, dust, chaff or flares.

Ball went for laser. 'The guy himself is not a big radar reflector but the rocks around him are.'

He did not want to risk hitting the rocks and not making a clean kill. On laser alone the missile would be delivered with pin-point accuracy.

'First we have to do the 9-Line,' Ball told the JTAC.

While the Telemark JTAC worked through the CAS Briefing Form with his field commander the unseen Tornado kept tabs on the man through its LITENING pod. Every time he moved the pod generated new coordinates that were fed into the missile. When it launched it would automatically go to the newest coordinate. Even if he started running along the ridge he could never move fast enough to get out of the way.

Staying in the wheel he was flying Ball began to do calculations in his head on how best to deliver the Brimstone. The ridge ran east to west so it would be best to tip in and run in from the west and drop the missile. That way he'd get good sight of both sides of the ridge as well as the top. If they came in from the north and the man stepped behind a rock down the south side or sat behind the sun, they would lose good sight of him. *You don't want to take a second shot; you want to do it right first time.*

At 4.20 Telemark's JTAC came back with the 9-Line complete.

There was no doubt that the commander on the ridge was embarked on a hostile act and posed an immediate threat to life.

Ball took his Tornado around in a gentle bank around his wheel to avoid masking the pod's camera with his wing. 'Okay,' he told Wilson, 'coming in from the west we are going to shoot and come off slightly to the right to the south so we get a good look in for firing.' He tipped out from the wheel and called the other jet. 'In. Hot. 090 degrees.'

There was no response. Over a crackling chat frequency by which the two jets were communicating it sounded as though the other was still trying to clear airspace.

Shit! Ball repeated: 'In. Hot.' he repeated, '090 degrees.'

He was now midway to the target and about to enter the bracket from where the missile would have to be launched. He had seconds to make a decision.

The other Dambuster jet was not responding.

'Coming off dry!' He had had no choice but to abort.

Pickersgill's Tornado was still trying to clear airspace with air traffic back at Camp Bastion but having to do so via radio-relay, which was taking an age.

Chris Ball's jet had the insurgent commander on its pod. He was still talking on his phone to his gunmen lower down the hill.

Jane Pickersgill's voice came on. Airspace over the target was now confirmed as clear.

'Okay,' Ball said, 'we'll teardrop round then spin back and come in east to west.'

Wilson agreed.

Running a few miles around Ball got into position, but then he looked down at the multi-function display screen between his knees and saw the images that his navigator was also seeing through the LITENING pod.

'The dude has moved on to the wrong side of the ridge.'

Ball was happy with the way he had set everything up. He was pretty certain he could have shot and come off left and it would have worked. One squeeze on the stick and the Brimstone would be on its way. But it just wasn't the nice clean picture that he wanted.

'It doesn't look good.'

He felt the adrenaline going. His pulse was racing. 'Hey, Wiz, let's give ourselves a moment.'

He aborted the second attempt.

Even though the seconds were ticking by Chris Ball was still flying at nine miles a minute. There was no time pressure. The insurgent commander had no idea the jet was above him and that he was as clear as polished glass on the pod which was feeding the Brimstone with updated coordinates every time he took a step. Down on the valley floor the JTAC was watching the same real-time video footage from the Tornado on his laptop with increasing anticipation.

Conscious that this was his very first sortie, Chris Ball was determined to get it right. Like most fast jet pilots he wanted it effective but not ugly. Their scramble mindset was 'slow is smooth, smooth is quick'. He wanted to keep it smooth and quick and keep that professional edge to it.

His pulse had slowed again. The commander was not aiming his weapon and even if he had started running down from the ridge to attack, Ball could still get into position fast enough for the Brimstone to get to him before he got within range of the Norwegian patrol.

'I'm going to wheel around to the north and re-attack from the west to the east.'

Wilson agreed.

At 4.28 p.m. their Tornado was in place. The other was now in over-watch; the lead jet taking a supporting role.

At 4.29 Squadron Leader Ball was happy to hit the gas. 'In. Hot. 090 degrees.'

This time there was no chatter on the radios. Inside the cockpit it was quiet; the engines behind them were barely audible. The only sensation of speed was the huge thrust of the jet that the crew felt in their backs, forcing them through the air. The anti-G trousers were squeezing their legs hard.

Just over three miles from the target. The commander stood back on top of the ridge. He was animated, talking again on his mobile, as though he was issuing final orders.

Chris Ball had his jet in a nice, easy approach.

At two point nine miles the laser locked on to the commander.

'Target captured,' Wilson said.

A dot appeared on Chris Ball's head-up display (HUD) screen.

This time Squadron Leader Ball instinctively knew that everything was right. At medium height he calmly squeezed the pickle button (trigger) on his stick and the 110 lb Brimstone sped from its rack underneath the jet at 1400 mph. Ball pulled the stick hard right and instantly put the Tornado into a steep turn.

Twenty seconds later down on the ridge the insurgent commander half turned his head as if he had heard something. He had. It was the sound of his impending demise.

The weapon impacted at 4.30 p.m. and 55 seconds.

The whole event had been recorded on the cockpit video and was being watched simultaneously by the JTAC. Now robbed of their leader, the insurgents cut and ran. The Telemark Battalion patrol was safe.

The JTAC called Chris Ball's jet. 'Thank you, thank you,' he said. 'You make me happy as a child.'

Before heading back Ball flew another sweep of the valley and saw six or seven men running down the mountainside, but they disappeared into a cave before he could get a decent fix on them. Wilson gave the coordinates to the JTAC. The Norwegians were on their way up there.

Ball landed back at Kandahar tired but elated, because 617's footprint was now planted on the map of Afghanistan. He paused to have a picture taken with Wiz, kneeling under their jet by the empty Brimstone rack with job-well-done grins on their faces. As Ballsy walked back from the ramp, 617's weapons instructor rushed out from the Squadron building towards him, grabbed the cockpit video and ran back inside with it. Ball and Wilson entered the engineers' room to be greeted enthusiastically by the engineers. As they signed the Tornado back into the Aircraft 700 book, adding in their mission details, there was particular professional satisfaction among the armourers, who liked to see jets come back with less than they went out with.

Ball took off his gear, hung up his helmet and went to the ops room, where he wrote a mission report (MISREP) which would be filed with the CAOC. This short summary had to be submitted for every single sortie within twenty-five minutes of the wheels coming down. Because there had been a weapons drop this would have to be followed by a more detailed significant report (SINCREP) and a weapons release form. Within the next twenty-four hours the relevant sections of the sortie video showing the deployment of the Brimstone would also be sent to the CAOC for review and scrutiny. There would also be video from the Tornado showing damage assessment of where the Brimstone had taken out the insurgent commander. Telemark's JTAC would also have submitted his MISREP to the CAOC describing how he went through the 9-Line process and justifying, in accordance with the rules of engagement, why he had called for the missile to be dropped.

By the time Chris Ball got to watch his cockpit video the weapons instructor had scrutinised it forensically five times.

Chris Ball and his navigator waited for the weapons instructor's critique and verdict. QWIs always liked to find one criticism of a sortie. Apart from suggesting that the sequence in which they had decided whether the missile would be launched laser or dual was a little clunky, it was, he smiled, 'a pretty good textbook attack'.

Chris Ball's conscience had been clear from the instant he had pickled the Brimstone.

'Me and Wiz are a bit old and bold and we were pretty confident with what we had done.'

The post-mission intelligence confirmed beyond doubt, and in the clinical bleached-out language demanded by post-bombing assessment, that the man on the ridge was able and about to take out a complete ISAF patrol.

Ballsy put it the Ballsy way: 'He was a bad dude who would no longer be spreading his badness around.'

10

ON THE MOVE

Late in the evening of 9 April the bulk of 617 Squadron boarded buses at RAF Lossiemouth. Joining the families to see them off was Josh Thompson. He wanted to support his mates but he was feeling a mixture of sadness and frustration that he was unable to join them in theatre. He stepped on to the aircrew bus, shook hands and said: 'Good luck. I hope to see you soon.' And then he stood there with the wives, girlfriends and children, feeling as empty and alone as they were as the Dambusters drove away out of RAF Lossiemouth to nearby RAF Kinloss to catch a flight down to RAF Brize Norton.

Flight Lieutenant Ollie Moncrieff took a shorter route having spent his last evening eating dinner with his parents near Bicester in Oxfordshire, a short drive from RAF Brize Norton. It was a pleasant evening but he could tell that his parents were tense. It had still not sunk in that inside twenty-four hours he would be in Afghanistan.

Twenty-eight-year-old Moncrieff had attended the same school as Guy Gibson and Douglas Bader, St Edward's, Oxford, and that had inspired him to join the RAF and fly fast jets. Commercial flying was of no interest. As he went through training the desire to join Gibson's old squadron grew stronger. He made it and during his first week with the Dambusters he attended a 617 reunion dinner at Woodhall Spa where Richard Todd, who had played Guy Gibson in the film *The Dam Busters*, was guest of honour. But movies could never convey the inner feelings of going to war. As Moncrieff left the pretty Cotswold town of Carterton behind him and drove through the Brize Norton gates it finally hit him that this was for real.

In the early hours of 10 April Keith Taylor and the engineering advance party boarded a Hercules at Camp Bastion for the 50-minute flight over to Kandahar. After two nights sleeping in a bunkhouse right next to a 24-hour helicopter pad Keith Taylor was not going to miss the claustrophobia of Bastion. As a squadron boss he was given a jump seat in the cockpit of the Hercules. They were airborne as dawn broke. A burning orange sun burst suddenly out of the half-light. Taylor felt his excitement and anticipation rise as the yellow and brown landscape of southern Afghanistan – parched desert earth with shards of green where water supported crops, people and their livestock – rolled out flat in front of him. Now he felt that he had actually arrived somewhere.

Four and a half hours behind Afghan time the rest of his squadron had hunkered down on benches and floors for a broken night's sleep at RAF Brize Norton before boarding a charter jet for a seven-hour flight to Al Minhad Air Base in the UAE.

The RAF outpost at Minhad, run by the 901 Expeditionary Air Wing, is a critical hub for coalition/ISAF partners in Afghanistan, including the Australians, Dutch, Canadians, Brits and New Zealanders.

After a ten-hour wait in a prefab transit lounge well away from the commercial terminal and sustained by anaemic coffee and sandwiches, the Dambusters and a large contingent from

3 Commando Brigade and The Rifles boarded the rear ramp of a C17 Globemaster for the two-hour flight to Camp Bastion. The interior of the heavy-lift C17 – which could carry three Apache helicopters or thirteen Land Rovers – was like a massive furniture truck with hanging straps, webbing and anchor points. Cargo and luggage was stashed at the rear on pallets under nets and scores of passengers were either squeezed into tight lateral rows or down each side of the aircraft. The pre-flight at-seat service consisted of ear plugs to dull the noise of four powerful engines and cans of fizzy drink. There was no movie. They passed the time chatting, listening to music or reading, but then about an hour out of Camp Bastion airfield there was a speaker announcement.

'Put on your helmets and body armour.'

They had been told that this would happen. They struggled into their armour and hitched helmet straps under their chins and then the cabin lights went out. All that could be seen in the dim orange glow of the emergency floor lighting were the silhouettes of row after row of helmets poking above seatbacks. All talking had stopped. This really was it. There was only the thrum of the engines to accompany their thoughts on what was the longest hour of a very long journey.

'All I could think about when they turned all the lights off was that we were going to land in something like the Vietnam War,' Joe Hourston confided later to Lucy Williams. Sitting in the darkened aircraft, next to his fiancé Caroline Day, navigator Jon Overton fully realised for the first time that he was going somewhere particularly unpleasant and that the lights were out to minimise the risk of being shot at. It made it worse that he could not see out.

'Aircrew always have a window to look out of but there were no windows and it was pretty much pitch-black. It was really quiet, noticeably quiet; people were not talking to each other. Everybody's mind was focused but we were a very inexperienced squadron. Nobody but the Execs and some of the engineers had been on ops before.'

Flight Lieutenant Alex Hutchison, 29, who would be flying with Overton, could not help his thoughts straying to his four-month-old twin sons back in Elgin who had been born prematurely just before Christmas.

'It was hard to leave them,' Hutch admitted. 'They are fine now but they are demanding boys. I think my wife Nicola [a primary school teacher] is going to be working a lot harder than I am. If I can I will phone every day.'

Hutch had 'nibbled' repeatedly at a former 617 boss to get on the Squadron. He had been a Dambuster for three years with more than a thousand hours on the clock and had done his tactical weapons training with the Canadian Air Force at a NATO flying training school in Cold Lake, Alberta.

'It's the pinnacle for a fast jet pilot,' he said.

Hutch was not alone in thinking that. The aircrew, and the majority of the engineers, were Dambusters first and last; not merely fast jet crew and engineers.

The Squadron flew on inside their big tube of darkness and when the C17's massive wheels lurched down on to the runway and the ramp was lowered they walked out into darkness. It was one o'clock in the morning of 11 April. Their journey into Afghanistan was like Alice falling down the rabbit hole and emerging somewhere that was very strange indeed. The only illumination on this new alien world came from the lights of big forklifts that were racing across the concrete loading and unloading cargo.

They had expected heat, but it was lashing down with rain as they walked in single file across an expanse of shale towards the terminal. A similar crocodile of uniforms was trudging out in the opposite direction towards the aircraft, led by a man holding a powerful torch above his head.

Camp Bastion is Britain's hub in Afghanistan and like Kandahar is a major artery kept supplied by endless personnel flying in and flying out. But its terminal isn't really a terminal at all in the Kandahar sense. More a series of prefab plywood structures and canvas aircraft shelters lashed and cobbled together shanty-style where soldiers, marines, aviators and a significant cast of civilian others were being shouted into lines by category to be processed in and processed out. The teak tans of theatre veterans were easy to spot alongside the sheer military buzz cuts and clean lily-white necks of recently arrived regular soldiers.

As the wave of arrivals moved slowly on the Squadron were able to huddle inside out of the weather and wait with their landing forms. Big TV screens beamed out BBC News 24 and coverage of events they had recently left behind, such as the impending royal wedding, which now seemed less important, strangely distant and not a little bizarre. There was coverage too from Afghanistan. Troops under fire, vehicles churning up dust, helicopters buzzing overhead. These were the routine images of daily bulletins to which so many back home were now immune, but the Dambusters were no longer on the outside of that story looking in. They were now part of the unfolding narrative.

Three Commando Brigade were checking in as well, presenting clearance forms so they could go and reclaim their weapons. Most of them looked about 17 or 18 years old. As they waited for their bags, helmets off but still wearing their body armour, Poppy Cormack-Loyd was not alone in realising once again how vital 617's job was going to be in protecting the guys on the ground. Even though flying fast jets in theatre was physically challenging there was little chance of sustaining the kind of injuries caused by IEDs.

The following day, 12 April, the Dambusters, who had spent the night in bunks in 50-person tents, joined a group of 150 new arrivals to begin their two days of RSOI training. During one session a medic from Camp Bastion's £10 million hospital asked for a male volunteer. A soldier stepped forward. The medic asked him to strip to his underwear and then outlined his major organs and arteries with a thick felt-tip. He asked the new arrivals to estimate how much blood would be lost when any of these suffered a wound and severe trauma. Everybody underestimated. In front of him the medic had a line of buckets filled with differing amounts of water. The medic picked up a bucket and emptied it on to the ground. It seemed to be half full.

'This is how much blood would be leaking from the body from a major abdominal injury,' he told them, 'and that is about as fast as you would lose it.'

Next he held up a leg-sized muslin bag that was dripping red and looked like a stump of blood.

'What are you going to do if you are in a firefight and your mate has had his legs blown off; what are you going to do straight away? The helicopter will arrive in twenty minutes.'

Somebody suggested morphine.

'Morphine won't kick in quick enough. They can do that when they pick him up. You've got to save his life! Stop the bleeding not the pain. Get the tourniquets on and the first field dressings.'

He made them practise against the clock.

The medic asked another volunteer to lie on the ground on his back and started pouring bottles of water over his face. As the man choked, the medic said: 'This is what it is going to be like if you are choking on your own blood. You've got to help him out. Roll him properly so he can breathe again. Quick fixes will save lives.'

On 14 April the 617 main party boarded three Hercules for the short flight to Kandahar. Again it was dark. They had still seen more of Afghanistan on television at home than they had since they had arrived in the country. Many of them reflected on the dangers that those going beyond the wire faced every day with every step they took. The training they had done with Amputees in Action during Lossiemouth War Week had been completely realistic and instructive, but there was an extra dimension to the rough-and-ready medical session they had received at Bastion. It was chastening.

15 April was the day of the handover from 12 Squadron to 617 and to mark it the two squadron bosses, Jim Frampton and Keith Taylor, flew a sortie together over Helmand. Taylor was amazed at how similar the lie of the land was to flying over Iraq. It was the same patchwork of walled compounds, waddies and strips of irrigated and cultivated land either side of the Helmand River that fed irrigation canals. The strips of green stood out vividly against a backdrop of arid desert where they stopped abruptly in the face of arid miles of brown and white. The airspace structure was very similar to flying over Baghdad and the process of contacting JTACs on the ground was just the same. And down below them was a familiar-looking string of British military vehicles led by two heavily-armoured Mastiffs, 6 × 6 wheel-drive patrol vehicles each carrying six soldiers and a crew of two.

The Mastiff's ability to resist explosions was increased by its

V-shaped hull which, unlike a flat hull, pushed the force of any explosion outwards. The soldiers from the Mastiffs were doing their own step-by-step route sweep, often by fingertip, stopping every time they feared for an IED or to investigate a potential pinch-point from where they could be ambushed. Some miles above them the job of the two squadron bosses was to fly on slightly ahead of the convoy to identify potential threats and alert the convoy's JTAC, and also be on hand to defend the convoy if it was about to be attacked.

There was no attack that day and the convoy made it to its destination, delivering supplies from a FOB to the first of an outlying series of patrol bases safely. But Keith Taylor was struck by what a painstaking and time-consuming business it was just getting around Afghanistan at ground level. In the four hours that he was on station the convoy had travelled barely ten miles. Probably originating from Bastion, it would then have to complete the same slo-mo journey in reverse.

For Taylor the first trip had been a reassuring start. He had got his eye in on a trouble-free sortie. Back at KAF he and Frampton shook hands in front of the Tornado for the official handover photograph. Then they went to Frampton's office, which would soon be Keith Taylor's, where the squadron bosses went through a final checklist.

Half an hour later, Frampton looked at his watch and said simply: 'You're in charge now.'

On Sunday 17 April a Merlin helicopter swept in over the rooftops of Lashkar Gah. Gazing out as it came in to land, Squadron Leader Tony Griffiths noticed immediate differences between Lash and Camp Bastion, which was a military base in the middle of nowhere, and KAF, which was close to Afghanistan's second-biggest city but was so separate and self-contained it may as well have been in the middle of nowhere.

Lashkar Gah, meaning army barracks in Persian, was a proper city of some 35,000 on the Helmand River. The capital of Helmand Province, it had paved roads, bustling markets, TV and radio stations, a university and new housing under construction. Griffiths touched down at the compact main operating base at Lash that was home to about 1400 people. Unlike Bastion and Kandahar it had some colour: a flower garden took the edge off military and desert hues.

Security for central Lashkar Gah was due to be handed over to the Afghan security forces in July; a critical step in the path to full transition of power to the Afghan National Army and the Afghan National Police when ISAF pulled out its combat troops in 2014. Key to that was 3 Commando Brigade's Operation Omid Haft, aimed at driving the Taliban further out of the parts of Helmand where they were still deeply embedded.

Prior to Omid Haft's launch Griffiths and Captain Adams were in Lash to talk to 3 Commando Brigade's air liaison officers to ensure that the close air support 617 would offer complemented Task Force Helmand's efforts on the ground and that the RAPTOR would provide the kind of visual intelligence the Brigade needed before pushing out from its bases.

'It is hugely, hugely valuable to the guys on the ground what RAPTOR can bring,' Flight Lieutenant Mark 'Phats' Taylor reassured Griffiths. Taylor was 3 Commando Brigade's fixed-wing adviser and was himself a former Tornado pilot. 'It's eyes that the insurgents cannot see. As soon as we get wind of insurgent potential at a *Shura* or a bazaar we send RAPTOR to get some images and have somebody in the safety of their own office decide what is going on.'

Griffiths' visit was the chance to put some faces to names. The Brigade's counter-IED specialist was an RAF flight lieutenant, as was the Intelligence, Surveillance, Target Acquisition and Reconnaissance (ISTAR) adviser. An early appreciation of how the other side worked and the external pressures they were under would reduce misunderstandings when ground and air were working together in the thick of Operation Omid Haft. Jock Adams would be in daily contact with 3 Commando Brigade via Phats Taylor so he could update aircrew at their daily met and intelligence brief on the latest from the front line.

After an intense two hours Griffiths and Adams flew back to Bastion for an onward flight back to KAF. As Lashkar Gah receded into the distance Griffiths was struck by a major difference in the style of operation between air and ground. Out in Helmand the marines and army units of the Task Force were only about 30 miles from their Brigade Headquarters. Except for the Battle of Britain the RAF was usually operating thousands of miles from its command-and-control HQ. Perhaps if the CAOC was 30 miles from Kandahar rather than in the Middle East then refuelling might not be such an issue.

11

DUCKLINGS TO WATER

Monday 18 April 2011 was the day that 617 started its full flying programme out of Kandahar Airfield and with a predominantly young aircrew Rocksy Sharrocks described the first sorties as 'taking the ducklings to water'. His first trip was with 29-year-old Flight Lieutenant Caroline Day. Educated at Gordonstoun, close by RAF Lossiemouth, and Loughborough, where she had studied politics and media communications, Caroline had once set her heart on becoming a fast jet pilot.

'All navigators do!' She passed all the aptitude tests but one. 'My arms are too short! They measure your functional reach around the cockpit once you are strapped into the front seat and I came out two mm below the cut-off line. The equipment is closer in the back seat.'

She would need to rely on the back-seat equipment totally because her first trip out of Kandahar was a night sortie; out into the inky blackness a long way north and east from Kandahar to provide over-watch for a raid on compounds that had been identified as insurgent strongholds. She said that a key skill for a navigator was patience. In theatre at night she would also need tenacity. When there was a big white full moon it was possible to see every compound and every waterway glinting without using night vision goggles; but when there was no moon, like tonight, the sky over Afghanistan, which is predominantly rural and kerosene powered, was an impenetrable black void.

The airspace was not as busy after dark but there were pilots flying around with covert lighting so the enemy could not own the night, which meant they could not be seen floating around in your airspace. As a flight commander Rocksy knew that Caroline, like the other rookies, had to get out there and get amongst it, prove that she could do it.

'It is scary,' he said. 'There are big bad mountains out there or you could be 20 feet away from a tanker and all you will see is the lights on the refuelling hose disappearing into the black. And then suddenly the tanker will bank right or left without warning and you have to react with it or lose it.'

As they headed north up towards Kabul it was like nothing Caroline had experienced before on night flights out of Lossiemouth. Out here the ambient light was many times less and she would be relying solely on instruments, radios, the computer and nous. In his mirror Sharrocks could see his navigator's bowed helmet. He knew Caroline would not flap – anybody who had organised her entire wedding as well as completing pre-deployment training had to be a good organiser – but he sensed how hard she was having to work.

For all first-timers in theatre the first few trips were like sensory overload. On the radios everybody was trying to tell somebody something all the time and all of it seemed important and to demand a response. The trick, Sharrocks advised her, 'is trying to work out which bits you need to listen to and which don't affect you and what the hell you need to do about it when they do'.

Like all aircrew Caroline carried A5 books stuffed into a front pocket of her anti-G trousers; these contained crib sheets known as gizzas. A gizza was like a revision note for easy reference in the cockpit, with diagrams and bullet points that covered flight profiles, weapons delivery and every other procedure and problem she was likely to encounter. For example, if she was at medium altitude and they were asked to do a show of force at 100 feet 10 miles away, the gizza would tell her at what point they would need to start their descent.

All the crib sheets in the world were no substitute for flying with somebody who was vastly experienced. A couple of times when he sensed that his navigator was finding it tough, Sharrocks said, 'Caroline, I'll just take the radios for two minutes,' to give her a break or allow her to catch up on something else. It was important to support but not undermine her.

'Those first two or three trips people are working very, very hard. As the pilot and the experienced guy, there are times when you have to say, "quiet, listen, we are at a good height, we're sorted."'

It wasn't only the younger aircrew who had problems, Rocksy said.

'Show me an experienced operator who early on in the deployment says that this is easy and I'll show you a liar.'

When they got back to KAF and climbed down from the aircraft, Sharrocks could already see a change in his navigator.

'Caroline has come back with eyes wide open. She has learned an awful lot, principally about herself. Not only can she do it; she can do the job at night.'

As they walked back to the Squadron block Rocksy Sharrocks noticed more of a spring in the step of his navigator than when they had walked out to the jet.

As the youngest pilot on 617, Flying Officer Al Spence's first sortie was a day trip. He had been through the process so many times before: the flight preparation, the briefings, the calculations; and as he sat in the jet doing his instrument checks prior to the see-off it was almost automatic. But this was not a training exercise. Even though he had Conan Mullineux, 'the padre', calmly going through all his navigational instrument checks, Al suddenly realised that junior as he was, he was still the captain of the ship.

He took extra time checking G-metres, the head-up display (HUD), head-down alpha gauges, the auto-pilot system, big buttons for making stuff go bang, throttles for shutting down engines, all his engine instruments on his right-hand side, and his early-warning panel, so if he was being shot at it would light up and let him know.

Also on the right-hand side of his seat he had a mixture of communications suites: terrain following radar (TFR), allowing the aircraft to fly automatically at low level when poor weather prevented visual flight, the tactical air navigation system (TACAN), which would give him bearing and distance to a ground station, and secure radios to talk to air traffic, tankers and JTACs, whose frequencies were always referred to by colours such as Lemon 11 or codes such as Alpha 12 so as not to give them away to the enemy.

On his left-hand side were all his back-up flight instruments, so if the HUD failed he could revert to those. Then he made sure that the landing-gear levers were set correctly as well as the wing-sweep and flap levers and indicators.

The multi-function display screen between his legs was an essential situational awareness builder, allowing him to toggle through maps of the areas he was flying over, look at the images from the targeting pod, ground-mapping navigational radar and forward-looking infrared (FLIR).

To the uninitiated the pilot's cockpit of a Tornado was a

bewildering grotto of sliders, switches, levers, knobs, winking lights and ranks of dials. Old hands said that on their first four trips young pilots took forty minutes to get the jet started and then suddenly a couple of months later they would hop in and suddenly know where everything was. Even when the cockpit was dark and they were flying on night vision goggles they had got pretty good at sticking their hand out, making a switch and knowing they had got the right one. They didn't even realise they were doing it.

As Sharrocks put it: 'They had been kissed by the Tornado fairy and that was it. But like a newly schooled horse it could still kick you if you got complacent.'

Which was why Al Spence was now being extra-methodical. Outside, the leader of the line crew, known as the crew chief, was connected to the jet via a communications cable plugged into the ground service panel on the starboard side of the fuselage, so he could talk to Spence and Mullineux. As they checked their instruments a computer on the floor of the aircraft shelter monitored all readings. The wing lights and those over the engine intakes were winking orange as the noise levels rose. The auxiliary power unit, a small jet engine and the equivalent of a starter motor, had kicked into life sending air into the main engines which were too big to start on their own.

Both turbofans were now going. The concrete vibrated underfoot. The wingtip lights came on red. The lineys began removing the long safety pins from the weapons – two Paveway IV 500 lb bombs and a Dual Mode Seeker (DMS) Brimstone held in racks under the belly of the jet. The noise of the engines intensified, building from a hiss to a whistle. The cable from the auxiliary power generator was removed from the Tornado as Spence flexed his flaps, slats, rudder and thrust-reverse buckets. The engines began to gust creating a heat haze at the back of the jet.

The crew chief made his way around and underneath the aircraft, doing a visual inspection of tyres and landing gear and patting the panels, a final check for leaks and cracks. He stepped back and held up both his thumbs and then disconnected himself from the jet.

The wing lights were now winking green. As the canopy began to go down the line crew took cover behind a blast wall in case the explosive charge that would blow it off the cockpit in the event of an ejection malfunctioned and sprayed them with shards of glass.

The crew chief now took up his position in front of the Tornado's nose and began to wave it out, beckoning with both hands above his chest. There was a momentary pause and then Al Spence moved his aircraft forward. He paused and then turned the Tornado left and moved off the ramp and down the flight line wall towards the taxiway. As he did so he raised his gloved thumb to the ground crew a final time.

Out on the taxiway the American voices of the air traffic controllers guided him ready for take-off and then he was hammering down the runway, afterburners on. He felt the jet lift up underneath him. At 250 feet he put his wheels in the well, checked his flaps were set clean and then accelerated away with the afterburners still in combat until he was more than three miles from KAF, when he cancelled the burners and took the Tornado into a strong 3G pull 20 degrees nose up to get as high as he could as quickly as possible and out of the ground-to-air threat zone.

Al Spence headed due south of Kandahar. The landscape initially was sandy and mountainous punctuated by rivers and strips of green vegetation. Then suddenly it changed as though he was crossing a coastline. Right to the far horizon all he could see were high waves of red sand that looked like an ocean. This was Afghanistan's Registan or Red Desert. Home to a few nomads, it was big, wide and empty, beautiful and threatening.

As they neared Pakistan the Red Desert ebbed out, replaced by scrub and mountains 6000 feet high. Their destination was a village called Bahram Chah right on the Pakistan border.

Some US marines stationed down there had requested air power that day to monitor any suspicious activity in and around the village. Spence looked down at the images that Conan was getting through the LITENING pod. Ten thousand feet up, Bahram Chah looked deserted, 'like something from a post-apocalyptic world', Spence said. It didn't look like anybody actually lived there. But then they saw some guys cutting around on motorcycles. Spence felt his adrenaline surge. Was this his first sight of the Taliban? Some insurgents sped around on Japanese motorbikes. They were called 'dickers'; lookouts who warned bombers and snipers of approaching ISAF troops and convoys. But these bikers did not seem in any hurry because they were stopping to talk to small groups of people and then splitting off at a leisurely pace. It was hardly the kind of intelligence that warranted invasive action. They passed the information to the JTAC on the ground who then asked for a show of presence. A show of presence wasn't as low or as intrusive as a show of force but Spence dropped down a few thousand feet. The Tornado made enough noise to tell anybody on the ground with bad intentions that it was there and watching them.

Spence and a second Tornado piloted by Flight Lieutenant Jake Fleming stayed on station for a while just in case the marines got attacked. When they got the all-clear they went to a tanker. Spence was first to the three-engine McDonnell Douglas KC-10 Extender, a grey whale of an aircraft 186 feet long with a 165-foot wingspan and loaded up with more than 42,000 gallons of fuel. Spence only took on a small amount because Fleming was tight on gas. He shifted along to the tanker's right wing to let Fleming, who had extended the refuelling probe on his Tornado, come in and lock on to the tanker drogue that dangled 30 feet beneath the tanker's stern.

'Do you have enough fuel for me to go to full?' Fleming asked Spence.

'Sure. Go ahead.' Spence stayed on the right of the tanker as Fleming filled up, but as he withdrew from the tanker it became unserviceable (U/S) and had to return to base.

Now Al Spence was very short of fuel. Unless they found another tanker soon he would be down to bingo fuel and have to head back to Kandahar. Bingo fuel was the minimum amount of gas needed in the tanks to get home safely without starving the engines, or to divert to another airfield if Kandahar runway was out of commission, and land with sufficient fuel remaining.

Calmly, Spence negotiated his way to another tanker and hoped that it would stay serviceable. He eased behind another KC-10 but this one had refuelling pods on the far extremes of its wings. His first time in theatre, Al Spence had never tanked off one of those before.

Sitting in the back seat Conan was impressed by his young pilot's steady nerve as he closed in on the tanker, extended the probe on the right side of the cockpit and plugged in perfectly. A few minutes later and he would have been forced to bingo back to KAF.

Although vastly more experienced and on his second deployment to Afghanistan, Conan's style was to let his young pilot get on with it and to offer advice where necessary rather than issue commands.

'Al appears to be a pretty laid-back character but he's always listening. Show him something once and he's up and running.'

For Al, having Conan in the back meant he could concentrate on flying in an alien airspace and on the radio traffic as well as those aircraft stacked above and beneath him.

Buoyed by the several tonnes of fuel he had taken on board, Al Spence headed back to join Jake Fleming over Bahram Chah village. He had passed a first test of nerve.

Three hours after taking off Flying Officer Spence came back into Kandahar air space. He knew to expect less turn performance from the aircraft and less power out of his engines than he would get at home so he nursed it around a wider, higher corner ready to be brought in for landing. Given the traffic he could see leaving and landing on the airfield he was expecting the approach into KAF to be chaotic. It looked even busier than Heathrow. But the control tower vectored him into position by radar, taking him down to the point about three miles out from where he would make his final approach to the threshold of the runway.

He had the jet in mid-flap initially because he needed a lot more power to stay airborne at slower speeds.

Spence selected emergency RAM-air – which was sucked in from the outside via various scoops and fans on the aircraft and was normally used to help cool the cockpit and equipment if the environmental control system was broken. As the environmental control system bled air from the engines, this meant that they produced a bit more thrust. Confident he was going to make the airfield he took full flap to achieve his landing speed. The tarmac came up to meet him. He was conscious that he must pile on some more power to smooth out and cushion his landing. If he slammed the jet straight down on to the deck he risked scraping the bombs and missiles all the way down the strip.

He landed much faster than he would at Lossiemouth because the air is thinner at KAF, 3330 feet above sea level. Al Spence's wheels licked the ground at 160 knots (185 mph).

'Expedite clear of the runway,' the control tower told him. 'Expedite clear of the runway.' Spence deployed the thrust-reverse buckets which covered the back of the engines to throw the thrust forwards. He felt the aircraft slow. Then relief. There would be no need to take the emergency braking cable. Just like the safety cable on an aircraft carrier, it ran the width of the runway and aircraft could drop a hook on to it to slow down if unable to do so normally. In 2009 the crew of a malfunctioning Tornado had to eject following a rejected take-off. It crashed in flames and the crew were rescued. These were rare events but they were always etched into the minds of those taking off and landing at KAF.

Ten minutes after landing cleanly and without incident Al Spence was back in the aircraft shelter. He climbed down from his Tornado and the ground under his feet felt good.

'One under the belt,' Conan congratulated him.

'Very happy to complete that one and get back safely,' Spence smiled. 'It's a good feeling.'

Al Spence was not the only Dambuster to have trouble with air-to-air refuelling on 617's first sorties in Afghanistan. On his very first mission it was Flight Lieutenant Stew Campbell's misfortune to have to refuel off a boom drogue adaptor (BDA), feared by all and known to all as the Iron Maiden. Keith Taylor was piloting the other jet when they both went to tank during a photographic surveillance sortie.

Campbell had refuelled off an Iron Maiden once in the UK and it had gone 'swimmingly well'. He approached the KC-135 tanker from behind and about 25 feet below. Hanging down from the back of the tanker was a rigid boom some 28 feet long and hanging limply from that was an additional 18 feet of inner fuel tube, which dangled down. On the end of that was a metal basket or drogue, 24 inches wide: the Iron Maiden.

Campbell knew that approaching an Iron Maiden demanded extreme caution. Unlike the hose drum systems used on other tankers the hose slack was not wound in on the BDA. Close in too fast and the hose would whip and most probably damage the receiving aircraft's refuelling probe. Keeping steady underneath, Campbell closed in gently and extended his five-foot probe into the centre of the drogue and locked into the pipe.

To actually get the fuel he now had to manoeuvre his aircraft to shift the hose up and sideways at least six feet, creating an S-shape, which would then open the fuel release mechanism.

Performing delicate positional adjustments behind a tanker at altitude in thin air was challenge enough but Campbell's Tornado was also carrying a RAPTOR photographic and surveillance pod underneath its belly, a twenty-foot-long beast weighing just over a tonne, which made the aircraft's manoeuvrability even more clunky.

If the tanker pilot banked suddenly without warning, which happened often, Campbell could lose connection and either break his probe or rip the drogue off if he did not react instantly and also bank. If he got too close or kinked his S-shape the fuel would be cut off.

This BDA was so tricky it was only used during daylight.

The advantage with this system was that when it worked the Maiden made refuelling quicker. Six tonnes could be delivered into the Tornado's fuel tanks, chiefly those that hung under the wings, in ten minutes.

Stew Campbell, a tall, softly spoken athletic Scot from Edinburgh, who had joined 617 in November 2010, had been told that the correct technique for docking with an Iron Maiden was to listen to his navigator's instructions and line up things on the HUD. If his navigator, Squadron Leader John 'Jonna' Howard, said move to the right he would move his HUD to the right and move in on the Maiden. What he must never do, so the experts said, was look at the basket.

Campbell manoeuvred the pipe into an S-shape and the fuel began to flow. But then the tanker banked without warning and he came out again. He managed to get back into the basket, but the tanker shifted in turbulence and he was out again. The problem wasn't getting the probe into the basket, it was staying in. Whatever Howard suggested Campbell could not make it work. As the minutes went by his nerves began to get the better of him. He feared that he was starting to spook his navigator. He was also worrying that he would not be able to complete all the mission tasks.

Thirty-one-year-old Campbell was a placid character normally. Now he was shitting himself.

'Ease back, take some time and try again,' said a calm voice over his radio. It was the Boss. Keith Taylor could see that Campbell was having problems. Experience told him that the more you hammered away at this kind of manoeuvre the greater the chance of doing damage to the jet or the tanker or both. He could also see that two F-18s had joined him in the fuel queue and he was running short himself.

Campbell dropped off the tanker and allowed Taylor and

the F-18s to dock and refuel. He watched how they stayed in the basket.

As he left the tanker, Taylor told him: 'Don't be afraid to engage visually as well as using the HUD.'

Next time Stew Campbell went to the KC-135 he went into the drogue and he stayed in. But this had taken forty-five minutes of sortie time which would have to be made up. And 3 Commando Brigade needed the highly detailed images he was taking of villages and compounds before launching operations.

Even though he had to tank a second time – this time on a reassuringly simple RAF VC10 that you just plugged straight into and flew along behind – Stew Campbell did complete all his mission tasks. He returned to KAF after five and a half physically and emotionally exhausting hours. When they studied the film he and Howard had taken it revealed two IEDs and a host of sites being made ready for ambush, along with visual details of how the marines could best get into compounds which may have been used for weapons caches.

Stew Campbell, who was inspired to fly by his mother's cousin who was a Lightning pilot, and as a small boy papered his bedroom walls with posters of every single RAF aircraft then in service, never again had a problem with an Iron Maiden.

'Now I always look at the basket. The probe stays in every time!'

'This is my eye on the world,' said Squadron Leader Sharrocks, staring at a constantly changing mass of text, figures, abbreviations and colours on a computer screen in the ops room. Sharrocks was taking his turn to be 617's authoriser – 'Duty Supervisor Flying, out here,' he corrected – and what he was looking at so intently was the real-time communications feed.

Run by the CAOC in Al-Udeid, it was watched round the clock by all air force elements in Afghanistan, ISAF military units and JTACs on the ground, the Air Support Operations Center (ASOC) in Kabul and the many air traffic agencies in Afghanistan. It summarised minute by minute everything that was going on in the battle space from troops in contact to the position of fast jets and all other aircraft.

In Guy Gibson's day the ops room would have consisted of cardboard aircraft being pushed across a large map by WRAFs with long sticks. As Duty Supervisor Flying Sharrocks could at any moment offer 617's Tornados to the CAOC to go to the aid of troops in trouble on the ground.

Whenever the bell rang crews in the crewroom instinctively sat up or stood and looked at the screen, hoping and in some cases praying that they would get the call.

'If I see something going on that is not being supported then I can offer our aircraft to the CAOC,' Rocksy said. 'I will then phone through to the crewroom to tell the guys to get ready. But only the CAOC can scramble them.'

At that moment a bell rang. Troops were coming under fire east of Camp Bastion.

'Here we go,' Rocksy said excitedly. 'That's fifteen minutes away. Let's see if we can get some of this.' He immediately offered 617 jets to the CAOC and phoned the crewroom to tell the GCAS crews to start walking to their jets.

'Shit,' he said, two minutes later. 'A pair of F-16s have been sent to it straight away and are soon to go on station. I guess they were already airborne.'

Sharrocks called the crewroom. 'Rest easy, guys. It's not for us.'

Sometimes watching the window on the world felt like voyeurism. Everybody else seemed to be in on the action.

'Because like all air assets we are run by the CAOC looking at the screen can be a bit like waiting for your lottery numbers to come up,' Rocksy said.

Rocksy saw some more ducklings emerge from the briefing room and walk towards the auth desk. Authorisers like Rocksy also gave the crews their final outbrief before they flew, running through the air tasking order and what was expected of 617 that sortie. He updated them on weather conditions, the status of other airfields in case they had to divert to them and the latest intelligence briefs from the ground over which they would be flying, so that when they were overhead they could look through their LITENING pods and compare what they actually saw with what they had been briefed to expect. He read out any special instructions (SPINS) issued by the CAOC and reminded them of the other aircraft that would be working in the same Kill Boxes. He was also on the phone constantly to the engineers to keep up to date on any mechanical problems and to avoid any time-wasting crew-outs where pilots and navigators had to jump out of a malfunctioning jet and run to a standby. Whoever was duty authoriser it was their job to ensure that the flying programme was running smoothly and that jets, whether already airborne or crews on GCAS readiness on the ground, could get to a TIC fast.

Sharrocks watched them exit the ops room.

'When people walk out to the jet after the mission brief and the authoriser's outbrief, I want them to walk out with snap, not saunter out thinking everything will be fine. It will be fine but it won't be crisp, sharp, and aggressive.'

12

THE UNSPOKEN FEAR

Joe Hourston and Lucy Williams were one of the crews where neither had flown on ops before and they were about to fly a mission in Nad-e Ali district, Helmand Province on 18 April.

They were both outwardly calm but Joe was thinking: 'We are going to get a missile fired at us two metres off the end of the runway, we are going to drop all our bombs and then we are going to get shot down, all in the first hour.' All completely unlikely, but he told himself that this thought process was keeping him on his toes.

Lucy was a cascading mix of emotions and nerves as she picked up her pistol. She holstered it and slipped a magazine of 9 mm ammunition into her pocket.

'Some people prefer to load their pistol before they take off,' she said, 'others only when they need it. It's a matter of personal choice.' Then she added reflectively: 'We have trained to fire a pistol, but this is the first time I have really faced the fact that I might have to use it.'

She would only need the Sig Sauer if something went badly wrong with the jet and Joe shouted '*Eject! Eject! Eject!*' and they had to defend themselves on the ground.

Combat rescue teams came in pretty fast to pick up aircrews that had ejected. They were usually recovered by road or picked up by helicopter very quickly in non-mountainous areas. In the north, where the terrain got steeper, communications were more difficult and landing was more challenging and hazardous, so rescue could take longer. The Dambusters didn't need telling that ejecting into mountains was physically hazardous.

Like all the aircrew Lucy carried not only a first aid kit containing dressings and painkillers for lesser injuries, but also a single-handed tourniquet and a first field dressing to stop major bleeding – which she had been shown how to use in both her pre-deployment work-up training and during RSOI in Camp Bastion – as well one auto-jet of morphine, enough to last until rescuers arrived.

Ensuring that a rescue team knew their exact location as soon as possible explained the extra weight of the lifejacket that Lucy was wearing over her flying suit. It was noticeably heavier than what she was used to back in the UK. The pouch pockets on the waistcoat were crammed with flares, torches, a heliograph, white plastic mine tape, used for marking a safe route through a minefield, a wrist GPS device, that would give the range and the bearing to a pick-up location, nightsticks, an old-style compass, a karabiner attachment so she could be hauled up by an Apache, a single lens night vision binocular, which had a compass attachment, and an infrared strobe light which rescuers could lock on to.

But the most important piece of kit for guiding the rescuers in was the emergency locater beacon that all the Dambusters also carried in their life jackets. Each device was assigned a unique serial number for their entire deployment so if it ever went off the Squadron would know exactly who was in danger. A hugely more sophisticated version of the beacons used by yachtsmen, these were programmable with two channels, loaded by the Squadron, for normal radio press-to-talk. Other channels were set to send out a beep that rescuers could home on to. Once contact had been established and a pick-up point had been agreed the locater would automatically give its range and bearing. It could also be used to send a situation report and had a texting device, including twenty-five pre-programmed messages such as 'moving to higher ground', 'signal weak', 'what is ETA for pick up?', and 'location of nearest threat'. Encryption codes and a unique radio identification number ensured that nobody hostile could listen in.

'If the locater beacon fails on them then they are pretty stuck,' said Sergeant Wayne Nicolson, who headed up 617's Survival Equipment Fitters, always referred to as Squippers. 'Like everything else they wear or use it has to be right every single time.'

As adept with a sewing machine as they were with setting encryption codes, the Squippers were responsible not only for keeping the locater beacons in good order but also for preparing and maintaining all bodily aircrew kit, starting with the boots, with special soles that would not melt in a fire, anti-G trousers, life jackets and all their contents, oxygen masks and equipment and helmets, one for day and one for night, fitted with night vision goggles. They also took care of the ejection seat parachutes and life rafts. While 617 were out battling the Taliban, Nicolson and his colleagues, who also looked after the Hercules crews at KAF, were fighting their own daily battle with the dust.

'It gets everywhere,' he said, shaking his head in resignation. 'It is fine and abrasive and it chafes material and ruins lenses. I guarantee that if we clean a helmet visor and put it back in its cover in its locker it will be covered again inside two hours.'

*

If there was one thing aircrew would only talk about reluctantly it was what happened if they were shot down or had to 'bang out' of a jet and 'hit the silk' due to mechanical failure. This was the great unspoken fear – one that training could never completely prepare you for. The Warlord looked uncharacteristically uncomfortable.

'For aircrew that's the most sensitive thing,' Griff said, shifting in his seat. It was not just mission security that drove their reticence; it was also to do with not wanting to tempt fate.

Of course all 617's pilots and navigators had not only been trained to evade capture if downed but also how to behave if they did fall into enemy hands. That training is delivered by the Defence Survival, Evasion, Resistance, Extraction (SERE) Training Organisation (DSTO) based at RAF St Mawgan near Newquay in Cornwall. DTSO's training teams of approximately 100 trainers are drawn from the Royal Navy, the Royal Marines, the RAF and the Army and they put on some twenty-three different types of course a year to train around 5000 service personnel in the arts of surviving.

The training is predictably tough and unremittingly intimidating. One of 617's squadron leaders still remembered it vividly. 'It lasted a week. Having taught us basic survival and evasion techniques we spent five days out on the moors and then got hungry, cold and wet, then they caught us, and took us back.' The squadron leader acknowledged the importance of the St Mawgan training in his professional preparation for all events.

When Lucy Williams and Joe Hourston signed out their aircraft and left the engineers to walk to their jet there was a quietness between them. There was nothing unusual in this.

Good friends socially outside work, they were never particularly talkative as a crew.

'I'll chat more, because girls generally do, and Joe is very quiet,' Lucy explained. 'And I go quiet when I am concentrating. Neither of us likes to break our concentrations.'

Today's sortie was to gather intelligence and fly surveillance for 3 Commando Brigade as it prepared to launch Operation Omid Haft, its big push into Nahr-e Saraj district in Helmand, which was still a Taliban stronghold. As 617's Squadron Intelligence Officer (SqintO) Flight Lieutenant Richard Smith put it:

'These are really the last strategic areas that the insurgency has got and they use the irrigation wadi system and canal crossings to come in from the desert, to infiltrate and intimidate the local population.'

Smith, a former air traffic controller who switched to the RAF intelligence branch, was an Afghan specialist having worked on the Afghanistan desk at RAF Waddington before coming to 617 Squadron in August 2010.

'The intimidation starts with threatening "night letters" pinned to doors, fixed with the seal of the "Islamic Emirate of Afghanistan". Then the locals are forced to pay extra taxes to fund the insurgency and those who refuse are beaten or killed or have their children kidnapped.'

But before British and Afghan troops left their FOBs to set up security checkpoints and pinch hard on insurgent crossing points they needed the kind of surveillance intelligence that cannot be got from the ground. Lucy and Joe's mission was to scan the routes coalition forces planned to take, looking for evidence of suspicious activity and patterns of behaviour such as unusual congregations of people or increased motorcycle activity, which would suggest that the Taliban was on the move.

Going through her pre-flight checks Lucy felt a deep empathy with the sacrifice made by female service personnel in Afghanistan. Sadly, she had learned that an Army colleague had been severly injured that very day.

Lucy turned her kit on, booting up the main computer. The three screens in front of her began to show signs of life. The largest central screen was a full-colour digital moving map and radar display known as TARDIS, which could also be accessed by Joe. The screens either side were TV tabs. The one on the left she set up to show images from the LITENING 3 pod and the one on the right she would use as the navigation screen, but she could also flip it to forward-looking infrared (FLIR) for strafe attack or use it as a Fix Attack screen for setting up a Paveway or a Brimstone. She had also loaded her mission data, carried on a device called a brick, which looked like a chunky video cassette, double-checking which Kill Box they were going to.

She started up the LITENING targeting pod and then checked that the Brimstone the jet was carrying was set up properly. During their outbrief Lucy and Joe had been told to expect more attacks on coalition forces in the very areas they would be flying over. Everything was working as it should.

For Lucy Williams and Joe Hourston the taxi-out to the runway was familiar yet surreal. The airfield looked just as it had in the simulator but now they sat there for real Lucy began to experience the same sensory overload: the radio chatter, the pistol, the live ammunition, the outbrief. And now here they were out on the runway for real. There would be no stepping out of a cockpit and finding herself back in the simulator building at Lossiemouth.

As they left KAF and headed off to Helmand, Lucy's biggest fear coursed through her mind. *I really don't want to mess this up. What if it all kicks off? Will I be able to handle it and help the guys on the ground?* It made her focus the sortie and concentrate only on doing the next thing next.

Their sortie was uneventful. They returned to KAF safely. But nobody was getting lulled into thinking that the Taliban were sitting back waiting for ISAF combat troops to pull out in 2014.

On 24 April insurgents who had dug a tunnel more than 1000 feet long into Sarpoza Prison in Kandahar City, bypassing military checkpoints, freed more than 470 insurgents including 100 Taliban, whisking them away to secure locations in a fleet of cars. 'This is a blow,' presidential spokesman Waheed Omar told the BBC and Reuters. 'A prison break of this magnitude of course points to a vulnerability.'

There was speculation as to how it had been possible to remove all the earth from the construction of the tunnel, which had taken five months to dig, without the security forces knowing. In June 2008 the Taliban had sprung over 850 prisoners out of the very same so-called high security prison.

13

RIGGERS, SOOTIES, LECKIES, FAIRIES AND PLUMBERS

Just as in Guy Gibson's day, it was Dambuster aircrew who dropped the bombs but it was Dambuster engineers who got them airborne. In Kandahar 617's engineers outnumbered aircrew 102 to 26 thanks to the complexity of the systems that made up a Tornado GR4. The engineers were now divided into two broad trades: mechanical and avionics. Traditionally they had been split into four: airframe, propulsion, electrical and avionics technicians. Even more traditionally they were still referred to, and referred to each other, by age-old nicknames: Riggers (airframe), Sooties (engines), Leckies (electricians) and Fairies (avionics). Then there were the armourers who put bombs and targeting pods on planes – always referred to as 'the stores' – loaded the gun and looked after the ejector seats. They were traditionally known as Plumbers.

Out on the ramp at any one time the Tornados could be divided into three groups. During two six-hour periods every day there would be two GCAS aircraft fully primed and ready to go, with a spare in case one of them developed problems pre-take-off. In front of each there was a yellow and black warning sign: 'GCAS AIRCRAFT ON STATE'. Then there were jets ready to fly on three waves of daily preordained sorties. These had warning signs placed in their cockpits: 'Aircraft ARMED'. The third category was jets that needed maintenance to keep them up to par in the heat and dust of Afghanistan. The workload on the engineers was unforgiving. At RAF Lossiemouth to lose a sortie was always frustrating. In Kandahar it could be catastrophic.

Whenever aircrew, who were sensitive to every rattle, hum and gauge reading, signed a jet back into the Aircraft 700 ledger, the engineers held their breath. Problems could range from replacing a cockpit bulb to removing an engine and fitting a new one, which could take six hours and more. And then there was an acronym that nobody wanted to see listed in the problem column – ECS. The environmental control system, which kept the crew and cockpit cool along with the computer and all the operating systems, was subjected to incredible strain in Afghanistan. Ground temperatures could be ruinous, along with the dust, and at altitude climbing or diving vertically through thin air did not do the system any favours either. The diagram for the Tornado ECS which snaked its way through the aircraft was complex enough; finding and sorting a fault required a mix of detective work and sheer good luck.

In addition to the unpredictable, the jets also had to undergo regular services to ensure flight safety. A primary service took two days. A primary star involved testing and checking the whole airframe and all the systems and took seven days with round-the-clock manning. At home a primary star would take two weeks.

When aircraft were taking off the engineers zipped around the ramp in their 'hit bus' seeing off jets or rushing to suddenly stricken aircraft when aircrew discovered a problem and had to decamp to a reserve. Once jets were in the air the pace on the ramp slowed as the engineers worked methodically on those jets that had longer-term problems. When aircraft had landed with more problems identified by the crew, the Riggers, Sooties, Leckies and Fairies poured out of the squadron building to begin the whole cycle again.

As they began work the Plumbers arrived to remove the missiles and ferry them on tractor-pulled trolleys back to the weapons store. SAC (Senior Aircraftwoman) Emma 'Ziggy' Zweig was one of two female armourers with 617 in Kandahar. The Squadron had sixteen armourers in all, eight on each shift, usually working in groups of four.

'As a woman you get the odd banter,' Ziggy said, working with a team removing a Brimstone that had returned to base, 'but if people see you can do the job then the guys are cool with having women on the squadron. There are certain things I cannot physically do just through sheer strength, but the guys don't mind that. It's nice to blend in.'

Ziggy, 26, came from a serving RAF family and had joined 617 in 2007. Her father, who is German, was a Warrant Officer on the catering squadron at Cranwell, and her brother was a corporal Sootie serving on 99 Squadron, which flies C17s out of RAF Brize Norton. Her mother, a Geordie, had also spent a short time in the RAF and Ziggy had been born in Lincoln. You couldn't get much more RAF.

'My dad's supportive but was a bit worried about me joining a technical trade. I've always been very tomboyish, taking things apart when I was a kid to see how they worked. Working on engines would have been okay, but weapons are very specialist and I wanted to give it a go and here I am ten years later.'

Ziggy, who had joined the Air Force at 16, had a constellation of blue and red stars tattooed up her right arm. A confident loner who prized her privacy, she could also join in and hold her own in what she called 'a big man's world'. She could look sulky or diffident one minute and be smiling radiantly the next. But one thing she really loved was her job. She had helped fit her first live rocket, a CRV7 originally designed to penetrate Warsaw Pact aircraft hangars, on to a Harrier on the second day of her first posting at RAF Cottesmore in Rutland. It was normal to have a three- or four-person load team with a corporal in charge.

'It was definitely exciting. You go through training and everything is replicas and duds, and all of a sudden it's wow, you're 17 years old and you have this highly explosive thing that you get to play with but at the same time the last thing you want to do is mess up.'

The engineers and armourers were working in two shifts, A and B, the day shift working 7 a.m. to 7 p.m. and the night shift clocking on at 7 p.m. and working through to 7 a.m. the following morning. Every 168-hour fortnight A and B would change over.

They were ferried to and from the Squadron's HQ in an elderly German *Bustouristik*, now known as the Dust Bus. In the whole time they were in Kandahar their only glimpse of the country would be from the Dust Bus, which was high enough to give a view over the blast walls, Hesco bastions, stacked ISO containers and razor wire to a flat landscape: to the south wheat fields and vegetable plots carved up by dirt roads and to the north Three Mile Mountain. Beyond the Afghans who delivered a curry lunch every day, this was the closest the engineers would ever get to a country that was never more than yards away. As soon as they stepped off the Dust Bus, either into work at 904 EAW or back home to Cambridge Lines, Afghanistan was gone again.

For the engineers every day was the same, punctuated at regular intervals by the rumbles and bangs of the ISAF forces patrolling the security zone around KAF, carrying out controlled explosions of unwanted munitions and suspicious objects. Even the weather was the same. Every morning at the 7 a.m. shift change Squadron Leader Stuart Clarke would walk into the engineering end of the Squadron's wing with the sun already beating down on his back and say, 'Turned out nice again'.

Several of the aircrew, including Jon Overton, Hutch and Al Spence – whose father had been an engineer in the RAF – sensed that the ground crew were living a kind of captive existence. They started taking pictures to show where they had flown sorties over vast swathes of Afghanistan, from the Red Desert in the south, over the green slash of fertility either side of the Helmand River, to the Martian landscape with vast lakes and boulder-strewn plateaus at 10,000 feet beyond Kabul and then the massive mountains and canyons of the north beyond.

'It is a beautiful country,' Joe Hourston said. 'One day when this is all over I want to come back here with a backpack and do some trekking. I will also read a lot more about Afghanistan before I return.'

Keith Taylor also encouraged the aircrew to go and talk to the engineers about the sorties they had flown. The Boss knew it was important that the engineers felt part of the deployment and that their contribution in keeping jets in the air was recognised.

Even so, for the engineers Groundhog Day effects were inevitable. Stuart Clarke and Warrant Officer Thomson were on the look-out for the first signs of claustrophobia.

'We did all the training at Lossie but here it is about focus and keeping our eye on what we are here for,' said Thomson. 'That's my biggest job. If people have problems they come to me; if they don't that's great but I still keep an eye on them. I go round the site every day, check everyone's okay; then I go round the blocks back at Cambridge Lines.'

To alleviate boredom most of the engineers hit the Squadron gym daily to boost stamina and upper-body definition.

'Suddenly there's a lot of skinny good-looking people out here; people with waistlines you didn't even know had waist-lines,' said thirty-three-year-old Corporal Ross Bowman, who worked on engines and airframes. 'With this work you are either totally maxed out, or waiting around for something to do. It's always extremes, so the gym comes into its own.'

Bowman, who came from Consett, County Durham, lived in Elgin with his Hawaiian girlfriend, Akemi Maruyama, who was an author and had just published her first novel. They had met when he was posted to Al-Udeid and she had been work-ing as an IT specialist with the US Navy. Groundhog Day was not getting to the cheerful Ross Bowman, because he had recently received some good news.

'I was nearing the end of a 12-year-contract. Then when I got out here I was told that the RAF had offered me a 22-year engagement, which means when I get home I've still got a job.'

He still wondered whether Lossiemouth could be closed and whether he would be relocated to RAF Marham. A decision on the bases had still not been made. There was nothing he could do about that but he could do something about keeping those broad shoulders in good shape.

'Back home everybody will get tubby again,' he grinned. 'I don't intend to be one of them.'

In fact most of KAF seemed to be sweating, pounding and pumping in the gyms. Apart from the Squadron's own mini-gym the base had two big work-out arenas open to all, one of them 24-hour. The NAAFI shop, like all the other stores on the base, had a section devoted to physical enhancement: buckets of bodybuilding pills, vitamin supplements, high-protein drinks, bars and powders, one which proclaimed to be 'the final round fat burner'. The engineers were also devoting their gym time to sponsored running or rowing, hoping to clock up the same mileage as that from Lossiemouth to Kandahar to raise money for SSAFA Forces Help (Soldiers, Sailors, Airmen and Families Association). In addition Stuart Clarke had put up a notice on the engineers' notice board headlined: 'CHALLENGE SENGO!' He posted his gym performances for each piece of apparatus on the notice and invited the lads, and the girls, to better him.

'Just a bit of fun,' he said, 'but keeping fit is very important here.'

It was not unusual to see one of his charges suddenly drop to the floor of the engineers' room and put in thirty or forty impromptu press-ups, which of course would be rubbished by everyone else. This was not something that was ever seen in the aircrew section of the Squadron building, although everybody was expected to keep up their fitness levels, which were assessed regularly, even on deployment.

Perhaps not the most enthusiastic visitor to the gym was the Junior Engineering Officer (JEngO) in charge of B Shift, Flight Lieutenant Rob Perry. A tall, straight man with freckles and ginger hair, Perry had been in the RAF just over five years, following a mechanical engineering degree and a stint working at British Aerospace developing the Typhoon. At 39 he was a late arrival to the Air Force, but it had always been his long-term goal to join from the time he had been to an air display in 1980 at St Mawgan in Cornwall, not far from where he was brought up in Devon and where his mother still had a smallholding.

'When my dad was alive he always teased me for reading war books, although I would call them histories,' Perry smiled. 'And then there was the inspiration of Leonard Cheshire. His VC was for continuous excellence, over 100 sorties and not just a single flight, followed by his charity work and his faith. Let's face it, a genuine, all-round nice guy.'

This was Perry's second visit to Kandahar Airfield and he was excited to be back. In 2009 he had been seconded to be executive officer to the then Commander of KAF, Air Commodore Malcolm Brecht. An RAF One Star, Brecht was responsible for an area of 650 square kilometres, which not only included running the airfield and feeding and watering its population but also the security zone beyond the perimeter wire, which was then patrolled by the Force Protection Team of the RAF Regiment but was now the responsibility of American forces.

It was Perry's job to run Brecht's diary and get him smoothly from place to place in a hectic schedule.

'I learned so much in those four months,' he said, settling into his new desk at Kandahar. 'I spent a day with a Slovak engineering detachment that was clearing mines within the wire. Because Kandahar has such a long history of being at war there are still minefields within the perimeter of the airfield. It may not be the high-risk clearance they do out in Helmand but it is sobering that on the edge of the base you are walking next to a minefield.'

In the short time he had been away from KAF Rob Perry could not believe how much bigger the base had got. He was also one of the few in 617 who had visited Kabul, accompanying Brecht to a meeting at ISAF HQ with General McChrystal.

'It's a 15-minute journey from Kabul Airport to ISAF and they run an armoured convoy shuttle which flies through crowded streets at 60 mph,' Perry recalled. 'I had read *The Kite Runner* and a lot of other books about Afghanistan and so I had this image of what Kabul was like and there it was just as described but on the other side of a narrow armoured window. Crowded streets, colour, apparent chaos, our driver stopping for nothing and no one, one's hand on a rifle, and then this old man who looked about ninety stepped straight out in front of us.'

The convoy screamed to a halt.

'Your mind starts rattling through the scenarios. Who is this old man? Is he a decoy? Are we vulnerable? Or is he really blind in one eye and just crossing the street?'

On his first visit to Kabul Perry had approached ISAF HQ down an avenue of pretty trees. 'On my next visit a massive car bomb had gone off outside the main gate. All the branches had been blown off the trees, walls had been flattened to the horizontal and there was a huge crater in the road.'

Now Perry's greatest fears were the dust that was as sharp as glass playing havoc on turbine blades and all the other stresses that climate and a full-on flying programme would have on the reliability of the Tornado fleet. He was responsible with his shift flight sergeant for making sure that all the engineering trades brought their skills to bear efficiently and in sequence to keep jets fit to fly and that they had an adequate supply of spares. Perry and his JEngO counterpart on A Shift, Flight Lieutenant Al Whitehead, authorised when work was needed and signed off jets when they had been fixed. They could decide if a jet was safe to fly with a fault that could wait to be fixed.

'As an engineer I guess you'd describe me as a resource manager,' Perry said. 'I don't turn spanners, I don't plug in avionic equipment; it's my job to deliver the aircraft to the SEngO and the Boss to meet the flight programme.'

Perry was underplaying the role as usual. Stuart Clarke reckoned that Perry should be more vocal about his talents.

'He's a gifted lad is Rob, excellent engineer, very committed, but sometimes I wish he'd push himself forward a bit more.'

It was not that Perry lacked emotion but gung-ho he was not. Back at Lossiemouth he lived in the Officers' Mess – 'because I'm ashamed to say that I am much too lazy to cook' – was generous to others with his bar tab and put good manners ahead of mouthing off about his talents. Because of his Kabul background and the fact that he tended towards the studious with a book never far from his side, the engineers dubbed Rob Perry, 'The Cultural Attaché'. On his desk at Kandahar were *Shackleton's Boat Journey* and *Hitler: A Study in Tyranny*. For new arrivals to KAF Perry recommended *The Bear Went Over the Mountain* about Soviet combat tactics in Afghanistan, especially in Kandahar City, 'where they got thumped because they did not understand that it was the Taliban's centre of resistance, ideologically as well as militarily'. Nearly fifteen years later maybe little had changed. Perry agreed that history could be persistently consistent.

'I'd love to go to Kandahar,' he said, and then added sadly, 'it's just under ten miles away, but I'll never get to go there.'

Warrant Officer Thomson, who shared an office with Rob Perry and Squadron Leader Stu Clarke, was pleased with the way the engineers were settling in.

'They have the breadth of skills to deal with what is likely to come their way. No worries on that score.' There had been very few occasions when the Warrant could be heard addressing somebody as 'Fellah!' 'Once or twice I have had to give them the odd tap,' he said, spectacles glinting, 'but everybody on this squadron knows what I want. I expect the highest standard and I expect everything to be done as expeditiously as possible.'

Another engineer who was keen on standards and systems was Sergeant Al Sharp, who was making one of his frequent visits to the senior engineering management office. 'Sharpy' had been to KAF before, in 2007, with 7 Squadron which flew Chinooks. This was his second stint on the Dambusters.

'I'm proud of being on 617 and what they achieved in the war and their legacy, but equally, the work we are doing today is very impressive,' he said.

A kind, easy-going man in his early forties, Al was the engineers' induction and training coordinator, but part of his job was to ensure that the RAF's Continuous Improvement programme was followed. This was a series of working practices and efficiency targets adopted by the Air Force from Toyota. It didn't matter that the Squadron was in a warzone, CI had to be followed. The station commander at RAF Lossiemouth, Group Captain Andrew Hine, was a passionate disciple of CI. It had to become part of the RAF's DNA.

Even though he had been mortared and rocketed many times at KAF, Al Sharp reckoned that it was nowhere near as unnerving as being harnessed to the battlements of Edinburgh Castle, as he had been when he was the lone piper at the 2009 Edinburgh Military Tattoo.

'The two spotlights coming on to me was a hundred more times terrifying than the lights going off inside the plane as we came into Camp Bastion.'

Sharpy had been piping for thirty years all around the RAF world. RAF pipers were a dying breed so as soon as 617 returned from Afghanistan he would be off down to Edinburgh to play in the massed pipe bands at the 2011 Tattoo. He had brought his chanters to Kandahar to practise, but not the full pipes.

'The pipes aren't so happy in the heat,' he said. The Warrant Officer was not a pipe fan either.

'I told Sharpy, "If you bring the whole set I'll make you fucking eat them",' Thomson chipped in with a malevolent smirk.

'Yes, Sir,' Sharp replied, feigning deference.

Thomson and Sharp. Sharpy and Mr T. The two Scots were like a double act. They were often to be seen walking around the place, Thomson taking stock, Sharp, his fixer, taking the notes. When Thomson was serious he would address Sharp as Al. When he was joking around and the banter was flying, he called him 'Boy'.

As they left the engineering office to do walkabout, Thomson was pleased that the aircrew and the engineers were in the same block. Instead of being in a separate building the engineers' room was just down the corridor from the crewroom and the ops room. Back home Keith Taylor made sure that a monthly 'beer call' in the Squadron's feeder (canteen) brought both sides together but it was not the same as being in the same place all day every day.

'If I could I'd wrap up this building and take it back to Lossie,' Thomson told Sharp. 'Back home I'm in the crew side all the time but for some of my guys the only time they see aircrew is when they sign out or return a jet. Here we are all part of the same mix.'

However, not all was present and correct in the Warrant Officer's eyes. The state of the pan left a lot to be desired. It offended Mr T's sense of order and efficiency.

'Al,' he said, 'we are definitely going to do something about *that!*'

'Would that "we" be meaning "*me*" Sir?' Sharp ventured.

'Teamwork, Sharpy,' the Warrant said. 'Remember, continuous improvement is all about teamwork.'

Three weeks into 617's detachment all the aircrew had flown at least twice. The pairings that Griff had chosen were bedding in.

'Jon and I get on well,' was Alex Hutchison's verdict on his navigator Jon Overton. 'We are of equal experience. He's a bit quieter than I am. He'll sit there and quietly contemplate things and come up with a plan. I'm more gung-ho; speak now, think later. Frequently I'm wrong and have to apologise!! I'm very confident that he does his job well. He very rarely asks me to do things. Stuff in the back gets done, stuff in the front gets done, we land and it seems to be all right.'

The mood in the Squadron was relaxed and collegiate. The social hub for the aircrew was the crewroom, which was next to the engineering management office. With two large seen-better-days sofas, pigeon holes for post, scores of DVDs, a couple of computers, a fridge stuffed with food with name labels attached to warn off random grazers, and an industrial-sized tin of coffee and assorted teabags, the crewroom was just like a student common room. On a wall there was a Pigz Board; an Air Force tradition where misdemeanours, usually embarrassing, were listed. 'Going to the wrong tanker' and 'turning up at the wrong briefing' were two that would take a long time to live down for those involved as would 'locking the ops room before the Boss needed to use it'. The Pigz Board was divided up into squares, one for each 'sin', and organised by Poppy Cormack-Loyd. Miscreants were fined £1 for every transgression, the cash going to charity.

Nobody in the crewroom ever needed reminding that the

war was never far away. The room was dominated by a huge screen which carried the real-time comms detailing the latest developments from the battlespace and on a row of pegs hung the helmets, sets of anti-G trousers, life vests and mission boxes of the crews on GCAS alert.

In his first monthly report Keith Taylor was confident. 'The Squadron has operated [successfully] with a variety of ISAF ground forces with the majority in support of Regional Command South West' – covering British forces in Helmand. The confidence in the younger aircrew was growing. The engineers were keeping the Tornados flying. Everything was going to plan. He had his squadron just where he wanted it to be; everybody was in the swim and nobody had drowned.

Taylor's aircrew also seemed happy with the way the Boss was leading the Squadron and so far Timmy Colebrooke had neither embarrassed the Boss nor let the Boss embarrass himself. Hutch had served under Taylor's predecessor, Wing Commander David Cooper.

Keith Taylor's laid-back demeanour was sorely tested on 29 April. While those off duty had draped the crewroom with Union Flags and bunting and settled down to watch the wedding of Prince William to Kate Middleton, two Tornados returned to KAF from a day sortie. The crews went back to the Squadron building and signed the jets back in with the engineers with no reported faults. It was only when the engineers went out on to the ramp to work on the aircraft that they noticed that one of them had a two-inch hole high up on its tail fin. An AIRCM flare from the other jet had been fired and had sped through the tail.

The Boss summoned both crews to his office for what one

of his predecessors calls a formal 'Hats on' meeting. The door was firmly shut.

'You made a mistake and then you didn't even notice the hole straight through the top of the fin,' he told them. 'It was a mistake that could have been disastrous. Two of you are lucky to be here.

'On top of that the engineers already have enough work on their plates without this.'

It was not Keith Taylor's style to shout or issue threats. He looked at them closely and shook his head. His air of disbelief was more chilling than a rant. The four of them could see the disappointment in his eyes.

Two chastened pilots and two weapon systems operators had to then take the long walk from the Boss's room, through the intelligence room, the ops room and then back down the corridor to the crewroom, walking past the bowed heads of colleagues who said nothing but knew everything.

'There was a positive side,' Taylor said. 'It is a wake-up call for the entire squadron and has come at a useful time when complacency can set in.'

Stu Clarke waited for the Riggers to assess the damage to the fin. Then he and his JEngOs would have to take a decision to either replace the tail fin, a job that would ground the jet for many hours and disrupt essential work on other aircraft, or hope that it was safe to fly with the hole patched.

If it was the former he did not relish having to break the news to the Boss.

14

UNDER THE BOARDWALK

The Squadron settled quickly into a routine of work, sleep, eat and gym, although not necessarily in that order. There was not time for much else. For the engineers the only time that those working on days saw those on nights was as they got on and off buses and pick-up trucks at shift change. It was the same for aircrews flying day waves and night waves. The only day when the pattern changed slightly was Sunday, which was a maintenance day and only GCAS sorties were flown if called for. It was the chance to take in one of the oddest 'sights' at Kandahar Airfield.

Right in the middle of KAF was an American corrugated iron church and a prefab building claiming to be 'Central College Texas'. Close by was one of several entrances to a huge open space 100 metres square, bordered on all sides by a raised covered wooden walkway. This was the Boardwalk. In one corner stood a tall black pole. Hammered into it were a score of yellow signposts pointing in all directions and indicating the number of kilometres to Denmark, Belgium, Estonia, Bulgaria, the UK, Slovenia, Germany and the other nations united in Kandahar Airfield. But the Boardwalk was unmistakeably home-from-home North America.

It was packed with American soldiers, male and female, all

ranks, and all carrying their rifles and machine guns as they always did. Beaming over them from a hoarding in what has been described as 'the apex of warzone escapism' was the familiar face of Colonel Sanders. Wall-to-wall retail outlets on all sides of the Boardwalk were home to KFC, ice cream parlours, juice bars, pizza, burger and hotdog outlets, an AT&T calling centre, a cyber café, currency exchanges and ATMs, a Choice Cuts Barbershop and T.G.I. Friday's, which proclaimed that 'every day is Friday'. An advertising board for Harley-Davidson Motor Cycles announced '"TEAM AFGHANISTAN" IS BACK SERVING YOU!' even though there did not seem to be any Harleys in KAF.

Afghan traders were allowed a slice of the Boardwalk retail action and were raking in the military dollar selling jewellery, souvenirs, fake designer sunglasses and classic flip-top lighters. There were electronics stores, cigarette kiosks displaying the famous smoking cowboy, wool and silk shops festooned with shawls and pashminas. Hand-made brief-cases, leather bags and Western-brand sports backpacks were lashed to the Boardwalk uprights. Grace Frame Shop promised 'a quick service for all styles and budgets'. A something-for-everyone bookstore sold travelogues and histories of the country that most would never see, religious tracts, yellowing pre-war postcards and racks of the latest Hollywood DVDs. An Afghan rug seller hunched down drinking a glass of sweet tea by the stretch of Boardwalk banisters that he had draped with kelims. The size of prayer mats, they were woven with maps of Afghanistan overlaid with images of Kalashnikovs, armoured troop carriers, helicopters and a single word: 'TANK'.

When General Stanley McChrystal was in charge of the war in Afghanistan he had tried to get the many Western fast-food outlets closed down, arguing that vital supply lines should not be used for shipping in food that made the troops too fat to fight. Some had gone but all the rest had outstayed him.

If Kandahar Airfield was like a frontier town that had mushroomed from nowhere into a strategic gateway and hub, there was something of the Klondike about the Boardwalk. It was Dawson City minus the gambling dens and the bars sold alcohol-free mocktails and near-beers instead of bourbon and rye. But like Dawson the Boardwalk was the last port of luxury for those about to step over the wire and into war and a first taste of Western civilisation for those coming back in from dusty, dirty patrol bases and a life of ration packs, septic foot problems and five-inch camel spiders. For those permanently based at KAF – like the thousands of military support personnel who spent their posting standing guard, issuing kit and stamping forms – the Boardwalk was a welcome distraction from the slow, featureless grind of Groundhog Day.

And it was not just an American home-from-home. The Dutch had a coffee shop and a tax-free retail outlet. The Canadians made for a Vanilla Cappuccino Supreme served 'always fresh' at iconic coffee and donut restaurant Tim Hortons.

The Canadians had also hired Afghan labour to make them a fast and true polished concrete hockey rink in one corner of the vast open space enclosed by the Boardwalk. There was little more surreal than seeing Canadian hockey players padded up and helmeted like the Toronto Maple Leafs or the Ottawa Senators ice hockey teams and chasing a puck in the surging heat of an Afghan afternoon. Next to them there was a basketball court and several games of baseball taking place, heels kicking up the dust as home runs were completed. Right by the signpost tree a tanned and trim American sergeant with a boogie-box was trying to coax his flabbier countrymen and women to join an aerobics session on a rustic wooden stage.

Bizarrely, in this far-flung corner of North American sporting endeavour a loudspeaker dangling from the roof at one corner of the Boardwalk was blasting out the commentary from an English Rugby League game between Leeds and St Helens.

Even though the insurgents fired rockets in frequently, forcing patrons to ditch their triple-fruit smoothies and hit the decks, the only hint that there was a war being fought between the West and the insurgents was a 'Terror Chess' set on sale in the German souvenir store. The board was the map of Afghanistan where the Americans – led by a Queen fashioned into the Statue of Liberty and a Barack Obama King – took on the dark forces with Osama bin Laden as their King.

Apart from rockets coming in from the north the only other airborne hazard wafting in on the wind blew in from the south west, carrying with it an unpleasant rotten egg smell that permeated the whole of KAF come rain or shine. This came from its other notable landmark, 'Poo Pond', KAF's sewage treatment lagoon. Dug out originally to handle the leavings of 10,000 residents and surrounded by wire and warning notices saying 'No Dumping Allowed', Poo Pond has struggled to keep up with the daily bowel movements of three times that number.

The distinctive faecal sweetness emanating from the fly-infested surface of Poo Pond was further laced with the diesel fume fallout from a nearby gas station, where the attendants shrouded their heads in shades and shawls to protect themselves from the heat and swirling dust as they pumped fuel into an unending line of dirty, thirsty vehicles.

However, KAF was nasal bliss for hay fever sufferers. No pollen.

*

178

Keith Taylor wanted to leave 617's mark on Kandahar Air Field in a different way. Driving into work early one morning he noticed a broken concrete blast wall in the yard of the cement works over the road from 904 EAW. He slowed down for a closer look. Most of the top half on the right-hand side had cracked off, revealing the rusting steel reinforcing rods. An idea hit him instantly. He parked his pick-up in front of the insignia boards of the other squadrons that stood in a line outside the Tornado Force building and went straight to find the SEngO.

'Stu, there's a damaged blast wall over the road. Rather than just having the squadron insignia on a wooden board in front of a perfect blast wall like the other squadrons we could use that damaged one to make ours into a dam.'

'Right.' The SEngO was already catching the Boss's drift.

'Why don't you pop over there and see if they'll give it to you? It's no use as it is.'

Squadron artwork in theatre is a tradition going back to the Second World War when British and American aircrew decorated the noses of their bombers and fighters, usually with pin-ups of women, the most famous being the *Memphis Belle*. Others featured animals, shark's teeth, cobras, dragons, Danger Mouse, sky pirates and grim reapers. During the Vietnam War squadron art began appearing on the flight lines where aircraft are stationed prior to take-off, often on aircraft carriers. The Squadron's engineers were already painting the Dambusters' 'Après Moi Le Déluge' insignia on the flight line wall at Kandahar, next to those of the other squadrons that had preceded them.

In the First Gulf War the pin-ups were back on the noses of British Buccaneers – riding broomsticks or wielding light-sabres and now minus their Second World War-style Rita

Hayworth swimsuits. There was also art on each bomb, with messages of dedication to Saddam! In the Second Gulf War 31 Squadron 'The Goldstars' painted a big gold star on one of the bombed hardened aircraft shelters on the northern end of the runway at Ali Al Salem Air Base in Kuwait.

'You can still see it on Google Earth,' Stu Clarke said.

Keith Taylor wanted something just as permanent for the Dambusters at Kandahar.

'Consider it done,' Clarke said, with his usual can-do optimism. 'I do like a challenge where I can influence someone to give me something that I am not entitled to.'

Later that morning the SEngO took a casual stroll over to the cement works. Having had an Indian housekeeper when he had been posted to Saudi Arabia, Clarke had picked up a few words of Hindi and Nepali and even some Pashto. His stabs at multilingualism won smiles from the Nepalis in the cement works and several glasses of hot, sweet black tea, but after four visits he had still not quite established who the manager was.

Finally on his fifth trip he befriended the general manager. Taking tea in his office, Clarke strode on to common ground, complimenting the superb contribution of the Ghurkhas to the British Army. Things were getting off on the right course.

Slowly the SEngO steered the conversation to the damaged blast wall.

'That blast wall,' he said casually. 'It's no use as it is; it's rubbish. We'll take it off your hands.'

'You want it so badly it can't be rubbish,' the general manager smiled sweetly. 'This is your fifth visit already,' he reminded Clarke, clearly in the mood to strike a financial deal.

Clarke was not going to cave in so easily.

The man shrugged. 'We could just break it up and recycle it.'

Clarke returned to base and found the Boss. 'This is going to take some time,' SEngO reported.

'I'm sure you'll prevail, Stu,' Taylor said.

Clarke made seven more visits to the general manager, to be greeted with: 'You want it so much; it must be worth something.'

Finally on his eighth trip it was the general manager who caved. Clarke could have the blast wall, but he would have to transport it over the road himself.

To move three tonnes of concrete was going to take a real truck. Undeterred, Clarke convinced 904's military transport to lend him a four-tonner, which he drove over to the cement works where he was greeted by his new Nepali best friends. It was *Namaste* all round as they winched it on to the flatbed and Clarke took it over the road to 904 EAW's site.

Here he encountered another problem. There was no crane to unload it.

Some weeks after making his first call at the cement works the SEngO entered the Boss's room with an air of triumph. 'I've got something for you to see.'

'How on earth did you get it off the truck without a crane?' Taylor asked, staring at the blast wall which now stood next to the insignia of 31 Squadron.

'Unloading the wall without a crane did prove to be another challenge,' SEngO agreed. 'However, Sir, how we did it must remain secret to save both my career and that of the RAF mover who "adapted" some equipment to fulfil the need. I used a mixture of charm and rank abuse to get it sorted!'

'Excellent,' Taylor said. 'Well done. Now all it needs is three lightning bolts, a big sign that says "Dambusters" and some paint.'

15

ENEMY KILLED IN ACTION

On 3 May all TV screens in 617's Squadron block at KAF were full of images of a high-walled compound surrounding a four-storey, flat-roof house in Pakistan. Under pictures of a familiar 54-year-old bearded man with deep brown eyes in white robes, for whom Kandahar had been home until a decade before, ran a ticker: 'BREAKING NEWS. BIN LADEN DEAD'.

Osama bin Laden had been killed in an airborne raid by US Navy Seals at his hideout in the army garrison town of Abbottabad, a Pakistani Aldershot, just 35 miles from Islamabad.

The news had come out first in a tweet from a witness who had heard an explosion and seen helicopters hovering. 'A huge window-shaking bang here in Abbottabad. I hope it's not the start of something nasty.'

Talking heads from around the globe were now lining up in TV studios to speculate. Whatever the full facts there was a spring in the step and many smiles among the Dambusters from Keith Taylor down that morning as the news unrolled and was digested. The outcome of the Abbottabad raid was the kind of mission that Rocksy Sharrocks as a former helicopter pilot would describe as 'a dream ticket'.

Even though bin Laden was now an enemy killed in action

(EKIA) they doubted whether a single fatal gunshot to the head of the world's most wanted man on the international terror chess-set had really changed anything in Afghanistan.

Rich Smith, 617's intelligence officer, was keen to point out that the Taliban was not one cohesive group as so often portrayed in Western media, but a catch-all for a number of loosely federated groups who, beyond having a shared hatred of the 'invaders', had little in common. Then there were other affiliated groups just as dangerous such as the Haqqani Network, with an estimated 10,000 fighters which operated both sides of the Afghan–Pakistani border. Like all intelligence men Smith was a close ally of precision and preferred the catch-all 'insurgent'.

While the pundits were still dissecting the implications of bin Laden's death, on 7 and 8 May insurgents mounted well-planned simultaneous attacks on key government sites in Kandahar City, including the National Directorate of Security Headquarters, the Provincial Governor's offices and the Afghan National Civil Order Police Headquarters. They were repelled and fourteen insurgents were shot dead, three wounded and thirty detained, but this was the biggest attack since the spring offensive had begun a week before. It was a statement of continued intent.

There was nothing that the Dambusters would have liked more than to have taken out some insurgents. It was over a month into 617's detachment and Chris Ball was still the only one who had dropped a bomb. As the younger crews' confidence of flying in Afghan airspace grew, so did their frustration at coming back to KAF with a full load of bombs and not a single Mauser shell spent. However, they realised that they must balance wanting to display all their skills, for which they had trained intensively, and taking pride in achieving the ultimate ISAF aim which was not to deploy munitions unless absolutely necessary.

The armourers had mixed emotions too.

'It's something we have discussed many times in the tea bar,' said 'Ziggy' Zweig. 'It would be good to see some weapons used, but if they are not and that means things are going well on the ground then that's really good.'

To the first-time pilots and navigators it seemed that every time other nations got airborne they went kinetic, while all the Dambusters did was fly over-watch missions. They overlooked the fact that this was statistically inevitable. There were hundreds of jets in Afghanistan flying thousands of missions. The RAF had eight Tornados.

Rocksy Sharrocks understood their frustration. Forty miles west of Kandahar, in the Canadian Area of Operations (AO) he and Caroline Day had positively identified two insurgents who had shot and injured Canadian troops that morning. They were hiding in an agricultural building known as a grape hut in the middle of a field. Sharrocks arrived on station as the helicopters were evacuating wounded troops and established contact with the JTAC.

With the insurgents positively identified and hiding in a location away from built-up areas the 9-Line with the coordinates for the bomb had been completed.

'Caroline, concentrate now,' Sharrocks said. 'Forget everything, calm down; put the coordinates in the kit.'

In seconds she had spun the Paveway IV up, ready to go to its target. All they needed was the ground commander to give them the instruction, 'Clear to drop.'

While they waited Sharrocks told Day, 'Let's work out how we are going to drop the bomb and what profile we are going to fly.' He banked the jet gently and did a practice run over the target.

While he did that he radioed air traffic 'Fellahs, I'm going to be dropping a bomb in the next five minutes. I need the airspace cleared. Get everyone away.'

The airspace was cleared. Back in position at the start of his bombing run and maintaining eyes on the target, Sharrocks waited on the ground commander.

'We have our airman's view of the battlefield but we do not have his view of the battlefield,' he told his navigator. 'We need him to say now is the right time.' For some reason the instruction did not come.

'Maybe he's busy still dealing with wounded guys.' The JTAC had gone silent.

Then on the LITENING pod Caroline saw the insurgents come out of the grape hut, climb on to a motorbike and speed off across the field. The coordinates in the bomb were now useless.

Rocksy spun away and tracked them. 'They've gone to this tree line,' Day told the JTAC. 'They are moving along a wooded road. We can't see them.' The Canadians couldn't see them either.

Without a positive identification they could not despatch a bomb.

The drop was aborted and needing to refuel Sharrocks handed over to two US Navy F-18 Hornets and an unmanned Predator.

'You can't go dropping bombs for the sake of it,' Sharrocks said back at KAF, 'but it was pretty frustrating to discover that the next day the exact location that we were overhead was bombed. *C'est la guerre.*

'Still probably those guys are not insurgents any more.'

*

Some said that it was typical that Chris Ball should be the first and so far the only Dambuster to get a bomb away in Afghanistan. Ballsy was chipper about his strike but he was no gunslinger. He remembered when he was flying with the Rocketeers in Afghanistan the whole squadron being called together at Christmas to watch videos. These were not seasonal movies. The squadron second-in-command, the job Ballsy now had on 617, had watched the video for every single sortie of the scores they had flown.

His navigator Jane Pickersgill, who had written her law dissertation at Durham on International Relations and Security, respected Chris Ball's Afghanistan experience as well as his ability as a pilot and felt privileged to be in the back seat of his jet. She also knew more about the rules of engagement and the legal conduct of war than most on 617 Squadron.

'I understand that if we go through a deployment without dropping it means that the war is being "won",' she said. 'The aircrew are all prepared to drop,' Jane said. 'Obviously within the ROE and zero civilian casualties.' The debate continued somewhere in the Squadron daily.

'There is no silver bullet in Afghanistan,' Ballsy insisted. 'One bomb is not going to win the war. It is not going to be won with bombs.'

Troops winning hearts and minds on the ground backed up with close air support; that was the story now.

'This is a fighting force,' Chris Ball said. 'In a squadron you need to have those who are prepared to do that otherwise they are worthless, but sometimes as aircrew we have to push back and say to a JTAC, "You know what? I am not comfortable deploying this weapon at the moment."'

*

There was one Dambuster who was dropping bombs; a lot of them. Determined to keep flying, Josh Thompson had hitched a ride with 15 Squadron on its heavy bombing exercise at the Royal Canadian Air Force's air base at Cold Lake, in Alberta. For over a month Josh was dropping Paveway IIs, Paveway IVs and strafing hundreds of 27 mm rounds. Cold Lake was a major F-18 base and it felt good to see his old aeroplane flying around as he flew off in a British jet on bombing runs. Afterwards he had flown his Tornado back to Lossiemouth via Bermuda and the Azores, hooking up with big refuelling tankers en route.

His first RAF Tornado detachment had been a great trip and it had more than filled his time.

16

SPIES IN THE SKY

The centrepiece of 3 Commando Brigade's leadership of Task Force Helmand was going to be Operation Omid Haft, a big push deep into the last remaining insurgent strongholds in central Helmand – especially Nahr-e Saraj and Nad-e Ali districts. Working alongside the Afghan Army's Kandak Battalion, Omid Haft (Hope Seven) would drive insurgents out of the Kopak, Malgir and Loy Mandeh Kalay areas in Nahr-e Saraj and bring an arc of security up to the Nahr-e Bughra or Neb Canal.

With security around Lashkar Gah to the south largely controlled by Afghan security forces, with ISAF troops in support, the Taliban and related insurgents were now coming in from the north via the irrigation tunnels built under the Neb Canal and across Route Neptune which ran parallel to it. If that door could be shut the insurgency could no longer be sustained.

Shutting that door was going to be a very complex challenge. Intelligence gathering and pinpointing enemy strength and activity in a built-up and highly populated area before any troops left their FOBs and patrol bases would be a crucial key to Omid Haft's success.

Where were the IED factories and the arms caches? Where

were the insurgents' safe houses? Behind high compound walls that all looked the same it was almost impossible to tell for sure from the ground who or what was inside and what threat they posed. It was only possible to tell the whole story from the sky. Three times a week for six weeks 617's armourers had wheeled out a twenty-foot-long, canoe-shaped torpedo weighing just over a tonne and attached it carefully to the underside of a Tornado. This was not a weapon but a photographic pod called the RAPTOR, one of the most advanced reconnaissance sensors in the world. The RAPTOR contained a camera so powerful that during its testing phase, prior to being used for the first time during the invasion of Iraq in 2003, it took a picture of the time on the face of Big Ben from the Isle of Wight, 75 miles away. That kind of detail and its ability to zoom in day or night on insurgents was of immeasurable value to troops on the ground.

In the lead-up to Omid Haft the Dambusters were flying RAPTOR sweeps over Helmand, zooming in on hundreds of points of interest and delivering stills to be analysed by the highly trained eyes of the Tactical Imagery-Intelligence Wing (TIW), who were working alongside them at 904 EAW in Kandahar. After each sortie the navigators rushed their footage to the coolest room on Kandahar Airfield, known as the TIW Exploitation Room. Banks of computer screens, the purr of the hard drives, subdued lighting, and rigidly controlled temperature made the low-ceilinged, windowless Exploitation Room like a set for the security service drama *Spooks*. It was one of the few dust-free rooms in the whole of KAF. The analysts of TIW and their spies in the sky were giving troops on the ground a vast amount of information about what lay in front of them.

The RAPTOR pod was capable of imaging hundreds of

separate targets on any one sortie and photographing an area the size of Cyprus.

'It could take an hour to analyse and break the intelligence out of just one still of a single compound,' said Sergeant Joolz Thorne, who was in the surreal position of somebody who had spent hours and days peering into the deepest nooks and crannies of Afghan life without ever having travelled beyond the confines of a semi-darkened room at Kandahar Airfield.

'We have been told by 3 Commando Brigade that this compound is a point of interest,' he said, bringing up an image that had been taken that morning by 617 over Loy Mandeh Kalay. Even though the RAPTOR had been flown at many thousands of feet the black and white image was so incredibly detailed it looked as though it had been taken from 50 feet. 'We can now see exactly what is inside,' Joolz said, pointing out where the living quarters were, how many people probably lived there and where the animals were kept. 'That is important because when troops go in they don't want to scare the goats and alert the inhabitants. There's an irrigation ditch that goes under the compound wall, east–west, right across the compound and out the other side, which could be a point of entry for troops, or a likely emergency exit for insurgents.'

Joolz donned a large pair of dark-rimmed stereo glasses. Because each frame of RAPTOR was set to slightly overlap he could place one image over another and get a 3D effect. What had looked like a smudge now stood out. It was clearly some kind of access tunnel. He could also measure the thickness and height of walls, doors and windows, the depth of the irrigation ditch and the undulations of the terrain around the compound.

Every image was broken down into its components, peppered with measurements, observations and comments and then emailed as a fully-fledged intelligence package to 3 Commando Brigade HQ in Lashkar Gah, who would then pass it on to their combat patrols. The RAPTOR images were always black-and-white, almost in negative, giving them the artistic quality of landscape photography.

'It is much easier to pick out detail and contrast in black-and-white than in colour,' Joolz revealed. 'I can't remember how many shades of grey there are but it's hundreds. Colour can restrict the ability to make a differentiation and to establish the kind of detail that a ground commander needs before going in.'

The RAPTOR sorties flown by 617 also meticulously swept the same areas and routes, flying in exact lines to collect imagery that could be compared to the archive of pictures added the week before. This enabled Joolz and the other TIW analysts to spot tell-tale changes in activity and human behaviour on the ground. The recent disturbance of earth near a culvert or locals suddenly shunning a well-worn footpath suggested that IEDs could have been planted in those locations. When Joolz brought up the imagery of a compound from an earlier sortie and compared it to the new footage of the same compound, he could see that there were repeated vehicle tracks going up to it and going into a barn. This might mean it was being used to store weapons and explosives. When evidence like this was uncovered TIW would issue threat and suspicious action warnings to troops on the ground.

'Understanding the pattern of life on the ground and knowing what is normal and what is not is vital,' said Keith Taylor, who had now flown several RAPTOR sorties and was convinced that 617's greatest contribution would be using the pod to find IEDs. Of particular interest was irrigation Tunnel 4 on the Neb Canal, which had been used by insurgents to come in and plant IEDs.

The RAF is the only air force to have a pod like RAPTOR and Flight Sergeant Sara Catterall, an intelligence analyst who headed up the TIW unit at KAF – TIW is headquartered at RAF Marham – was impressed with the commitment 617 had brought to its RAPTOR sorties.

'When the cloud is bad some squadrons will come back and say that the conditions were not right. Twice last week we had bad weather and Wing Commander Taylor and some other crews flew down lower to get the imagery we needed of possible IED sites.'

In Taylor's weekly squadron reports the tally of TIW targets captured by the 617's RAPTOR sorties was never less than impressive. Particularly so, given that aircrews had only had a couple of training sorties with the pod at Lossiemouth. TIW had also briefed 3 Commando Brigade, 617's customer in theatre, on the versatility and depth of intelligence that the RAPTOR could provide. As Omid Haft neared kick-off the requests for imagery were growing daily.

'In the fourteen years I have been doing this job I have never seen the level of interest in the imagery they have taken as I have from this squadron,' Joolz said, as six weeks into the deployment Lucy Williams came in to see what images she had captured of Nad-e Ali on the removable memory module she had loaded into her RAPTOR for a sortie that morning.

'It's good to know we covered all the target points,' she said, looking over Joolz's shoulder. 'You never get to see what you've got until you come in here.'

She looked at a series of images that showed a man who had stopped his motorbike along a main route in Nad-e Ali and was clearly digging a hole.

'I think we have an IED emplacer,' said Joolz, as he 'interrogated' the picture to try and get more detail on the man.

'This is very exciting,' Lucy said, staring at the incredibly detailed but eerie black-and-white images of the bomber against the gentle hum of the computer. 'This is what you hope for every time you do one of these sorties. When we hear at the intelligence briefs of somebody else who has had their leg or arm blown off or been killed it has an effect. When you first get out here you think it's awful and shocking, but your perspective changes and you start to think, "I hope they only had one leg blown off, that they're okay." '

Unlike their predecessors having to avoid tracer and anti-aircraft guns over Germany or missiles in Iraq and Bosnia, this was the closest that this generation of Dambusters would come to contact with the enemy in Afghanistan. And unlike a state-on-state war, in a counter-insurgency conflict such as this, the enemy was at his most dangerous when you couldn't see him. In a game of stealth the aircraft's frog's-eye glimpse of warfare was even more important in protecting and forewarning the boots on the ground.

That afternoon TIW issued the imagery that Lucy Williams had brought in with a threat warning to 3 Commando Brigade, who identified the man, a known IED emplacer, and arrested him.

'When you find an IED, it is not like dropping a bomb where there is an immediate measurable effect,' Lucy said. 'You never know for sure if you have prevented a life being taken or whether the person who planted it is free to then plant more. That is why this case was so rewarding. They got the guy.'

'There's a lot of competition between the navs to get the best imagery,' Sara Catterall said, which is why she had introduced a 'Nav of the Week' trophy. 'We gave it to Caroline Day last week because she got some absolutely superb imagery and worked really hard to get it, plus her fiancé Jon Overton was flying on the Thursday so we just wanted to wind him up a little bit!'

RAPTOR was also being used to identify potential helicopter landing sites and drop zones for Omid Haft and because it was an ISAF asset other coalition forces also requested TIW's Tornado-captured imagery.

'Nobody has anything as good as RAPTOR for high quality, over-arching situational awareness,' Sara Catterall said. 'The imagery is superior and the interpretation with human eyes is second to none. However good the technology is for capturing an image, you can't beat the eyes for interpretation.'

While eyes and analytical skills told TIW intelligence analysts if earth had been disturbed by insurgents burying IEDs, the aircrews knew that the RAPTOR pod could be temperamental. It was a delicate piece of avionic equipment containing some sensitive software, and was kept in an air-conditioned shelter at one end of the ramp. For pilots the challenge was on landing the jet with a RAPTOR slung underneath. The pod was so heavy and bulky that there was minimal ground clearance. Bang the Tornado down too hard and several million pounds' worth of sleuthing camera would be damaged.

Chris Ball reckoned RAPTOR missions, with the huge number of targets to be photographed inside a few hours, were some of the most demanding and precise flying in theatre, especially when a TIC meant that the airspace you were trying to fly was suddenly cleared of all but essential combat aircraft. Not all 617 pilots liked RAPTOR missions. Gary Montgomery said that chugging up and down in straight lines on a predetermined flight path painstakingly harvesting up points of interest (POIs) was vitally important, but it was about as exciting as mowing the lawn.

*

Not all crews were being short-changed on the excitement front. Flight Lieutenant Alex Hutchison was just completing tortuous negotiations with two different air traffic control agencies to clear the airspace to get to a tanker when his navigator Flight Lieutenant Jon Overton, who had been talking to a JTAC, cut in.

'Stand by, Hutch! Stop doing that. We've got to do a show of force. The guy really needs an SOF.'

The 'guy' was a JTAC with a 42 Commando patrol in Upper Gereshk Valley, way below them in Helmand. The marines had noticed a crowd of people running to a compound, an unusual sight in the raking heat of the middle of the day, when life mostly slowed to a crawl. They could have been trying to find a goat or have gone to grab their guns. The JTAC wanted them to disperse before the patrol moved on.

Hutchison and Overton quickly discussed their options. They had five minutes before they had to go and refuel but the other Tornado with Al Spence and Conan Mullineux that was returning from the tanker would not be back on station in time to do a show of force.

'These guys don't ask for an SOF unless they need it,' Overton said.

And it was always possible to tell from the voice if a JTAC was potentially in trouble. This one's ground commander wanted to get his men into a position of cover and greater safety in case something erupted from the compound.

Hutchison opted to delay going to the tanker and take the risk of burning down to below diversion fuel. That meant that if he missed his plug on that tanker and could not find another he would have to use his reserves and go back to Kandahar and if the runway there was closed for any reason he would no longer have enough fuel to divert to Bastion or anywhere else. They would be forced to bang out over the desert and lose the jet. Normally a crew would never burn down to below diversion fuel unless they were supporting a TIC. These troops were not in contact but potentially they were in danger.

'Let's go,' Hutchison said.

'It's to this fixed point here,' Overton said, putting a marker on the screen for Hutchison to see on his display.

Getting down into the valley was not as simple as dropping the nose, shoving the throttles forward into combat and zooming in. The valley was littered with aerostat balloons, lower level spies in the sky, anchored to the ground every half mile. Although they were marked on a map their steel anchor cables were not always easy to see especially if the wind changed direction. The marines and other units in the area also had a dozen mortars in place. They were not firing but they were active. The JTAC would have to confirm that all had been made safe before the Tornado could descend.

While Overton was talking to the JTAC and getting a 9-Line to authorise the show of force, Hutchison was on the radio to air traffic at Bastion to get the airspace cleared. There were several helicopters and other aircraft, including a UAV, in their section of the Kill Box that needed to move aside.

Within five minutes of being asked to do a show of force everything was in place. Hutchison took the jet down to 500 feet in seconds, then 250. He was flying below the balloons. Close up, their cables seemed just feet from their wing tips, as close as slalom markers.

As they sped towards the compound 150 feet off the ground a female voice suddenly filled the cockpit. 'Obstruction! Obstruction!' she implored them.

This was the ground proximity warning system (GPWS), always referred to as Bitching Betty. Using data from the Tornado's radar altimeter, inertial navigation system, GPS and flight control system, Betty could predict the flight path of the jet up to five miles away and warn of collision. Her other warning was 'Pull up! Pull up!' Betty had sensed an observation balloon. It had just been put up and was not on the Tornado's maps.

Hutch pitched his jet hard to the right. One wing dipped, the other shot up skywards. Their heads were now flying parallel to the ground at 495 knots (570 mph). He straightened her up, the ground catapulted back underneath them and he brought the Tornado screaming in low over the compound at 120 feet close to 520 knots (600 mph) and with enough force to ripple the ridge tiles. Those inside would not have seen them coming until the very last minute. Like all pilots Hutchison knew a show of force was all about getting in fast and getting out quicker. Clear of the compound he piled on the Gs, climbing, climbing to get his jet as high as possible and out of range of anybody with an RPG. The Tornado could withstand a certain amount of battle damage but it was not armoured.

Back up at altitude Hutchison looked at his fuel gauges. They had to get to a tanker fast. The air controllers sent him to a KC-135, a dreaded Iron Maiden.

'If you really need fuel badly it is the worst tanker you can have; an added pressure you don't need.'

He lined the basket up, plugged in, kinked the fuel tube and took on 300 kilos. But then turbulence threw him out again. Now he had enough fuel to feel comforted that he would not have to throw the jet in the desert. He still needed more to get home safely and to avoid the engines flaming out from fuel starvation. He waited for the tanker to settle then came up just underneath and plugged in again. This time he filled to full.

Hutchison and Overton returned to Gereshk Valley and hooked up with the other Tornado, which was now back flying over the marines. They took a look at the compound they had recently buzzed. There was now no sign of anybody inside, hostile or otherwise. The show of force had done its job. The marine patrol could go about its business unhindered.

In the debrief back at KAF Hutchison was asked to explain why he and Overton had decided to do the show of force when they were so low on fuel.

'By the letter of the law we should have said to them we don't have the fuel to do it,' Hutchison admitted, 'but if those guys in the compound were hostile they could have posed an immediate threat to the patrol, so we had no business being away at a tanker, leaving them in danger. We scared them off and reassured our guys on the ground that we can support and protect them.'

Conan may have been the senior man on the two-ship sortie in terms of flying experience but it was Hutchison who had authorised action that day as skipper of the lead jet. When it came to taking action the RAF was not rank-bound. 'I'm the one who put pen to paper because I judged that eroding our fuel safety margins was a risk that we had to take.'

17

SIXTY-EIGHT YEARS ON

14 May 2011, Petwood Hotel, Woodhall Spa

On a sunny Saturday afternoon men of a certain age began arriving at the half-timbered Petwood Hotel in Woodhall Spa. They might have lost the gait of youth but they still strode purposefully into the dark panelled lobby to check in. Petwood had been built in the early years of the twentieth century in the Tudor and Jacobean style for the daughter of the founder of the Maples furniture company. Set in 30 acres of green lawn, statues, terraces and winding rhododendron walks covered in big pink and scarlet blooms, Petwood was the opposite end of the colour spectrum from the brown upon brown of Kandahar, but it had a special place in the Squadron's history.

Requisitioned by the RAF in 1942, Petwood was the Dambusters' Officers' Mess and every year on the closest weekend to the 17 May Dams Raid, the 617 Squadron Aircrew Association meets for the annual Dambusters Reunion Dinner. Squadron history is everywhere at Petwood. Outside in the car park is a bouncing bomb. Inside the interminable corridors and creaky landings are adorned with oil paintings, drawings and framed photographs of Guy Gibson, Leonard Cheshire and other aviators who have flown with the Dambusters during the sixty-eight years that have passed since the Dams Raid.

The veterans walked to their rooms past framed groups of pensive and formal faces staring out of the walls. Other pictures captured the smiles and grins of young men clutching drinks and smoking pipes and cigarettes on the terrace. The place of pilgrimage was the Squadron Bar. It was not the main hotel bar; its interior was more a place of contemplation, with more pictures and framed press cuttings cataloguing the Dams raids, the sinking of the *Tirpitz* and other famous missions.

Some eighty people, including Aircrew Association historian Robert Owen, assembled for dinner that evening. Serving officers in their No. 5B Mess dress and the rest in dinner jackets and ladies in evening dresses were welcomed by Group Captain David Robertson, Chairman of the Association. As OC 617 from 2000 to 2003, Robertson had led the pioneering Storm Shadow raids on Baghdad in which David 'Noddy' Knowles and Andy Turk had their close encounter with a missile. Now he was Group Captain Operational Training at Air Command in High Wycombe, responsible for ensuring that RAF squadrons going on operations were fully exercised before deploying. When 617 were in America a couple of years earlier on an annual Red Flag exercise on ranges north of Las Vegas – involving heavy weapons, electronic warfare and air-to-air combat against F-15s and F-16s – it had been put together by Robertson's team.

'Today's 617 aircrew are much better than we were when we joined the Air Force because we ask so much more of them these days,' he said. 'They probably don't have the depth of knowledge of the equipment that we had then – they pumped so much into us we probably could have built the equipment that we operated – but you don't need that level of expertise now. Aircrew today are very intelligent and committed to doing a really good job. And they are personable – amongst the best.'

Robertson welcomed guest of honour Mary Stopes-Roe, the daughter of Sir Barnes Wallis, and said he was delighted to present her with associate membership of the Association. In her eighties but robust and straight to the point she rose to make a short speech.

'I accept this honour in the name of my father but I think everybody here knows what he thought of the Squadron. As he said to us: "any fool can invent something but it takes those that use it to make it work". That is the Squadron.'

Normally the Officer Commanding 617 would give one of the main speeches but because Keith Taylor was in Afghanistan he had asked his wife Lizee to stand in for him. As a teacher she was well used to standing in front of audiences who were far more unruly than this one, but she looked nervous when she got up to speak.

'Like many I was inspired by *The Dam Busters* book and I was determined to become a pilot,' she began. 'My parents got all the recruiting office publications but I was disappointed that the WRAFs as they were then seemed to spend their time playing netball and driving senior officers around in shiny cars, neither of which really appealed to me. So I dropped the idea and my career went in a different direction, but it does strike me now that I come to think of it how life has a habit of coming full circle. Only a couple of weeks ago I applied to join my local netball team and often have to pick Keith up after he's been to Happy Hour!'

The ice was broken. She told them how she had met Keith at a party for single officers when he had been stationed at RAF Brüggen in West Germany. She spoke of the strain on families left behind when squadrons went on ops but praised the fortnightly briefings laid on by 617's rear party at Lossiemouth, which kept them up to date, and the squadron online forum where every day new pictures were being added showing their loved ones at work in Kandahar.

She also read out a progress report from Keith. The first month had been relatively quiet as he had wished, he wrote. The Squadron had bedded in and was performing well supporting troops on the ground. Seventy-five per cent of the Dambusters' work had been supporting British troops on the ground.

'We have flown reconnaissance missions using a pod called RAPTOR which is saving army lives as it detects mines and IEDs laid by insurgents. We have also flown several shows of force, which involve flying low and fast over known insurgent positions for maximum shock effect to dissuade them from attacking coalition forces.

'The Squadron has yet to drop any weapons,' Lizee read out, 'but with the Taliban's Spring Offensive, "Operation Badr", which kicked off on May 1, this is only a matter of time.

'The one aggravation on base is the rocket attacks,' Keith Taylor said. 'They predominantly happen at night to cause maximum disruption by disturbing sleep patterns of the majority. Still, they do keep us on our toes; or on our faces actually.'

So far there had been two salvos of 107 mm rockets fired into KAF, the first just after the main squadron party had arrived at Kandahar.

It all seemed so far removed from the half-timbered familiarity of the Petwood Hotel where Al Monkman then marked the twentieth anniversary of another conflict, the First Gulf War, in typically ebullient style.

'Combat is a visceral, an intensely emotional experience,' he began, 'and I remember watching spellbound as the flak and the missiles arched up from the black desert at night for the first time. Those sphincter moments are not forgotten quickly. I was hugely excited, feeling that pulse of history, that adrenaline rush that has fuelled my addiction to operational flying throughout my entire career.'

Then, as the final toasts neared, Monkman's thoughts and those of everyone in the room turned both to the former glories the Dambusters hold dear and to the conflicts of the present.

'The standards and values that were laid down during the Second World War of professional excellence, a total trust in others, an utter commitment to the task at hand; they are timeless and they underpin the great sense of Squadron spirit and pride which continues to this day.'

In the bar after the dinner, talk soon turned to squadron spirits of another kind and the keen rivalry between the Dambusters and 9 Squadron. This was manifested most strongly in the disagreement as to whose bomb had actually sunk the *Tirpitz*. Both squadrons had flown on that mission. Both had dropped bombs. To this day each squadron claims that it was their Tallboy that had sunk the mighty German battleship at Tromsø Fjord in 1944. Alfred Zuba, who had been a sailor on watch on *Tirpitz* when the Lancasters attacked, described the attack vividly in the 617 Squadron Aircrew Association's newsletter *Après Moi* in 2010.

'Now things hit us. The ship jumps up. A further two hits; everything flies about the ship. The ship rocks as if it's being shaken by gigantic fists. The resonant sound of the hits is like cloud in the room. Now the ship begins to list, slowly and relentlessly. In horror I stare at the gauge. It is now showing 18 degrees.' Only 900 of the 1900 crew survived.

Diplomatically not taking sides on who did for the *Tirpitz*, the official telegram of congratulations was sent to both 617 and 9. Strangely, this only stoked the rivalry. Five years later the Norwegian salvage team found an engine room bulkhead on which one of the *Tirpitz* crew had painted a picture of the ship powering through a choppy sea and bearing the legend *Gegen England* (Against England). In 1950 this was presented by the Royal Norwegian Air Force to Bomber Command and put on display at RAF Binbrook in Lincolnshire, where both squadrons were then based.

The trouble started when the squadrons relocated to different bases – for years afterwards there had been repeated raids by one or the other to appropriate the *Tirpitz* bulkhead and reclaim it as their own.

'Of course it was ours,' Tony Iveson insisted, as the drinks flowed in time to the stories. 'If you look at the timings of each of the aircraft on that mission 9 Squadron did not drop any bombs until we had let go all of ours. Nine of our aircraft had dropped within ninety seconds, the other nine within a couple more minutes. Within eleven minutes the *Tirpitz* was sunk.'

Robert Owen gave the historian's view. 'The difference was that 617 had a precision bomb sight while 9 had the standard Bomber Command sight. Given the equipment 9 had they put up an admirable performance.'

Balance is not something that often features in this spirited debate. At the bottom of the main staircase at Cranwell there hangs a large oil on canvas of Iveson's Lancaster at 15,000 feet bombing *Tirpitz*. The drama of the raid is captured for ever between the blueness of a cloudless sky and the ice below, as the ship's heavy guns blast shells up at Iveson's Lancaster. Today's 617 aircrew would have walked past it most days on their initial officer training.

The members of 9 Squadron – formed in the First World

War as No. IX (Bomber) and also known as IX(B) Squadron – disagreed vehemently with Iveson's interpretation and took the *Tirpitz* bulkhead to their headquarters and claimed it as their own. By 1991 it had become part of the fabric of 9's crew-room, then at RAF Brüggen, 27 miles west of Düsseldorf. The Dambusters were safely on the other side of the water at RAF Marham and for years had shown no interest in it. The older squadron assumed that possession was nine tenths of the law and history was on their side.

'However, one 617 navigator called Andy began to hatch a plot to get the bulkhead back to its rightful squadron and kick-start the old rivalry,' explained Wing Commander Jock Cochrane, warming to a favourite story.

Cochrane, a navigator, served two stints on 617, first as a flying officer and then as a squadron leader. A regular attendee at 617 reunion dinners, he was now based in Bristol working on the UK Military Flying Training Project to bring together all flying training for the three services from 2017 onwards for the following 25 years. He had also been adviser to the Chief of the Iraqi Air Force, but back then when Andy was plotting to repatriate the *Tirpitz* bulkhead he was just a flying officer.

'Andy was always talking about getting the bulkhead back, but we never thought he'd do it, but then we went on an exchange visit to Volkel Air Base in Holland. Andy had done a lot of research and he knew Volkel was just an hour's drive over the German border from Brüggen. As soon as we arrived he went off to the local hardware store and on the first weekend in June he and this other navigator turned up in a minibus full of hammers and drills.'

Andy said the 'mission' was on. 'Let's go, guys!'

'There were nine of us pretty hung-over and we still didn't think he'd go through with it until we pulled up at the Brüggen main gate. He blagged us through and we parked up around the corner of 9 Squadron's site. It was all locked up. There was a German worker painting lines in the car park.

'I thought, *this is not going to happen*. Andy took a sledgehammer and got us through the front door. We piled in, found our way into the crewroom and set up the equipment.'

The bulkhead was set into the wall in what looked like a fireplace.

'We set about trying to drill it out. We turned the radio on to mask the noise. Getting the thing out of the wall proved to be a difficult task. I am not sure the tools were up to the job.'

But in the end they were successful and they jubilantly made off with the disputed trophy.

Wing Commander Bob Iveson (no relation to Tony), 617's commanding officer, took the rap, put on his No.1s and flew to Germany for a bollocking, but the bulkhead stayed at RAF Marham, buried in the floor of 617's crewroom, covered in glass and protected by motion sensors, courtesy of the RAF Police.

About a year later Cochrane went into an early met briefing and discovered that the crewroom door was locked. It had been sealed with nails from the inside. It appeared that 9 Squadron had made an abortive attempt to seize the bulkhead back and had left things in a somewhat untidy state. Four days later the Queen was due to visit 617. All was spick and span when she arrived but it had been at the cost of much frantic effort! When 617 moved to Lossiemouth the *Tirpitz* bulkhead went with them but in 2002 it was presented to the Bomber Command Museum at Hendon in London as a memorial to 617 and 9 and replicas were given to the squabbling squadrons.

These days the rivalry continues in the shape of a bombing competition between 617 and 9 held every three years. They first fought for the large solid silver trophy on the bombing ranges on the Wash on 12 November 2009 to commemorate the sixty-fifth anniversary of the sinking of the *Tirpitz*.

'We won that too,' Tony Iveson smiled, making his way to bed.

History was also on Flight Lieutenant Gary Montgomery's mind in Kandahar, where the Squadron were having a barbecue to commemorate the sixty-eighth anniversary of the Dams Raids. As a modern Dambuster he was fascinated by 617's heritage and had asked to be the Squadron's history rep. He dealt with enquiries and requests for information from the public and academics, referring them on to Robert Owen – 'he's a great guy; knows everything' – when he did not know the answer. It was appropriate that it fell to Monty to say a few words on the most important date in 617's history.

'I want to get over a little bit of the ethos of this squadron. A lot of the younger engineers may not have come across the history before, certainly not briefed by the aircrew.'

It was also halfway through the tour and a chance to make sure that morale stayed topped up. Monty spoke for ten minutes about the design of the Barnes Wallis bomb, the huge engineering challenge of adapting the Lancasters to carry it and how every single member of each crew was doing something they had never done before.

'The Lancaster was being asked to do something it had not been designed to do, a bit like the Tornado,' he explained. 'The Dams Raids have been written about a huge amount and a lot of it is about Guy Gibson. He was a remarkable pilot; but this wasn't just a one-person event,' Monty emphasised. 'It was science, engineering and pilot, aircrew and ground crew skills that came together; a big combined effort to do something crazy, something outrageous. It was a remarkable mission and it is all our history.'

The Squadron's history was also a source of pride to Corporal Stephen 'Beany' Doyle, who had been in the RAF twenty years and worked on engines and airframes. He had visited the dams several times.

'The experience was very poignant,' he said. The previous November when Keith Taylor had been laying the Squadron wreath at Woodhall Spa, Beany had been laying his own wreath on two graves that lie side by side in the cemetery of the small Dutch town of Steenbergen in the south of the Netherlands.

'They are the only flyers in a civvie graveyard. Their graves are surrounded by a small hedge and there is a book of remembrance.'

These are the graves of Guy Gibson and Squadron Leader Jim Warwick, who crashed near Steenbergen in a Mosquito and were killed on 19 September 1944.

'After the Dams Raids Gibson got sent to the US to do a goodwill lecture tour and then he was given a planning desk job,' Beany explained. 'I guess they wanted to keep a war hero out of harm's way, but you can imagine how boring he found that.' While the station boss at RAF Woodhall Spa was away Gibson fixed to fly a Mosquito that was directing a bombing raid near Mönchengladbach. There is no doubt that if the station boss had been on duty Gibson would never have been allowed to go on the mission. He was too valuable to lose.

Bombing raid completed, Gibson, gung-ho and press-on to the last, decided to make the return journey to Woodhall at low level against official briefing instructions. What happened as Gibson flew over Steenbergen is still debated today. No official reason was ever given for the fatal crash. Some reckoned it was unforeseen mechanical failure that had caused the Mosquito to splutter. There was a jet of flame and then the aircraft dived into the ground and exploded. Another theory is that Gibson and Warwick, who was responsible for managing the fuel, were inexperienced on the Mosquito and ran out of gas in one tank and switched to the other too late. The sudden rush of fuel into a now dry engine probably caused the fire and even though the second engine was running Gibson had lost control of the aircraft.

Whatever the reason, Gibson had been partly responsible for his own death by being somewhere he was not supposed to be. Initially the Dutch rescuers thought they had found just one body. After a subsequent search they realised that two graves had to be dug. 'In Steenbergen there's a Gibsonstraat and a Warwickstraat,' Beany Doyle said, with pride in his voice, 'and also a Lancasterstraat.'

In the town's Dambusters Memorial Park a propeller from a Lancaster is mounted on a stone obelisk, a monument to all aircrew who helped liberate the Netherlands.

Barnes Wallis said Gibson, who had flown more than 170 bomber and fighter sorties and won a DFC and Bar, a DSO and Bar and the VC by the age of 24, 'had pushed his luck beyond all limits and he knew it. But that was the kind of man he was … a man of great courage, inspiration and leadership. [He was] a man born for war but born to fall in war.'

When Guy Gibson was killed he was just 26 years old, the same age as Al Spence, the youngest Dambuster pilot now serving with 617 in Kandahar.

On the evening of 17 May, sixty-eight years after the nineteen Lancasters of 617 Squadron flew east to the dams, two Tornados took off into the night sky from Kandahar Airfield.

They flew to the outskirts of Kandahar City and took their place in a huge stack of aircraft. Below them were attack helicopters and an AC130 gunship, above them a UAV. Flight Lieutenant Stew Campbell watched as two Chinooks swept in and landed a Canadian team, which set up a cordon some way off from a compound, where they could not be seen.

Then Campbell's navigator spotted a motorbike and a car heading to the compound. He immediately alerted the JTAC. 'Got 'em! PID.' The people in charge of the vehicles, perhaps thinking better of it, then turned back.

An hour later another Chinook arrived and landed much nearer the compound. Through his NVGs Campbell watched in shades of green as an ISAF team of about a dozen jumped down and were inside in the compound in minutes. There was no resistance.

Like the Dams Raids this operation had been carefully pre-planned. Perhaps 617's sortie in support of it may not have been as dramatic as Chastise but the Canadians had found an IED factory in the heart of Taliban country. Three men were detained. One of them had explosive residue on his hands.

'I didn't think about the Dams while we were on the sortie because there was too much to do,' Campbell said, 'but it had been on our minds earlier. It was good to be airborne on that particular day.'

On 21 May another chapter of 617's history closed when Squadron Leader Chris Ball landed at Kandahar, his last flight as a Dambuster before returning to England to take up a desk job in High Wycombe. Climbing out of the Tornado he was surprised to see so many people there to mark this landmark in his RAF career. Even those who were not on shift had come in. It was a mark of how much Ballsy was liked and respected. However, he was also slightly suspicious. It was traditional to see off those leaving the Squadron by dumping them in the deep, dark and freezing emergency water tanks at Lossiemouth. Ballsy knew that in a desert he was going to be spared that. Keith Taylor and a few others were clutching bottles of water and as he got on the ground he got sprayed. On a hot Afghan evening it was pleasant, but as he stood there chatting to his soon-to-be ex-colleagues somebody came up behind him and dumped a bin of filthy water over him. Suitably drenched and drowned in laughter he walked with the others from the ramp to the engineers' backyard for a few near-beers. Somebody produced a camera and asked him to stand next to Keith Taylor for a picture. Too late, he saw an even bigger bin of oily water being carried aloft by 'Big Stu', Corporal Stuart Young, a mechanical engineer who was a mountain of a man whose rock band played at Squadron gigs in the HAS shelters and the feeder (canteen) back at Lossiemouth. Seeing what was about happen and knowing there was no escaping Big Stu's imminent delivery, Ballsy tried to grab Keith Taylor close to get him soaked as well but the Boss was too quick and shot sideways out of his embrace.

Always one to enter into the spirit, Ballsy deemed it 'a pretty good see-off'. Four hours later he had cleared his paperwork, packed his bags and skipping sleep was sitting on the Boardwalk having a coffee, the surreal beginning of a journey back to Bastion and then out of Afghanistan to a future in the gentle Buckinghamshire countryside, where he would be posting new young fast jet pilots to their first squadrons. Rocksy Sharrocks would take Chris Ball's place as 2iC 617.

*

Meanwhile Josh Thompson had recently returned from Canada. If Josh could still not support 617 Squadron in theatre, he could support their families back in Lossiemouth and was encouraged to do so by Squadron Leader Ball when he returned from theatre. Ballsy was 617's link with a full programme of social events and get-togethers organised by wives, husbands, partners and children, both on the base and in Elgin, that was in full swing. These included visits to swimming pools and wildlife parks, drinks, dinners and raffles. Both the Squadron and RAF Lossiemouth had family open days. A Dambusters website forum 'Air Space' was filling up with photographs of the Squadron in Kandahar, many taken by Caroline Day and Flight Sergeant Paul Peden, whose idea it had been for bringing families closer together. He had also asked the families back home to put in requests for posed pictures of their loved ones, especially silly ones. He was now inundated.

SEngO Clarke had a nice line in camp poses, several were sporting very dodgy moustaches that they were growing for charity while Keith Taylor was captured underneath his *Toy Story* duvet, chosen by his eldest daughter Lucy. His mother-in-law had dubbed him 'Boss Lightyear'. Boss Lightyear was showing an increasing liking for the camera; Lightyear grinning as he leapt down from the wings of a jet, creeping up behind Rocksy Sharrocks as his new 2iC was marking a wall-map and mock-strangling him. However, a shot of him pointing at dirt on the crewroom floor while the female aircrew did the sweeping did not go down well with his girls at home. He would have to answer to that one when he got back.

Lucy Taylor had found the months before her father had deployed much more distressing than his being in Afghanistan. During a history lesson on the First World War she had been upset when a teacher had said it was unlikely that anybody in the class would know what it was like to have someone close go to war and not know if they would ever see them again.

'I worried about what if something went wrong, if he didn't come back? Once I heard from him and could see pictures and emails I knew it would be all right.'

Keith's youngest daughter Hannah had kept her spirits up by visiting the Dambusters' crewroom at RAF Lossiemouth to do the research for her school history presentation on the Squadron.

Sergeant Al Sharp's wife Emma had decided to set up a fund-raising project with three other wives and girlfriends called Operation Halfway, encouraging everyone to swim, cycle, row, run or walk sponsored miles until they had accumulated 2800 – halfway to Kandahar. The money they raised would go to the Royal Air Force Association, a charity that supports RAF personnel and their families who are experiencing hardship, and the appeal launched by the 617 Squadron Aircrew Association to build a new monument in Woodhall Spa to those who had been killed in action since the Second World War. Emma's four-year-old son Calum was clocking up six miles a day walking to and from his nursery school.

Emma, who also had a six-year-old daughter, Caitlin, and was about to start the final year of a three-year nursing degree, had found the beginning of Al's deployment very hard. Apart from studying and having two small children to look after, her car, washing machine, fridge freezer and iron had all broken in the first week Al was away. And then one day she looked out of her window and saw a car driving very slowly up her road. Inside were two RAF uniforms obviously looking for a house number. She hadn't heard from Al for a couple of days. This was how bad news arrived. Instinctively her hands grabbed the window sill and did not loosen until the car had turned the corner and had not returned.

'Still,' she said, 'if you are married to a blue suit you just have to get on with it.'

Helping each other to just get on with it was bringing the wives and girlfriends, boyfriends and husbands closer together. Lizee Taylor did not have the central role that wives of the officer commanding of years before had had, such were the support services now laid on by the RAF, but she did sit on the wives' committee and tried to get to as many social events as she could, including the coffee mornings and drop-ins.

'Carving out a role as the Boss's wife is not easy,' she admitted. 'You don't want to become pivotal to everything, as though you are bossing the wives, nor do you want to appear uninterested.' She concentrated on the practical things she could do too. 'Keith phoned to say that one of the Squadron's wives was in hospital for an operation so I sent flowers and fixed lifts for her when she came out because she was unable to drive.' She also contacted Nicola Hutchison to see if she could do anything to help with the twins.

In addition to the social events there was a fortnightly briefing at RAF Lossiemouth given by the Squadron to update families on the latest events from theatre. Josh Thompson now volunteered to do these.

In the early days of the deployment some of the engineers' wives felt self-conscious in the presence of uniformed officers. Some of those who lived in Elgin or Lossiemouth had never been on the base before without their other halves. Josh's easy manner and the fact that he was American immediately brought a more relaxed atmosphere. He turned up with a PowerPoint he had put together.

'I've got as much information as I can from the guys in

theatre and included any experiences I have had in the past to help you understand what the Squadron are dealing with in theatre,' he explained. After the presentation they came up to talk to Josh and ask questions. 'I like to think they really appreciated that and had a better understanding of what was happening,' he said. The film star looks and impeccable manners went down well too.

Emma Sharp spoke for many when she said: 'not only was it interesting but because there was food and the children were taken care of in a crèche for the evening, it was a chance for me just to be me.'

'I enjoyed it too,' Josh said. 'It made me feel I was being helpful.'

Stalk's report was upbeat. He did not mention that into the second half of May insurgent activity had increased markedly. The poppy harvest which traditionally finishes in Helmand in early May had released farmers of fighting age, the '$10-a-day Taliban', to join the insurgency. It followed a classic pattern. On 15 May, a 19-year-old marine of Lima Company, 42 Commando, Royal Marines, was killed by an improvised explosive device in the Loy Mandeh wadi area in Nad-e Ali district, Helmand. He had landed by helicopter in a cordon and search operation of 'compounds suspected of being associated with IED facilitation', according to the MoD. 'The location of these compounds allows insurgent commanders to operate with a degree of impunity.'

On 19 May there were multiple direct fire attacks on ISAF patrol bases along Helmand River Valley. A suicide bomber had attempted to target Lashkar Gah, 3 Commando Brigade Headquarters, and there had been a rocket attack on Camp Bastion, the first since February 2010. On 21 May a suicide bomber had attacked the National Military Hospital in Kabul, killing eight medical students. The next day gunmen and suicide bombers hit Khost Bazaar and the governor's compound in Khost province, east Afghanistan, resulting in an eight-hour firefight in which five Afghan National Army soldiers were killed. Meanwhile a truck taking workers into Kandahar City had driven over a pressure plate IED killing twenty and injuring a score more. The list of fatalities and injuries was detailed in Rich Smith's daily intelligence briefings to the Dambusters in Kandahar.

18

OPERATION OMID HAFT

On 24 May Royal Marines from Juliet Company, 42 Commando with ANA troops moved into south Loy Mandeh Kalay to create a diversion and draw the enemy away from Malgir, which was to be the main focus of Omid Haft. Two days later, in the early hours of 26 May and in poor weather, 300 soldiers from the Afghan National Army (ANA) and 1st Battalion, The Rifles, landed by helicopter in the town of Alikozai in Helmand. It was one of the largest air assaults seen in Afghanistan. Protecting the helicopters were gunners from 29 Commando Regiment Royal Artillery, who fired illumination rounds to flush out any insurgents lurking in the darkness. Operation Omid Haft had begun.

By 9 a.m. the ANA soldiers and those from 1 Rifles had got to Malgir and secured several checkpoints and crossings over the Neb Canal. The Sappers of 39 Armoured Engineer Squadron (39AES) carried out the initial clearance of the strategically important Route Neptune. With other routes also cleared, tonnes of supplies could be flown in by helicopter and brought in by road to sustain the hundreds of troops now on the ground. By the end of the first day a cordon had been secured around Malgir and five new checkpoints were in place.

So far there had been very little resistance.

The next day, 27 May, Juliet Company moved towards the village of Loy Mandeh from the west, which was still controlled by the Taliban. The Task Force regarded Loy Mandeh as the 'last ulcer' in its area of operations. Juliet Company's mission was to clear out the insurgents and then set up checkpoints to create the conditions for the Royal Engineers to clear the hundreds of IEDs that had been planted in and around the village. Juliet Company were soon involved in very heavy fighting and were battling their way from compound to compound. Lima Company, 42 Commando and Afghan troops pushed in towards Loy Mandeh Kalay from the east to hit the insurgents and provide support.

On the afternoon of 27 May a Juliet Company patrol led by a 23-year-old lieutenant as troop commander on a Clear, Hold, Build Operation were searching a compound in the village when an IED exploded, killing him and a 28-year-old marine, a heavy weapons specialist who was the father of a son who had not reached his first birthday, and the winner of the Military Cross for gallantry in Afghanistan for saving the life of a colleague on Operation Herrick 9 in 2009. The troop commander had only passed fit for duty after officer training in December 2010.

The news of their deaths did not take long to reach Kandahar. As 617's linkman with 3 Commando Brigade Jock Adams knew in minutes. As yet more sorties took off from KAF and headed for Helmand to support Omid Haft, special signs went up on all the phone-booths and public computers and in all British military and civilian offices, 617 included. They carried two words: Operation Minimise. Op Minimise meant that all British communication from Afghanistan with the outside world had been cut to give the MoD the chance to tell the families of deaths and serious injuries before the press or anybody else could. When the families of 617 squadron suddenly could not get an email connection or the phone did not ring at the appointed time they knew too what it meant, and although logic told them that the RAF suffered few casualties in Afghanistan they still dreaded every knock on the door until the phones were back up again and they knew finally the identities of the service personnel that were being repatriated to RAF Lyneham.

The KAF airbase was rocketed a week later. Nobody was killed but six missiles fired from a crescent of villages about five miles north east of the airbase closed down the runway. Rocksy Sharrocks and Caroline Day, returning to KAF and very low on fuel after supporting American ground forces north east of Herat, who had been taking persistent fire for twenty-four hours, were within minutes of landing when the KAF tower told them the airfield had gone black.

Looking at his fuel gauge, Sharrocks realised: *This is all going to be over in fifteen minutes one way or the other because I'm either going to be landed somewhere else or flying a glider.*

He managed to get clearance to go to Bastion and touched down with the minimum fuel. He taxied clear of the runway and when the fuel tanker came out to refuel he left Caroline with the jet while he went off to the airfield ops room to get the clearance he needed to fly back to KAF. Nobody could just go flying in Afghanistan until they were listed on an air tasking order. Once he had sorted that he returned to the jet and waited for everything to calm down in Kandahar so they could fly back home.

Warrant Officer Thomson twitched when he heard the news that Sharrocks had been forced to divert. He was never happy when Tornados had to land at other airfields. If Rocksy's aircraft developed problems at Bastion or flamed out on landing he would have to lead a six-man action team of his best engineers to go and repair it.

'Bastion is a short hop from here but it has no Tornado engineers.'

Thomson had performed this flying engineers' service many times in Iraq, loading up a Hercules with new engines, hydraulic lifting gear, auxiliary power units and all the tools necessary to fix stricken jets stranded at remote airfields and then working twenty hours a day and sleeping underneath the aircraft.

'I take the A team,' said Thomson, who kept a backpack with three days' kit close by. 'I can pick up my bag, pick up a gun, pick up my body armour and be out the door in ten minutes, heading for a Herc.'

He once spent five days fixing a Tornado in Basra and while they were testing the new engine they had fitted at full pelt one night the rockets came flying in.

'Focuses the mind,' he said. 'We'd had three hours' sleep in forty hours. Exciting times.'

Thomson would not be grabbing his pack and his weapon that day. Sharrocks and Day returned to KAF that evening.

By 1 June Task Force Helmand had forced the insurgents out of Loy Mandeh. While ISAF commander General David Petraeus dropped into Patrol Base Wahid in Nad-e Ali North to congratulate 42 Commando on the progress Operation Omid Haft was making, Flight Lieutenant Mark 'Phats' Taylor, 3 Commando Brigade's fixed-wing adviser based in Lashkar Gah, flew into KAF on 4 June to update Jock Adams. Taylor admitted that 42 and 45 Commando and others were taking horrendous injuries, mainly to IEDs. A Royal Marine and a soldier from The Rifles had suffered severe injuries.

On 3 June – a day after the flag-draped coffins of the two

Juliet Company Royal Marines were driven through the streets of Wootton Bassett, lined both sides by hundreds of bowed heads – 'Another Marine had suffered serious injuries,' Phats Taylor said.

The intensity of the fighting in Helmand was increasing. Not only were the $10-a-day Taliban planting IEDs instead of harvesting poppy, after taking up their guns, their commanders were actively rallying the troops. The fighting had also ramped up because Omid Haft had now hit full stride.

As a former Tornado man himself Phats Taylor knew that however good the RAPTOR pod was – 'and we are getting fantastic imagery coming over our desks every single day' – the Dambusters were not going to find all IEDs. 'Our Brigadier's take on it at the moment is that our front-footedness, our going forward has put them on their back foot and has stopped them carrying out even more attacks. Thanks to fast air power bringing us the intelligence in advance we have gone into areas the insurgents did not expect us to go into.'

Phats Taylor reported that Task Force Helmand had also seized large quantities of drugs, including 900 kg of opium near Lashkar Gah with a street value of around £160 million. Hitting them in the pocket and harming their ability to rearm and recruit 'has just as good an effect as actively engaging bad guys doing bad deeds,' Taylor said. 'The Tornados' role in that is just as important as our guys on the ground.'

On 5 June a 22-year-old Lance Corporal from Kilo Company, 42 Commando was killed by small-arms fire from a compound while on patrol in Nahr-e Saraj (South). Also in Nahr-e Saraj (South) on the same day a 27-year-old Rifleman of 1st Battalion The Rifles, who had been supporting locals in the fight against insurgents and had established a checkpoint in Alikozai, was killed by an IED.

Elsewhere the insurgents were also ramping up their targeting of significant Afghan security leaders. On 28 May General Mohammad Daud Daud, the Afghan National Police Commander for Northern Afghanistan and a Deputy Interior Minister for Counter Narcotics, one of the most effective opponents of the Taliban, had been killed by a suicide bomber wearing a police uniform who infiltrated the governor's office in Takhar Province in the north east of the country following a meeting Daud had attended between Afghan and coalition forces.

As Omid Haft pushed on, 60 per cent of Dambuster missions were over Helmand, feeding LITENING video pictures down to the 3 Commando JTACs. As well as flying over-watch and RAPTOR missions 617's younger aircrew were equally ready, able and very willing to kick off with some ordnance. Many of them had friends in the army and the marines.

Sitting in the crewroom both Jane Pickersgill and Monty Montgomery agreed; 'Surely there is something more we could do than over-watch and RAPTOR missions.'

Keith Taylor understood their frustration. 'When I flew recce missions over Southern Iraq in 1994 as Saddam Hussein tried to wipe out the Marsh Arabs by draining their land and poisoning the water, all we were allowed to do was report the number of villages that were on fire.'

Phats Taylor reminded them: 'This is counter-insurgency and we cannot go around flattening the place.'

Early on in June Keith Taylor was flying along the Neb Canal when he noticed somebody suspicious at the notorious Tunnel 4. The Dambusters had been called in by 3 Commando Brigade, who had spotted several men who looked as though they were planting IEDs to try and disrupt Operation Omid Haft. They wanted the Tornados to take a look at them. By the time Taylor got to Tunnel 4 the group had gone but there was a man making repeated visits up to the canal road and then going back across Route Neptune to take cover in a ditch under some trees. There were definite signs of digging in the canal bank and on the side of the road.

Taylor's Weapon Systems Operator confirmed with the British JTAC: 'We are convinced that he's up to something.'

The JTAC was looking at the same pictures. 'Agree and confirm.' There was a group of young men on the north side of the canal.

'They don't look like combatants,' Taylor confirmed.

Nor would they be in danger when a Brimstone went in on the target that was on the south side. The canal was 60 feet wide and was raised on the south side so the road was substantially lower than the water line. The north side was higher so a missile would have been 20 feet below the civilians, who would have also been protected from any fragmentation by a dense body of water.

With a surgical weapon like Brimstone the civilians on the other side of the canal were not in danger. It was safe to remove the IED planter.

Under the rules of engagement the JTAC read out a pre-emptive 9-Line to the Tornado. 'I am now seeking higher command authority for you to strike. Over.'

The word *Yes!* flashed through Keith Taylor's mind. A 9-Line at last.

A pre-emptive 9-Line meant that all the paperwork had been done and as soon as the ground commander gave the go-ahead Keith Taylor could unleash a Brimstone at the suspicious figure, with the other jet to back up with strafe. While they waited Taylor sent the other Tornado with Stew Campbell and John Howard on board to get fuel. Still he waited. Now the marines were having problems getting positive identification on the suspected bomber. Hiding somewhere under the tree line he was also out of sight from Taylor's LITENING pod. Campbell and Howard returned and Taylor went to refuel.

When he got back to the Neb Canal the JTAC was still very keen that the Dambusters should take the suspicious figure out. 'I could get support from others for this but you found the IED emplacer. This is going to be your strike.'

A couple of hours passed. Still nothing happened. Taylor flew as wide a fuel-saving wheel as he could over Tunnel 4 and the tree line but eventually had to go and refuel again. This time when he got back the JTAC told him:

'I'm really sorry, guys, but you have been ripped. You're going to have to RTB.'

The air traffic controller had brought in American jets to replace the Tornados. The Dambusters spun around and routed back to Kandahar. Their mood was subdued. RIP (relief in place, or ripped) and RTB (return to base) were any pilot's least favourite acronyms.

But it was not all over. Later on in the afternoon Rocksy Sharrocks led a two-ship back to Tunnel 4 and hooked up with a 12-man Royal Marines/Afghan National Army patrol that was now following the suspected insurgent. The Tornados trained their pods down on the man and kept the JTAC up to speed. Thanks to the spy in the sky the patrol could follow him out of sight.

Sharrocks and Day watched the man arriving at a shop 20 metres from the Neb Canal. He stood outside, looking intently up and down the road, as though he knew he was being followed and was maybe luring the patrol towards an IED.

'We think he's a dicker,' Day reported. Dickers, often on motorbikes, provided a steady flow of intelligence on the movements of ISAF forces to insurgents. 'He's stopped outside,' she said, 'he's looking up and down the road you are about to come down.'

Then the man knocked on the door and slipped inside. Another man arrived and he too went into the shop.

Day alerted the JTAC.

Sharrocks flew on to check the patrol's route ahead to make sure that there were no signs of IEDs or ambushes set.

'Your route is clear,' Caroline Day reported.

After being thrown straight into weeks of night flying, she was showing signs of experience, keeping conversation with the patrol minimal and relevant. Early on in the detachment she, like all the young navigators, had reported everything that she could see on the ground; all human life, every car and motorbike. To troops on the ground too much information got in the way of making fast and accurate assessments of what lay ahead. The Tornado's job was to help enhance a JTAC's situational awareness of what was happening on the ground, not crowd the picture with trivia. Now Caroline knew the difference between what looked like a suspicious gathering or movement of motorbikes and what was the normal pattern of life.

Spotting changing patterns of life on the ground was vital intelligence.

'When you see something and the hairs stand up on the back of your neck, you just know it's time to call it in to the ground,' Sharrocks had told her.

He took up position at 14,000 feet over the shop as the patrol arrived and knocked on the door. The shopkeeper came out and stood outside while the patrol questioned him.

'He says he's here all alone,' the JTAC told Day.

'There's definitely two more dudes in that building,' she said. 'We've seen them go in and they haven't come out.'

'We're putting a search team in.'

As several members of the patrol entered the shop Rocksy Sharrocks flew his Tornado in a lozenge-shaped wheel to the north of the building where the entrance was, positioning his wings so as not to mask the LITENING pod, enabling Caroline Day to keep her eyes constantly on what was happening on the ground. He was also in a good position to respond with a weapon if anything hostile happened.

In a room behind the shop the search team found two men hiding. One of them was identified as the same man that Keith Taylor had been asked to target that morning. The other was his father, a known mid-ranking Taliban commander. They arrested both.

'It's what I call a soft kill,' Sharrocks said. 'Air and ground working in perfect harmony.'

Back at KAF Keith Taylor's frustration had been replaced by satisfaction. 'To get as far as a 9-Line and then have nothing happen might be frustrating but in the end though it's a good result,' he admitted.

Two for one was not full compensation for the loss of the Juliet Company marines and the others but it was two more insurgents taken out of the battle space who would not be able to plant any more IEDs.

On 12 June British engineers from 39 Armoured Engineer Squadron (39AES), 24 Engineer Regiment and 3 Commando Brigade had completed a 147-foot-long bridge over the Neb Canal near the border of Nahr-e Saraj and Nad-e Ali. The largest bridge built in Helmand, it had taken six days to construct in temperatures that reached 54 degrees Celsius. Without Operation Omid Haft it would not have been possible. Not only would the bridge convey troops, supplies and heavy vehicles further north in their quest of the Taliban, it was also being used by the locals to move livestock and goods from one side of the canal to the other without fear of being ambushed or blown up by the Taliban. The dangerous tunnels had been closed, denying the insurgents access and the Afghan National Army, working with 39AES, had also built four new checkpoints along Route Neptune and cleared the route of scores of IEDs.

Brigadier Ed Davis declared that 'Omid Haft is the latest in a series of Afghan Army led operations to remove the insurgent as an evil force in the daily lives of the people of Nahr-e Saraj. For several weeks now, the combined Afghan and ISAF force has shown great courage and resolve in clearing one of the most dangerous areas in central Helmand. Much hard work remains to be done,' he admitted, [but] 'as the operation draws to a close the people of Nahr-e Saraj are one step closer to a life free from insurgents. I salute the supreme professionalism and unfailing bravery of the Afghan and ISAF heroes whose sacrifice has made this possible.'

In the complex military jigsaw that was Operation Omid Haft, the Tornados of 617 Squadron not only commanded the sky, they had also helped prepare the ground.

19

DOWNTIME

As the drive against insurgents in Helmand continued there was precious little leisure time for 617, although Poppy Cormack-Loyd had managed to bring out balloons, party hats and banners to decorate Lucy and Caroline's bedroom and had organised cakes and candles to mark their thirtieth birthdays. Those not flying went to the Dutch Café to celebrate.

'A bit OTT, maybe,' Poppy said, 'but somehow birthdays seem to matter more out here, so we always go out to celebrate at the Dutch Café or T.G.I. Friday's.'

The Squadron also had visitors from other air forces. The French considered anything other than a Mirage to be lesser hardware. The Dutch who flew F-16s were impressive pilots but they were conscious that they were a fast-diminishing presence at KAF. They were due to stop flying out of Kandahar altogether in October 2011, after five years and clocking up 18,000 hours. They would go back to Holland and the Dutch air presence would shift north to support the Netherlands' Police Training Mission in Mazar-e-Sharif. Rocksy Sharrocks particularly liked the Americans, especially the pilots who flew the A-10 Thunderbolt, a kind of armoured bomb carrier with a Gatling gun strapped to it, known as the Warthog. Several of them had rows of teeth painted on their snouts.

'They call themselves Hog Drivers and they all try to fit a caricature of being five feet six with a neck five foot six wide, chewing tobacco and talking out the side of their mouths, like Texas Rangers. Great pilots though. Very front-foot.'

The American F-16 pilots all talked like Chuck Yeager, the legendary test pilot who was the first to break the sound barrier in 1947 and who was portrayed by the eloquently cool Sam Shepard in the film of Tom Wolfe's book *The Right Stuff*. If they ever remade the film these contemporary Right Stuff pilots would have been in the audition queue.

One of them said, 'Show us over your *Tornardo*.'

'It's Tornado,' Rocksy explained.

'Like the ones that rip through towns?'

'That's the ones.'

On Saturday mornings those with any time off headed for another strange cross-cultural event: the KAF Bazaar. Every Saturday Afghanistan was allowed on to the base. Afghan traders who had been carefully screened set up their stalls on a site near Tim Hortons, selling carpets, hand-spun pashminas, jewellery, silver, lapis, wristwatches, waistcoats and oils. In every way it was a typical Asian market with jangling colours, spicy smells and lots of noise, except the bartering was done in much-needed dollars. Everyone called it the 'jingly market' and jingle it did. Richard Smith was not alone in shopping early for Christmas, returning to the squadron building with an armful of stuff but not quite knowing if the transaction he had just completed had been to his advantage or not.

Even more surprising, there was also a KAF Bazaar School, which was held every Saturday morning for the sons and nephews of traders, in a wooden building alongside the market that had been erected by Slovak engineers in 2010. Volunteers from various ISAF forces joined the boys to do arts and crafts projects while Afghan teachers taught them Pashto and English in formal lessons. Every session finished with a chaotic and fiercely contested soccer game involving the military and the boys.

Security was tight around this little glimpse of reality at KAF but for the residents of the base the bazaar was a welcome distraction, a small and exotic punctuation mark in a sentence of monotony. For the traders hard currency and some free education in a country where both were scarce was an obvious draw, but there was no doubting their bravery in coming on to ISAF territory. They were risking their lives.

The few waking hours that the Squadron had off were taken up by eating at one of the seven huge dining facilities dotted around the airfield. Known as DFACS (pronounced *deefacs*) they could seat hundreds at a time and offered an array of cuisines from Thai curry to Yorkshire Pudding and the culinary specialities of Luxembourg. There was no shortage of fresh fruit and vegetables, some sourced locally, but most flown in. After dinner most went to one of the secure phone and email booths to call home although the Operation Minimise signs were going up. British troops were still taking casualties in Helmand.

Some of the squadron had TVs in their rooms and relaxed watching DVDs. Others were avid readers. Ollie Moncrieff had stormed his way through *The Lord of the Rings* and was now reading *The Hobbit*, with Roald Dahl's *My Uncle Oswald* to come. Poppy Cormack-Loyd was on to her ninth book.

'I read a random selection,' she said, 'most recently two chick lits and a book about Dunkirk because I like history. And an Ian McEwan; good but a little bit weird.'

With weddings fast approaching Poppy and Caroline Day were also avid readers of a bridal magazine that their families had sent over. Both had fixed every detail of their weddings before the Squadron had deployed. Now they just had to decide on the frocks they would wear to each other's.

'I'd love to say it was me organising it, but it is all Caroline's doing,' Jon Overton admitted. 'I think I have taken a very traditional role.'

Overton was worried that Timmy Colebrooke was planning to bring his unburned glitter-covered white wedding piano to set ablaze at their ceremony in Nairn.

Even though Caroline had decorated it, 'I really hope he doesn't.'

Among the other dog-eared magazines lying around the crewroom was a copy of *Country Life*, incongruous in a war zone maybe, but everyone pored over well-appointed houses in Dorset, Suffolk and Shropshire which they could only dream of owning. Keith Taylor liked to see his pilots and navigators grabbing downtime when they could and he was happy to sit and watch a movie with them, even if it was in ten-minute snatches over a few days. Even so he was not going to let people's concentrations lapse, reminding one of the junior flight lieutenants, for example, that he should not be in the crewroom sending personal emails and surfing the net until he had completed some official paperwork that he had just discovered had been left unattended in the ops room.

Everybody took more than a passing interest in the continuing debate going on back home on the severity of SDSR cuts.

'There's no point worrying,' Lucy Williams shrugged. 'It's a bit like the future of Lossiemouth; what can we do about it? We just have to get on with the job here.'

Ever practical, Tony Griffiths was hunting down a copy of the Military Covenant. Those like Griff, who were due to leave 617 immediately at the end of the deployment for new postings, were spending much of their spare time online to their partners trying to sort out accommodation and new schools for their children. Griff was due to take up a new job in Bristol and his wife Angela, a podiatrist, had found a house to rent and had hoped to educate their children at the same school nearby, but the local authority had allocated them to different schools in completely opposite directions, miles away from where they were living.

While Angela Griffiths, who was not by nature prepared to accept no for an answer, launched an appeal against the local authority decision, Griff was going to lobby his new MP.

Some people's leisure interests may not have been universally enjoyed, but unlikely common interests were discovered within the close confines of the Tornado detachment. Al Sharp was passing one of the briefing rooms when he swore he could hear a familiar and heart-warming sound. He pressed his ear to the door. Bagpipes! He opened the door to find Flight Lieutenant Stew Campbell practising an air. For the first time, Sharpy realised that he was not the only piper on 617. And Campbell had a full set too!

Sharp was in the room quicker than a raid on an insurgent's compound. Stew Campbell had once been in a pipe band and was due to play at a friend's wedding in Poland in September and at Joe Hourston's in November. He was having problems with the pipes. It was worse than trying to tank on an Iron Maiden.

'I am afraid I've rather lapsed,' he admitted to Sharp.

'Let me have a look, Sir,' said Sharp, taking the pipes from him and giving them a practised visual examination.

'You'll need to seal the joints in the chanter for a start,' he advised Campbell. 'I'll have some hemp sent over,' Sharp said, 'and you'll need some reeds.' He handed the pipes back. 'I hope you keep your jet in better condition than these pipes.'

Campbell smiled sheepishly.

'Never mind,' said the sergeant, 'once we've cleaned them up and sealed those joints I'll give you some tips on playing if you like.'

'Al, that would be great.'

'It'll be no problem, Sir.' Sharpy had a smile on his face too. He was imagining the Warrant's expression when he caught him playing the full set.

Another Scot was not enjoying Rich Smith's passion for cricket. Smith liked to have the Test Match on the TV while he worked, much to the irritation of Jock Adams, who shared the same office.

'Pointless English game,' he muttered, as England kept knocking over Sri Lankan wickets.

'At least when Wimbledon starts we'll have a Scot to watch,' he said.

'Andy Murray is only Scottish when he's losing,' Squadron Leader Clarke suggested, popping in to catch up on the score, 'as long as he's winning, he's a Brit.'

The SEngO's favourite read was anything by Charles Handy, the Irish philosopher and management thinker. Over the next week he would have to delve deep into one of the guru's inspirational tomes as 617's organisational management was about to face huge challenges.

20

UNDER PRESSURE

The fact that 617's aircrew were able to play such a major role in Operation Omid Haft and still support other ISAF forces all over Afghanistan was equally down to the engineers giving them the jets to do the job. While the aircrew battled insurgents, the engineers deployed their dedication, skills and high standards to win daily victories over the bugs, gremlins and incredible wear and tear that could rise up anywhere within a Tornado airframe. Now, overhalf way through 617's detachment to Kandahar the engineers' excellence would be challenged as never before.

A Tornado GR4 is a multi-million-pound aircraft and is known by all as a *Platform*. This platform is a complex collection of systems: the airframe, the power units, defensive aids, the navigation suite, the hydraulic system, the undercarriage, the flight systems, the communications suite, environmental control and the weapons system. Getting all of these disparate components to work together is not far removed from rocket science. Engineers refer to this as Systems Integration. Keeping everything going was like spinning plates. By way of contrast a mid-range family car has only one engine, one electronic control, a small air-con and a passenger cabin with a radio and possibly GPS. It has no weapons, no re-heat, no laser, no radar, no swept wings, no supersonic intakes, and it does not consume five tonnes of fuel per hour.

A Tornado GR4 costs £35,000 an hour to fly and the 138-strong fleet is supported by prime contractor BAE Systems to the tune of £1.5 billion until 2016 with a further £690 million to Rolls-Royce for the operational contract for engines until 2025, its planned out-of-service date.

With their panels removed these formidable bombing platforms suddenly look vulnerable, reduced to looms of different coloured electronic cables many miles long. Every cable comprises a group of wiring strands. Each loom is like a motorway, every cable an A-road. There are hundreds of switches, bulbs, circuits, vents and valves.

Squadron Leader Sharrocks admitted that while the jet was easy to fly – 'push the stick forward, houses get bigger, pull it back, houses get smaller' – and its eighties-style cockpit was the 'gentleman's club of cockpits', he did not like to see 'the jet undressed'. It made him feel uneasy.

The aircrew were eagle-eyed to the quirks of an aircraft at the best of times but in a war zone they were sensitive to every unusual noise in the jet and queasy about taking a good look inside. They pored over the Aircraft 700 ledger before signing jets out and reported every single niggle and snag when they signed them back in again.

In spite of the demands of the flying programme in Afghanistan and the adverse climatic conditions, over the first six weeks of the Squadron's detachment the engineers provided Keith Taylor and his aircrew with more than enough aircraft to meet the air tasking orders from the CAOC and GCAS.

Sometimes it was a Herculean effort. Now over halfway through the Dambusters' deployment and with a secondary phase of Omid Haft to get underway, Squadron Leader

Sharrocks was about to see a lot of undressed Tornados.

The problems had begun when Flight Lieutenant Ollie Moncrieff and Squadron Leader Griffiths returned from a sortie and reported that the Pitot probe on the nose of their jet was not working properly. The Pitot probe measures airspeed, height and air pressure. Along with other sensors on the nose of the aircraft, it also tells the cockpit instruments if the jet is turning right, left or flying upside down. Without it the Tornado could not fly.

As they raced out to the aircraft the engineers were entering a period of extreme stress.

The first to arrive at Moncrieff's jet were the Leckies and the Fairies. Inside the cockpit there was a burning smell that seemed to be coming from somewhere under the pilot's feet. There was no choice but to take off the canopy and remove the ejector seat, both charged with explosive. A three-strong team of armourers (Plumbers) set to work. To render the explosive charges inert and remove the canopy and seat would take ten hours. At 7 p.m. the night shift arrived to carry on the task.

The next day when the SEngO clocked in at 7 a.m. he went out to look at the jet. The canopy was off and the seat was out. He climbed up the steps and peered down inside. A loom of thirty cables had been rubbing against the airframe and had been damaged. Of the thirty some went to the Pitot probe and others went to every corner of the aircraft, some carrying signals, others power. On operations it was permissible to shortcut some procedures to achieve a temporary fix on an aircraft until spares arrived, so long as it remained airworthy. Clarke knew this was not an option. A four-inch section of the loom had to be replaced.

On 30 May an order was placed with RAF Marham for

a new loom and given the highest priority: D State. It would arrive in two days.

To make the repair the throttle box would also have to be removed by the Riggers and the Leckies. As JEngO Rob Perry planned out the work for the aircraft he knew that to remove and then reinstate the canopy, the seat and the throttle box, install the new loom and carry out all the safety inspections before the jet was serviceable again would take three days. So far they had done half the job. Now it was a case of waiting for the part to arrive.

'The trouble with jets is that they like to fly,' Perry said. 'The longer they don't the longer it takes to get them up again.'

On one wall of the engineers' room was a large whiteboard divided into eight vertical columns, with the silhouette of the rear view of a Tornado at the top of each one. Each column represented one of the Squadron's aircraft and was subdivided into four sections, each one filled with a mass of coloured counters, acronym stickers and magic marker notes that described the current serviceability of that aircraft, whether it was armed and the armaments it was carrying.

This was the all-important rectifications board and the man in charge of it was the Rectifications Controller, Chief Technician George Allen. On hearing the news about Moncrieff's jet from Clarke and Perry he reached up to the top of its column and replaced a green plastic sticker with a black 'S' for serviceable on it with a red one bearing the letters 'U/S'. Unserviceable.

It was George Allen's challenge to ensure that all routine primary and primary star servicing and maintenance checks were carried out and to amend the timetable, often at minutes' notice, to fix the variety and number of unforeseen problems that hit the jets daily. The key was making sure that all the trades worked on an aircraft in the most effective sequence. With the squadron's flying schedule there was no time for hanging about.

'Trades tend to automatically concentrate on the major job, but sometimes fixing something smaller first will enable the bigger task to be completed quicker,' George explained. 'That's where I come in.'

A small ('not that small!') man with watchful eyes and a ready smile, George was like a project manager on a complex building programme. There was constant traffic to and from his desk. Every time a shift changed or Keith Taylor, the SEngO, one of the JEngOs or the Warrant Officer came in, or an aircrew member passed through to sign out an aircraft, all eyes would automatically look to George's board to see how many jets were green and how many red. George was the man who knew everything about the jets and how near to being airworthy they were. All knowledge was pooled with him. All questions came to him. Genial by day, it would have been no surprise if George had dreamed in red and green at night.

'The more jets that go down the more pressure gets put on the others, and the more pressure you put on an aircraft the greater the chance of something going wrong,' George said. 'To achieve our flight programme we always need a spare jet to provide additional resilience in case another aircraft goes U/S.' Way before that happened George would be heads down with the SEngO, the Warrant and the relevant shift JEngO to make sure that the engineers were focused on where they were most urgently needed. Whatever problems flared up through missions or during routine servicing the squadron's flying programme had to be achieved 100 per cent. That was the non-negotiable grail.

*

So far the Dambusters had missed just one sortie. On the evening of 21 May a Tornado caught fire on the runway. Throughout the detachment the altitude, the ambient air temperature and the dust had made starting engines harder.

'The ideal conditions for starting a Tornado are at sea level in a fridge,' Rob Perry explained. 'Here we are on top of a mountain in a cooker. We've had a lot of challenges just getting the balance of the engines correct with problems from over-fuelling or under-fuelling.'

When the pilot of this jet, Kiwi Spencer, who was guesting with 617 from 15 Squadron, throttled up to combat, ready for take-off, he got a surge of fuel through one engine. He immediately brought it back to idle and shut it down, hoping he could restart. It was then that he noticed his Turbine Blade Temperature gauges soaring to critical. There was only one thing in an engine that generated that kind of heat, and that was fire. He saw smoke coming out from the back of his aircraft. Spencer deployed the engine's fire bottle, hoping to put it out. Then for some reason the other engine failed. He was now stuck on the runway at the head of a queue of traffic.

As soon as they heard the alarm the 617 engineers' crash team jumped in a van and drove out to the stranded Tornado with an auxiliary power unit to kick-start the jet's engines. When Spencer tried to fire up, a bigger cloud of smoke belched out from the back of the jet. Even when the engines had shut down they were still flooded with fuel from when he had been sitting at combat ready to take off. The igniters in the engines were clicking like spark plugs and had set it ablaze.

The Squadron now had a Tornado loaded with live weapons and 7000 kg of fuel with flames shooting out of the exhaust pipes of both of its engines.

It posed a major threat to other aircraft and ground crew. Air traffic instantly declared the KAF runway black. Whenever an incident like this happened the airport authorities had only one priority: get the runway open as soon as possible to avoid having to divert incoming aircraft elsewhere, which would have a major impact on the effectiveness of air operations throughout Afghanistan. If that meant the KAF Fire Response Team drowning the Tornado in foam and then bulldozing the aircraft off the runway then so be it.

The last thing 617 needed was to lose a jet completely but this was turning nastier by the second and the aircrew were showing signs of wanting out. A piece of quick thinking was to save the aircraft. When the crash team had grabbed their tools to race to the jet Corporal Ben Cook, a propulsion engineer, had instinctively picked up a fire extinguisher. While JEngO Flight Lieutenant Al Whitehead was on the radio to the fire response team leader, trying to persuade him that his services and those of the bulldozer were not needed, and reassuring Spencer that everything was under control, Corporal Cook calmly dealt with the fire.

Once the weapons had been put into safety mode the Tornado was towed back to the ramp, where the damage to the engines and the airframe was found to be superficial.

There was one day when all eight jets were ready to fly.

'Whether here or at Lossie that is incredibly unusual,' George Allen said. 'So unusual I took a photograph of the rects board, which is a bit sad, but it seemed like a momentous occasion. Short flights or long flights they break; there's no pattern to it, beyond the fact you will never have them all working for long.'

Today George Allen's board showed that 617 now had two

jets down. In addition to the aircraft waiting for the new wiring loom, the Tornado had a persistent engine problem.

'We are fitting yet another new engine to that,' he said calmly.

Whether he was at his board, seeking out the latest progress from the Riggers, Plumbers, Leckies and Fairies or reassuring the Boss that 617's flying programme would be achieved, George never seemed to flap or get spiky, unlike some others. Banter could fly between the trades like hand grenades, but between them and Chief Technician Allen, never. No wonder they called him Gentleman George.

Corporal Andy 'Mitch' Mitchell appeared from under the Tornado and straightened up. Suitably for a propulsion engineer or Sootie, he was covered in grease and oil up to his elbows and he had a resigned look as he wiped his thin face with a sweat rag. He nodded to two other engineers, who gently began the inch-by-inch task of winching the right engine down out of its bay and on to a trolley.

'This is the fourth engine we've changed on this jet,' Mitch said, rubbing the back of his shaved head with his fist. 'This one's only been in two weeks. It's always the right-hand engine and every time it is a different fault.'

Mitch was brandishing the latest culprit, which looked like a six-inch piece of wire. It was part of a sensor called a Turbot (Turbine Rear Bearing Over Temperature), which measured the temperature at the back end of the engine. An engine had four and could run on three, two or even one. But this engine was down to the last one and it was broken. If a pilot could not accurately determine the performance of his high-pressure turbine engines, especially during re-heat when temperatures reached 1600 degrees Celsius, the aircraft could catch fire.

The Tornado should not have even been in Kandahar at all.

It and another jet had been due to fly back to RAF Marham at the beginning of May for a major service, to be replaced by two newly-serviced Tornados, known in RAF parlance as a roulement, but they and their VC10 tanker had both broken down and had been forced to land in France for repairs. The delays while they were being fixed meant that the diplomatic clearances to fly across Europe, the Middle East and Pakistan had lapsed and would have to be negotiated all over again. This would take more time. They had now returned to RAF Marham.

The Tornado's engine was only held in place by three attachment points, two pins and a large nut. But to disconnect the fuel pipes, power take-off shaft, all the electrical plugs and the air pipes and then remove an RB199 Mk 103 turbofan engine weighing 1250 kg and costing £1.5 million and replace it with a new one and then run that engine until it met serviceability tests took between twelve and fifteen hours. Even peering into the depths of an engine with a borescope – a magnifying optical device like a medical endoscope with a camera fitted on the end of a flexible tube – or running sophisticated function tests on a computer did not reveal all faults. It was only when engines were fired up that small but vital components showed themselves not up to the task.

Those with serious faults were flown back to Rolls-Royce in Bristol for repair. Until recently major engine overhauls had been done by RAF Tornado engineers at Marham. So far six engines had been returned to Rolls-Royce during 617's tenure at Kandahar. Mitch, originally from Troon, had been fourteen years in the RAF and ten on the Dambusters. He had signed on for twenty-two. Quick-witted and with an occasionally sharp tongue, Mitch was good at his job but this jet was trying his patience.

'It's pretty soul destroying really,' he admitted, keeping a firm eye on the engine as it neared the trolley.

Mitch was a 'top man' according to the Warrant Officer. There was a natural confidence in the way he worked on the jet. He had completed two operational tours in Kuwait and four at Al-Udeid in Qatar, all with 617. Married with a four-year-old son and a two-year-old daughter, Mitch looked like the kind of guy who in his youth could have handled himself in a scrap.

As the new engine was eased up into the aircraft Mitch explained that this was the second time it had been in the jet.

'Inside the engine is a centrifugal breather that separates oil and air and re-circulates some of the oil,' he explained. 'As soon as we fitted it, it started leaking oil so we had to reject it. On top of that the engines don't seem to like it here,' he said, raising his voice as a pair of serviceable jets headed for the taxi-way. 'When we were in the Gulf it was okay. It was hot there but here it is the altitude as well as the heat and the engines really struggle.'

A jet engine does little more than take ambient temperature air in the front end, squeeze it, heat it up by adding ignited fuel and then throw it out of the jet pipe far faster to achieve thrust. Because the input ambient air in an Afghan summer was 30 degrees warmer than in Lossiemouth the exhaust gases in the jet pipe were equally warmer and the engines had to run hotter to get the Tornados into the air. If their engines had been made entirely of steel – rather than their vulnerable parts being made of high-temperature metals like nickel alloy and titanium – they would have melted. Even so, the temperatures were bordering on the very limits of the engines.

It was a continuation of a 617 tradition to make planes do the opposite of what they had been intended for. As a high-level bomber, the Lancaster was never designed to fly at 60 feet as they did on the Dams Raid. The Tornado had been specifically designed to do just that in damp, dense northern European air.

Underneath the aircraft shelters the temperature was kept within bounds by air conditioning pipes pumping out cold air overhead as the engineers pored, crawled and climbed over, under and inside the jets. Birds flew into the roofs of the shelters to take refuge. Another team running some tests on a Tornado outside put a thermometer against the aircraft's skin. The temperature was 80 degrees Celsius.

While the other trades tried to fix broken jets, the armourers went about their business unflustered. Ziggy Zweig and Corporal Graham Wylie were carefully winching a heavy three-foot square steel ammunition box containing belted rounds of 27 mm shells into the belly of the aircraft to arm the Mauser cannon.

'I like doing the gun work the best. It's meaty,' Ziggy said, as she cranked the tank inch by inch up into the jet. Once it was in place she threaded the ammunition belt through to the gun and then using a lever and gear moved the first round, a dummy, towards the chamber. Once in place she shouted 'Cocking!' then released the gear and the round was in place. After three rounds the gun was fully armed.

Each round was five inches long and yellow tipped with a red band, meaning it was high explosive. Armour-piercing shells were black with a red band. The outer casing was made out of sintered iron, Wylie explained. It was stronger than steel, which was liable to split and explode. When the pilot hit the trigger the shell would expand to fill the chamber to stop gas escaping and exploding in the aircraft. If a round jammed then a circular chamber of cartridges would fire a round to clear it. Firing at the rate of 1700 rounds a minute, expended shells were then spewed out of the gun into a tube that fed into a collection box.

The loading process had taken around twenty minutes, requiring strength and a high degree of finesse. When she had finished, Ziggy blew on her fingers.

'If this was an F-16, you'd do this with the touch of a button,' said Wylie, who had fitted the first Storm Shadow missiles to Dambuster jets during the invasion of Iraq in 2003.

'The other trades say we just turn up to put the jewellery on the jets,' said Ziggy. 'There's more to it than just clicking bombs on to the pylons,' she explained. 'There's the electronics side of things, the ejector seat, the flares the cockpit, the explosive charge in the canopy. Every day's different.'

In the heat of Afghanistan the weapons also had a shorter shelf-life and had to be stored and handled with even greater care than normal. Even though they had put the 'Aircraft ARMED' warning sign in the cockpit the armourers' work was not done. Taking weapons off and de-arming required skill and when weapons or flares were fired they left behind hazardous chemical residues on the jet which the armourers had to clean off.

Being an armourer on a front-line squadron was certainly more interesting than Ziggy's last time in Afghanistan in 2006 when she had worked for three months in Kabul, seconded from the armoury at RAF Benson, 'handing out flares and bullets'.

Another verbal joust from the other trades was that armourers always hung out together, went everywhere together.

'The other trades have to talk and interact with each other more than us,' Ziggy said, clearing away some tools. 'When we go away we tend to stick together more. It's more of a family thing. You look after your own. And anyway you can't load a bomb by yourself.'

Two days after ordering the replacement loom it duly arrived in Camp Bastion on Wednesday 1 June and was now on its way down to Kandahar.

'Until a few months ago the British airbridge from Brize Norton was direct to Kandahar but now it is to Bastion since they opened a new runway,' Stu Clarke explained. 'That adds another delay but they assure us it will be here at two o'clock this afternoon.'

The new loom arrived on time and the engineers took it out to the aircraft. A few minutes later they were back. The wrong part had been sent. Given the time difference it was now late evening in the UK. Nothing more could be done until the night shift came in that evening and Marham opened for business next day, around 4 a.m. local time.

When things got frustrating SEngO Clarke liked to quote the serenity prayer. The bit he was having trouble with now was: 'God, grant me the serenity to accept the things I cannot change.'

He felt like kicking something.

In contrast with the mounting tension around him Warrant Officer Thomson was unusually serene. He looked up over his computer and then back to what he was doing. He was playing Patience.

Having spent an hour running the new engine at different speeds and building up to max dry power, Mitch Mitchell took the readings into the engineering room and ran them through the computer against Roll-Royce tolerances.

...rk goes on around the clock, with the engineers working in 12-hour shifts
...er Rapid Erect Shelters (RES) to keep the jets flying. Only about one or
... in five Tornados ever returned from a sortie with no problems at all.

617's female navigators: (from left) Flight Lieutenants Jane Pickersgill, Poppy Cormac Loyd, Caroline Day and Lucy Williams.

A Tornado GR4 is a £70 million collection of complex systems: the airframe, the power units, defensive aids, the navigation suite, the hydraulics, the undercarriage, flight systems, communications suite, environmental control and weapons. Getting these to work together is not far removed from rocket science.

A stickler for order and not a spanner out of place, Warrant Officer Stew Thomson on his weekly walk of inspection along the Tornado flight line. When he called people 'Fellah!' it was not a good time to be around. He argued that tidiness meant no accidents to aircrew or engineers.

During its deployment to Kandahar 617 Squadron clocked up the one-millionth flying hour of the Tornado since it entered RAF service in 1981, equivalent to flying to the sun and back or 16,000 times around the globe. Since the First Gulf War it had been on daily operational service for 20 years.

An engineer grabs a moment on the Hesko-bastion anti-blast wall that protects the Tornado ramp. The Hesko-bastion, filled with sand and rubble, is the ubiquitous military building block in Afghanistan.

The engineers' rec room and welcome respite from the heat on the Tornado ramp, where temperatures could reach more than 50 degrees C, even under the shelters.

A pair of Tornados taxi out the runway at Kandahar. All 617 sorties in Afghanistan were flown as 'two-ship' missions.

...ting the fires. A pilot puts
...jet into combat setting,
...king the twin engines with
...l to fire up the afterburners,
...ich produces enough forward
...ust for take-off. The flame
...sting out of the jet is also
...own as 'the carrot'.

...e of the 617's two female
...ourers in Kandahar, SAC
...ma 'Ziggy' Zweig prepares
...ser-guided Paveway IV bomb
...or to a sortie. The orange
...sels are attached to safety
...s which when removed means
...apons are live. The armourers
...o loaded the GR4's cannon
...l serviced the ejector seats.

...adron Leader Chris 'Ballsy' Ball
...t) and his navigator from 12
...adron, Squadron leader Carl
...z' Wilson, pose by the empty
...apons rack from which they
...d the Brimstone missile that
...k out an insurgent commander
...o was about to mortar a
...rwegian infantry patrol.

Flight Lieutenant Rob Perry, one of 617's two Junior Engineering Officers (JEngO), inspects a rudder. It is the JEngO's job to provide enough jets to fulfil the flying programme.

Highly experienced Squadron Leader Ian 'Rocksy' Sharrocks and his navigator Flight Lieutenant Caroline Day, on ops for the first time, walk to their jet. Sharroc likened early sorties with the rookies to taking ducklings to water.

A Survival Equipment Fitter ('Squipper'), responsible for all aircrew and safety kit from boots to helmets and radio transmitters, checks out a set of night-vision goggles.

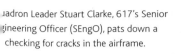

...uadron Leader Stuart Clarke, 617's Senior ...gineering Officer (SEngO), pats down a ...checking for cracks in the airframe.

...ht Lieutenant Timmy Colebrooke ...nning a sortie. For a routine sortie ...planning and pre-flight briefings ...ld take up to three hours. In ...hanistan few sorties were routine.

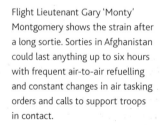

Flight Lieutenant Gary 'Monty' Montgomery shows the strain after a long sortie. Sorties in Afghanistan could last anything up to six hours with frequent air-to-air refuelling and constant changes in air tasking orders and calls to support troops in contact.

A Tornado returns from a sortie at dawn.

'It's running slow,' he sighed heavily. 'There's some obscure problem with fuel supply to the engine. Fixing it is a bit like tweaking a carburettor but on a very complex scale. We might need to take a look inside.'

The aircraft could not be taken out and run on full power with the pilot soaking the engines as he would for take-off until this problem was solved.

'Whatever it is, it's not going to be finished this shift,' Mitch said, shoving his anti-ballistic glasses down over his eyes and stepping back out into the heat.

The good news when Stu Clarke came on shift next morning was that the new engine on the Tornado was at last ready to go. A new loom for the other Tornado had also been ordered and the engineers would be able to fit it on Friday. As Clarke looked at George's board he saw the pleasing sight of seven green jets ready to go, one short of full complement.

It would not stay that way for long. Later that day Poppy Cormack-Loyd came back into the engineers' building, after completing a RAPTOR mission, looking as though she had just flown a sortie in a sauna. Far from her normal jolly self, she was flushed and exhausted.

'We were out in the North West at about 24,000 feet and there was a funny noise and a red warning caption came on in the cockpit,' she said, draining a bottle of water. 'The ECS has totally packed up.'

The environmental control system (ECS) on her jet ensured that the operating temperature of the aircraft and its systems, such as the computer, adjusted to the ambient air pressure outside, whether the Tornado was climbing at 500 knots (575 mph) or diving at 500 knots.

'Sometimes you can get it to work if you fiddle with the buttons and even if it is saying it is hot the cold air will flow; but all we got was hot,' Poppy said. 'We had no choice but to head for home. We missed our last two RAPTOR points of interest, although these were picked up by another jet, so not all is lost.'

From about 150 miles out of Kandahar, the journey back would normally have been about twenty minutes.

'With the ECS down we were limited to 250 knots [290 mph] so we pretty much chugged home.'

The ECS was one of the most complex systems on the aircraft, and in Afghanistan temperatures it had to work extra hard. In Lossiemouth there might be one ECS problem a week; in Kandahar they were running at up to seven. Finding the solution could take hours. A jet in Lossiemouth had once been grounded for three months. When Keith Taylor filed his weekly aircraft assessment report with the CAOC in Al-Udeid and with Air Command back in the UK the only system on the aircraft that had its own section on the form was ECS. This week he would be able to add his own experience for added emphasis. On Thursday he had his own ECS failure just before landing. His frustration increased when he returned to the crewroom to discover that Lucy Williams and Joe Hourston had come in to land but were stuck out on the far end of the runway.

'What's the problem?' he asked George Allen.

'They reckon the brakes are overheating.'

'I doubt that,' Taylor said. 'No way would they get so hot that they would have to just stop, unless he hit the runway with the RAPTOR which has very little clearance and slammed them on.'

Due to radio dead spots on the airfield not only were the

engineers having problems getting accurate information from Joe and Lucy but they also could not get clearance to drive down to help them. Eventually George managed to talk to the control tower on a landline and relay messages by radio to the engineers in the van.

On landing Joe Hourston had deployed the thrust-reverse buckets but the aircraft was not slowing down as it should. If there was a problem he should have seen an 'attention getter' message in his cockpit. No warning light had come on. Joe applied the brakes harder than he would if the thrust buckets had been working. Because it was a long taxi back Lucy called air traffic and asked if they could check the temperature of their brakes. Joe brought the jet to a halt clear of the runway and three fire engines and three fire crews arrived, a mixture of Canadians, Brits and Americans, and scurried around under the jet. They told Joe and Lucy that the brakes were hot but were not a fire risk. However, more seriously they had also had a hydraulic leak on landing and hydraulic fluid was now dripping on to the brakes and smoking. That could have caused a fire.

The fire crews readied their hoses. Joe tried to tell them to stand off but he had lost radio contact with them. With frantic hand signals and scribbling out a sign saying STOP! he managed to prevent them drenching the jet.

'I didn't want it doused unless there really was a fire,' Hourston said, 'because we had the RAPTOR pod on and we had taken a load of imagery which we didn't want to lose. All I wanted was for them to be ready to put out the fire if the hydraulic fluid ignited.'

With the temperature mounting in the cockpit Hourston and Williams climbed out of their aircraft and were putting the safety pins in the weapons and fuel tanks to neutralise them as the Squadron engineers drew up and secured the aircraft. After waiting two hours on the airfield a towing tractor arrived to haul them home. Three hours after they had landed they arrived, sodden and exhausted, back at 617's ramp.

At the start of the day shift on Friday 3 June the Squadron was way down on serviceable jets. The Tornado with the engine problem needed another new engine, its fifth. Even Gentleman George was showing signs of stress. Not once during that day did he sit on his chair.

Aircrew were frequently forced to leap out of jets that suddenly went U/S pre-departure and run, dripping with sweat, to reserve aircraft.

Unlike the Lancaster days when pilots and crews flew the same aircraft and gave them names, to today's Dambusters a jet was a jet, no more than a number. You just wanted one that worked. Tony Iveson described poignantly the fate of his Lancaster.

'In 1946 my brother Peter, who was at officer cadet school stationed in Elgin, was on a route march in Morayshire and he came across a scrapyard full of Lancasters. He recognised one by the cartoon character painted below the cockpit on the pilot's side of the aircraft.'

It was F-Fox, Tony's Lancaster in which he had flown just two years earlier on the *Tirpitz* raid, its finest hour captured in oils on the staircase at Cranwell.

'F-Fox cost the country somewhere in the region of £58,000,' he said. 'Now it was worth £250 as scrap.'

Were 617's Tornados characters? 'No,' George Allen said, 'they have idiosyncrasies,' then he added, 'which I guess when they go wrong makes them *bad* characters.'

*

The Warlord was having his own engineering issues. The previous Sunday, Griffiths had noticed that the pressure was low in a hydraulic hand pump on the side of a jet that powered the mechanism that raised the cockpit canopy. It was a niggling problem, like a slow puncture, that would eventually have to be fixed permanently but which would take days – and given that other jets were going U/S, it was not flight critical. For GCAS launches it was vital that the engineers kept the pressure pumped up so when the aircrew ran out to the jet the canopy would open instantly. It was not possible to leave the canopy open on a GCAS jet because the cockpit would fill up with dust. The hydraulic fluid had leaked and Griff and Moncrieff had to pump it up to get sufficient pressure for the canopy to open.

Griff reported the problem to the line controller and the flight sergeant. On Monday the same jet had the same pressure drop. The engineers had not kept it pumped up. Between Sunday and Monday the shifts had rotated. When Griff mentioned the pressure problem to the new day shift he got blank looks. He sensed instantly a communication breakdown between A Shift and B Shift. He went to see the SEngO.

'Somebody needs to be detailed to go out every few hours and keep it pumped up,' he told Stu Clarke. 'As managers we have to up our game and our supervision.

'As the Warlord I not only look after the aircrew; I am also the major conduit between the aircrew and the engineers and my job is to make sure that the engineering standards we have on day one are the same standards we have on the very last day.'

Clarke briefed his JEngOs and flight sergeants in the engineering management room they shared between the aircrew room and the engineering trades' room. 'See to it that it's done,' he said. 'Nothing is more important than GCAS and the ability to launch in minutes.'

Clarke decided that starting the next day he would have Griff step into the engineers' rest room to brief them on his role as the Warlord and on recent sorties and the current state of ground operations.

'There's no point in me passing on what I learn from the intelligence briefing; that's just me bumping my gums,' SEngO said, nosing his wagon out into the slow crawl back to Cambridge Lines.

'I want them to hear it from the guy who was overhead; what did he see through his pod; what was the conversation with the guy on the ground? It's the human side of a war that we are pretty well sheltered from here. What I am trying to engender is pride. An attitude that we didn't come here just to fix aeroplanes. We came here to save lives.'

On the Friday of an increasingly fraught week the good news was that the replacement cable loom had arrived in Afghanistan. The bad news was that it had been sent to Kabul.

The engineers may have had seven days and seven nights of major technical problems to overcome but thanks to round-the-clock teamwork incredibly the Dambusters did not miss a single sortie that week.

Sunday 5 June was a maintenance day. The Warrant Officer had organised a party of volunteers among the aircrew and the engineers to go out and give one of the jets a good wash. Corporal Mitchell was in the back of the engineers' room, busy not with spanners, wrenches or borescopes but a jigsaw, sweat dripping off him as he and others worked at some planking. A couple of hours later he appeared inside carrying three lightning bolts five feet long that he had just cut out for the Dambuster dam outside the Squadron building.

Keith Taylor came out to inspect as Mitch held up the bolts against the blast wall that was transforming into a dam. A guide for the painters had been chalked on to the concrete.

'Excellent,' Taylor said. 'What do you think for the lettering?'

'I think they should be mounted on a piece of board across the top,' Mitch suggested.

'Sounds good to me,' the SEngO chipped in, who had come out to join them. Taylor agreed.

'I'll carry on then,' said Mitch.

All jets had been fixed. The Squadron had overcome what the Warrant Officer called a 'crump'. Gentleman George, tucked up safely in his bed on the night of Sunday 5 June and through into Monday 6 June would be able to dream of a rects board where all jets were green to go.

21

'OUR DOG IS BIGGER
THAN THEIR DOG'

Towards the end of May Keith Taylor walked into the crewroom with a smile on his face. Nobody noticed. Poppy and Caroline were off duty, sitting side by side on one of the sofas comparing bridal magazines and putting the finishing touches to their weddings. Tony Griffiths was working at his emails, while Lucy Williams and Joe Hourston were kitted up for a sortie.

The Boss made himself a coffee, sat down calmly, took a sip, and said: 'I've just heard that we are down to go to Operation Ellamy.'

At the mention of flying missions over Libya all chatter stopped. Griff spun round on his chair. Other members of the aircrew arrived seemingly from nowhere at the news. Suddenly the silence broke and Taylor was dealing with an onslaught of enthusiastic questions.

'This is provisional,' he warned, 'but as of now we are down to go in January, which means that our next deployment to Afghanistan in March will be put back until November 2012.'

When the Boss formally briefed the aircrew at met briefs and the engineers at the next shift handover, the reaction was 100 per cent upbeat. The TV screens in the squadron building and the dining facilities showed rolling News 24 footage of Tornados destroying the ammunition bunkers, tanks, heavy guns, barracks and fuel supply lines of pro-Gaddafi forces with Storm Shadow missiles and Brimstones.

The decision to put 617 Squadron on standby for Libya came from another legendary former Dambuster, Group Captain Pete 'Rocky' Rochelle OBE DFC. Rochelle was station commander at RAF Marham and Tornado Force Commander. From January 2006 until January 2008 Rochelle had been OC 617 Squadron and for his command had been awarded the OBE.

Rocky was a navigator who had served on several Tornado squadrons but 617 held a special place in his affections. He had even spent his honeymoon in 1990 with his wife Pam in a castle overlooking the Eder Dam. Lizee Taylor had been a bridesmaid at their wedding. Stocky, fearless and forthright, Rochelle bore the facial evidence of a former rugby open side flanker – 'it was my job to get in and destroy their game'.

Rocky won his DFC for a series of under-fire raids in the Kosovo campaign, where he was the Warlord on 14 Squadron flying out of RAF Brüggen, notably attacking and taking out SA3 missile sites in Obrovac in Serbia. The air was full of the Russian-made warheads as the Tornados went in. An American F117 Nighthawk had been shot down. While other Tornado crews were 'going defensive, banging off fuel tanks and escaping out low with missiles going off all around them, my pilot, Squadron Leader Hugh Smith, who is now a group captain, was dead calm. We stayed pretty steadfast and continued with our target run.'

Bizarrely, when they came out of the combat zone and refuelled over the Hungarian border they were told that 14 Squadron's mascot, Eric the Burmese Python, was on board the tanker.

Over Iraq in 1991 Rocky, flying with 31 Squadron during Operation Desert Storm, had been in a Tornado that was hit by an SA3 over an area occupied by the Republican Guard and had just made it back to base at Dhahran Airbase in Saudi Arabia. On landing they found the jet had been so peppered it looked like a cheese grater. There was shrapnel under Rocky's ejection seat and a hole in the right tail-plane that was big enough to fit a man through.

'These things happen,' he shrugged, throwing off his favoured leather pilot jacket in his large office at RAF Marham and displaying that press-on spirit that seemed to be essential DNA in all 617 bosses however different the remainder of their character set-up.

Mapping out the Tornado rota for the Operation Ellamy campaign was becoming a real juggle between the demands of counter-insurgency flying in Afghanistan and the kinetic challenges of protecting the rebels trying to oust Gaddafi in Libya.

Defence cuts meant that Rochelle had just the five remaining front-line Tornado squadrons at his disposal to do both jobs. Rocky had 2 and 9 squadrons from Marham concentrating on Ellamy, backed with elements of 15 Squadron from Lossiemouth. The Dambusters were heading into the back end of their deployment in Kandahar and 31 were well on into their pre-deployment training programme to replace them, so could not be spared for Ellamy, while 12 Squadron were slotted to take over from 31 and beginning their training cycle. His only flexibility was to send 617 to fly over Libya.

In spite of the logistical headaches of getting squadrons trained for, and then transported to and from, theatres of war, Rocky couldn't help but feel a tinge of envy for 617's current crop of aircrew. In his flying career he had been renowned for taking young un-blooded operators into combat. That was so much more exhilarating than having a flag on the bonnet of your car, being saluted by everyone and spending ten hours a day and more in meetings and conference calls.

'If you have ever been in combat and on operations you hate to miss out,' he said. 'During Op Telic in 2003 I was at Staff College and I was sitting with 380 international students in a lecture theatre while it was all going on in Iraq and it was torture, absolute bloody torture. I knew where I'd rather have been. Sitting in the back seat of a Tornado jet. It's in your blood.'

Being in the thick of things was in Keith Taylor's blood too. He also liked precision. He had pinned a sheet of paper to his office wall in Kandahar on which he was recording details of every sortie he had flown so far over Afghanistan. Tuesday 31 May stood out because it was finally a GCAS launch. It was minutes from the end of their three-hour GCAS hold and Taylor had been waiting and patiently hoping for some action when at just before 12.30 p.m. his attention was drawn to the real-time comms screen. Bagram airfield had been closed by a dust-storm, grounding all aircraft. The phone rang in the crewroom. The authoriser's desk had immediately offered 617 to pick up one of the Bagram sorties. The offer had been accepted. Taylor was to fly 50 miles north east of Kandahar and make contact with an American JTAC.

Running out on the ramp, Taylor boarded the lead jet. Running to the second Tornado that day was 38-year-old Squadron Leader Kiwi Spencer from 15 Squadron. They were likely to be airborne for five hours but Taylor and Spencer would remember the day for very different reasons.

When the jets arrived at the Kill Box Taylor's navigator could not make contact with the JTAC. They were wasting a lot of fuel flying around in circles with him unable to hear them. While Taylor kept trying, Spencer switched to air traffic frequency. 'We're having difficulty getting hold of the JTAC.'

'Stand by. We have new tasking. Route north immediately to a TIC west of Kabul.' An American convoy had a broken axle and as the soldiers had tried to fix it they had come under small-arms fire. 'Two ISAF soldiers have been shot. Enemy forces are still in the area.'

Daryā-ye Meydān Valley, south west of Kabul and around 230 miles north east of Kandahar, is over 7000 feet above sea level, hemmed in on both sides by 5000-foot mountains. The two Dambuster jets were there in fourteen minutes and took over from a US Navy F-18 that had been keeping watch over the convoy but was being sent to another TIC. As was normal for the lead aircraft Keith Taylor went into a wheel with Kiwi Spencer about 1000 feet above him. That way they did not have to worry about where the other aircraft was or risk banging into each other. Beneath him he could see the eight wagons in the valley below, still at a standstill on a large, winding bend with compounds either side. A medical team had landed and was evacuating two casualties to a helicopter. He could not tell if they were alive or dead.

Taylor tried to make contact with the American JTAC but it was not easy. The deep valley bends and the jagged crags above were mugging radio signals. Eventually Taylor's navigator did connect with him but the conversation was tortuous. Not only was the high mountain valley not conducive to communication but the JTAC had to keep getting in and out of a vehicle. When he was inside the signal was strong but his voice was drowned by the noise of the running engine. When he stepped out he started to break up.

'One of my guys has probably been killed and one is seriously wounded,' he said. The medical helicopter swirled dust as it rose up into the air.

While they continued to fix the axle the JTAC wanted the Tornados to watch a number of potential ambush points and look out for signs of further attacks. Spencer, with Poppy Cormack-Loyd in the back seat, spotted a motorcyclist and tracked him, but he was over a kilometre away and heading away from the convoy. Then they saw a group of people in a field and went to take a look.

'They bad dudes?' the JTAC asked.

'They look like farmers to us,' Poppy replied. Through her pod she could see clearly that they were bent over, working with tools.

'You sure they're farmers?' The JTAC was understandably jumpy and keen to act.

The continual surveillance meant that Spencer had to increase his bank to ensure that his wing did not mask the pod's view of the ground and this increased fuel consumption. To try and eke it out he rolled out of a turn, let the jet accelerate in a straight line which used less fuel, and then entered the turn again. But it was now about an hour and fifteen minutes since he had last refuelled and he was bleeding energy.

'There's a tanker coming to you about 90 miles away,' air traffic told him, 'but you need to stay overhead until the tanker is on task.'

Spencer looked at his gauges. 'If we don't leave for the tanker now we are on emergency fuel.'

Then he heard on another frequency: 'You have a tanker behind you.' Spencer looked up. He could see it a few thousand feet above and not more than five miles away. He broke out of his wheel and headed fast for it, leaving Keith Taylor to stay over the convoy. Kiwi reckoned he could be there, topped up and back inside twenty minutes.

Now the casualties had been evacuated by helicopter and were on their way to hospital and the axle was just about fixed, the JTAC asked Taylor to fly ahead of the patrol and identify any other insurgents who might try and stop them getting to their forward operating base.

Even though the road through the valley was good the patrol moved at a sedate speed while Taylor flew forward-looking for the tell-tale signs of insurgents about to attack; single guys on motorbikes, racing up and down, and people running to the safety of compounds. All was quiet.

Three hours into the sortie and still flying over the convoy, Keith Taylor heard Kiwi's voice come over the radio.

'I can't get any fuel. I'm on a bingo back to KAF.'

Taylor realised that when it was his turn to go and refuel he would be forced to leave the convoy with no protection.

'We think the guys who attacked us are holed up in a village to the south of us,' the JTAC broke in. 'See if you can find them.'

The village was a sizeable maze of buildings shrouded in trees which cast shadows that even with the LITENING pod were difficult to see into. A lot of people and vehicles were on the move but they looked as though they were going about their daily business. It was impossible to pick out any as insurgents. Nor were there any compounds where ambush parties were massing.

Even so the convoy stopped short of the village. Figures began dismounting from the army wagons.

'We're sending in a party to find and apprehend the guys that attacked us,' the JTAC said.

High above Taylor circled and watched admiringly the guts of infantrymen walking into the unknown.

Suddenly his radio crackled to life. 'Something's happening! We need a show of force.'

If you couldn't bomb or strafe what you couldn't see, the show of force was the next best thing to spook an enemy. The 9-Line all complete, Keith Taylor banked his Tornado and looped down to the south west of the village. At about four miles out he eased the jet into a thirty-degree dive. He dropped down from high above the valley floor to just 150 feet in seconds. That close to the ground the Tornado unfurled its true speed. With the afterburners blazing flame out of the back of the twin turbofans, fields, roofs, compound walls, ditches and trees swept under the belly of the jet.

Two minutes after the JTAC's call for help, Keith Taylor's Tornado was right on top of the village at more than 520 knots (600 mph). Nobody feeling the ground begin to shake would have heard anything until the jet was above them. The suddenness of the screaming, churning, ear-splitting din of twenty-nine tonnes of Tornado about to rip the roof off was as terrifying as it was meant to be: terrifying beyond imagination. People ran and cowered, animals scattered.

Yet inside the cockpit all was quiet and calm.

No other air force flew as low as the Tornados. Thanks to the heritage and design of a Cold War aircraft, the Tornado was at its happiest wings back and zipping low and nasty over a landmass, pumping out flame, flares and noise and generally making its presence felt.

Thirty seconds later Taylor pulled his Tornado up into a steep climb straight into the sun. Anybody on the ground with an RPG or a surface-to-air missile would be dazzled and with heat-seeking missiles there was no safer place to be hiding than the greatest heat source of all.

Back up high and out of range Taylor radioed down to the JTAC. 'Did the ground commander get the effect he wanted?'

'You bet he did!' the JTAC said, all tension gone from his voice. Keith Taylor had driven several insurgents straight into the custody of the US infantry patrol that was in the village looking for them.

'Man, it was great to show the enemy that our dog is bigger than their dog.'

22

WALKING THE LINE

Every morning at 7.15 after the engineers' shift handover briefing SEngO Stu Clarke, Warrant Officer Thomson and Sergeant Al Sharp would get into a left-hand-drive pick-up and drive to the American Dining Facility for what they called the 'Gentlemen's Breakfast'.

The trio would take it in turns to drive to breakfast and whoever was at the wheel would depress the clutch when they got to within 100 metres of the American DFAC and see if they could freewheel the rest of the way over rough, undulating open ground and park with precision exactly in line with the other vehicles. They were keeping score.

'Stupid things, but they become monumentally important on ops,' the Warrant said as the SEngO feathered the steering wheel and eased the wagon into a space with the last little bit of momentum.

'Yes! How about that?'

'Not bad, not bad,' Mr T agreed. 'I'm afraid Al's got some catching up to do. I wouldn't let him park my car.'

The always cheerful Sharpy was used to being the butt of Stew Thomson's jokes and being referred to as 'the boy', even though he was well into his forties. Apart from the joshing the Gentlemen's Breakfast was also the chance for Stu Clarke to tap into issues on the engineering side and get a steer from Thomson and Sharp on any shop floor problems he ought to be knowing about.

Stepping into the coolness of the dining facility they washed and sanitised their hands – obligatory in a place where everybody was terrified of D&V (diarrhoea and vomiting). Inside they swiped their meal cards, grabbed a tray and prepared to breakfast in America.

The American DFAC was like a vast diner. Constructed of pristine white dustproof plastic it was the size of two aircraft hangars and as high. A dazzling array of stainless steel and glass self-service counters were heaped with fresh fruit, cereals, breads, bacon, sausages and hash browns. The queues snaked around juice, smoothie and yoghurt bars, coffee machines, milk dispensers and five types of tea. Uniforms stood in line at the hot bars where cooks tossed pancakes and scrambled or fried eggs any style. The only difference was that the cooks were from Sri Lanka and playing Hindi movie tunes on a small cassette player as they worked. Just in case anybody forgot that they were not in a branch of the US of A, big wall-mounted flat TV screens ran the length and both sides of the DFAC, relaying basketball highlights from the LA Lakers and the New York Knicks and moving moments from the *Oprah Show*.

The SEngO arrived at the table where they were sitting with a plate of bacon and a pile of toast. 'Porridge again, Mr T?' Clarke nodded in Thomson's direction.

'Absolutely, Sir.'

Every day the Warrant and Al Sharp ate the same thing. 'I like to ring the changes,' the SEngO said sitting down.

For Al Sharp every day began with yoghurt, a croissant and chocolate spread.

'You and your fancy roll, Sharpy,' Thomson said, stirring fruit into his oats. Between mouthfuls he looked around at the landscape of diners. Most of them were heavily armed. It baffled Thomson.

'In the unlikely event of the Taliban breaking into our compound we'll be ready. If a missile comes down while you are eating breakfast you've got fuck all chance against it with a rifle.'

Al Sharp seemed preoccupied.

'You are looking a little peaky, Al,' the SEngO suggested.

Sharp's usually firm smile was looking untypically wan. 'It's Friday,' he said, and pushed his Nutella to one side. Suddenly he didn't fancy it any more.

'Say no more,' the SEngO said, smiling at Thomson.

For most of the week every day was just like any other as Sharp busied himself about the base. The only one that was different was the fifth day of the week when Warrant Officer Thomson walked the aircraft line.

'You ready, Sharpy?' Thomson said back at 904, replete with porridge and rubbing his hands. 'Let's see what we have out there today.'

It was the first Friday in June and Sergeant Sharp grabbed his clipboard and followed Thomson out to the aircraft shelters to begin the weekly tour of inspection. For two hours Thomson would peek, peer, sniff and feel every inch of that Tornado pan, awarding marks out of ten. He wanted it spotless. It was Sharp's job to record the scores and the comments and get ugly, hazardous and sloppy practices sorted before the morning was out.

Striding into the first shelter which was empty, Thomson looked into a stack of metal drip trays that sat under the jets to catch leaking oil or fuel. These were smeared with engine oil.

He picked them up and hurled them across the floor. Sharp winced.

'Not good enough, Al,' he said, as the trays slithered across the concrete. 'Get someone out here to clean them up.' A spool of cable left lying around was also despatched across the floor.

Next he spotted a toolbox that had not been padlocked. 'Al, I am quarantining this box. Boxes should be locked. Four out of ten.'

And so the Warrant went on his Friday line prowl from aircraft shelter to aircraft shelter. 'That trolley is in the wrong place!' 'Get that towing tractor parked where it should be!' He stopped, stooped and tapped his keys on a waste oil drum. 'This needs emptying!' A smear here, a spillage there. On he went. 'Get somebody out here to clear that up!' 'How many times have I told them?'

The faithful Sharpy scuttled along behind scratching notes on to his clipboard.

Suddenly Thomson's attention was diverted. He had spotted an engineer slouching across the far side of the ramp.

'High-viz belt,' the Warrant bellowed. 'I can't see your high-viz belt!'

She tucked her T-shirt into her trousers and her fluorescent yellow high-visibility belt was once more present and correct as she marched off back to the squadron block.

'The Warrant is definitely old school,' said Rocksy Sharrocks, 'but I'm all for old school. Most of the aircrew have come through university and then intensive training and have had a lot of rough edges smoothed off, although not all. Many of the engineers have come straight from school and to succeed in this business they need strong figures to guide them.'

At the end of his inspection Warrant Officer Thomson had pronounced all but one of the shelters seven or eight out of ten.

'That is a hell of a lot better than what we inherited when we came out here,' he said. 'The guys are by and large doing a first-rate job,' although Mr T was a bit too old school to dish out too many compliments directly.

'Not the worst Friday we've had, Sir,' Al Sharp agreed, now wishing he had eaten all his Nutella.

'People think I am a bit OCD about this,' Thomson said, walking down to the edge of the ramp to check one of the weapons stores. One could feel all the engineers' heads nodding as one as he said it. He admitted that he did have a shadow board in his workshop at home so he could see instantly if tools were not hanging in their right place.

'I believe that Mrs Thomson once used a screwdriver to stir a tin of paint when you were on ops, Sir?' Sergeant Sharp offered, confidence and relief raging through his veins.

'That she did, Sharpy, that she did.' Thomson bristled as if the crime had only been committed yesterday. 'But there is a serious side to all this,' he insisted, kneeling down to pick up a couple of pieces of grit off the concrete.

Visitors from other squadrons based at KAF always remarked in admiration that the British Tornado ramp was the cleanest they had seen on the airfield.

'If stuff is left lying around or the ramp is dirty then jets can get damaged,' Thomson said. 'If they suck up debris and don't fly we cannot be there for the guys on the ground. I am not going to allow that to happen because some prat leaves something in the wrong place.'

Back home Thomson had once taken some young engineers to a hangar that contained the mangled unrecognisable wreckage of a Tornado that had crashed, killing its crew. It was a wake-up call for anybody in the fast jet world.

'I tell them to *Get a grip!* because we are in a war and we need our jets and our crews to do their jobs supporting Omid Haft and all the other operations and get home safely.' As far as Thomson was concerned if small seemingly insignificant mistakes were prevented then the chances of big bad things happening were reduced significantly. 'If that's OCD then, okay, hands up, I'm guilty as charged.'

Ironically Stew Thomson had not always been so precise and tidy himself. On joining the service in January 1976 he had been described in reports as 'scruffy and over-confident whose servicing tasks were not always completed satisfactorily'. He was now referred to as a 'strong charismatic leader' with 'a reputation for excellence and professionalism'.

Had there been a Damascene moment?

'Today they call it career counselling,' Thomson smiled. 'In those days they'd take you somewhere quiet and tell you to *Get a fucking grip!*'

Stew Thomson got his grip. Working on the Jaguar servicing team Mr T became 'an enthusiastic, valued operator' and came full circle from scruff to scrupulous. Thirty-five years later Warrant Officer Thomson's guiding motivation as he walked the line was simple. 'I want to help the guys not make the mistakes that I did.'

That evening around 6.30 Warrant Officer Thomson tried to find a space to park his pick-up on the south side of the airfield but there were many others trying to do the same. 'That's not going to move,' he said, squeezing it into a tiny space. He got out, put on his beret and joined scores of others making for the runway apron. Alongside the Warrant was Chief Technician Andrew 'Abo' Alexander. Hair shaved into submission and bristling with tensile strength, Abo was one of the fittest guys on 617. This evening both men were subdued.

The edge was going off the heat of the day as Abo and Thomson mingled with 200 other uniforms that had assembled and were greeting one another in several languages. Their conversations were uncharacteristically muted. A hundred metres away across the tarmac a big transport plane stood with its back ramp yawning open. Its vaulted interior was cave-like and empty.

At a predetermined signal a regimental sergeant major came striding over.

'From the aircraft you will line up in two lines, four deep, facing one another,' he instructed. He was Australian. 'Australian forces personnel will line up in the front rows,' he continued. 'ISAF and other forces personnel will line up in the second and third rows. Civilians will form up at the rear.' He paused and looked around. 'You will follow salutes as instructed. No sunglasses to be worn.'

This was the ramp ceremony and repatriation of a twenty-seven-year-old lieutenant who had been killed when the Chinook in which he was a passenger had crashed near Tarin Kowt in Zabul Province, southern Afghanistan, on 30 May. His body was about to begin the long journey home. He was a qualified helicopter pilot and serving with the 6th Aviation Regiment, based in Sydney. He was less than a month into his first front-line tour of Afghanistan where he was due to operate unmanned UAVs, and was the twenty-sixth Australian soldier to have been killed in Afghanistan since 2001.

This was the eighth repatriation Thomson had attended since he had been in Kandahar. He took at least one of the engineers to each one.

'We live in a false environment here,' he said. 'We are not in the same danger that the army is under and it is the chance to re-emphasise to my guys that this is what we are here for. And we are not just here for the British forces; we are here for every other nation's soldiers as well.'

The previous week Thomson had taken a group of engineers to a ramp ceremony when nine American coffins had been put on a plane: two air force and seven infantry. The youngest was just under 18 years old and the two oldest were 35.

'When you are watching a young person's coffin carried past it is not easy.'

His eldest son, Scott, who was an oil production engineer with BP and his other son Kris, who was a physics teacher, were both in their twenties.

At a shouted command two lines formed up and marched slowly out towards the aircraft. They formed up facing one another all the way from the ramp of the Hercules back to the apron. The majority were Australian, but there were also many French, British, American, Canadian, Dutch and Bulgarian servicemen and women standing with them and a good sprinkling of civilians at their backs. They stood in silence, staring directly ahead, straight-backed, index fingers pointing down trouser seams.

In the distance there was the sound of a lone bagpiper playing. The strains of 'Waltzing Matilda' hovered across a light hot breeze. The music stopped. A flurry of shouted commands. Right hands shot briskly up to temples. A flurry of salutes went down the lines, some with palms facing out, others palm down and some angled. The words of a priest over a malfunctioning speaker were hard to make out. The pipes started up again and the cortège moved on. Now the piper was in view. He stood to one side and played 'Amazing Grace' as the coffin passed. Thomson could see the shape out of the corner of his eye. And then it was right in front of him. The metal coffin was borne on eight shoulders and draped with the Australian flag. On the top was a wreath of yellow roses, greenery and daffodils with gold and green ribbons to match. In front of that was a lone dark blue beret.

The priest walked behind clutching a bible, his crisp white robes the cleanest thing in this dirty, dust-ridden place.

At the tailgate the simple cortège stopped for a prayer. The mourners removed their berets and bowed their heads. An 'Amen' rippled through the ranks. Then silence. Even the din and drone from the runway seemed to have stopped. When 'The Last Post' played Thomson looked up. The coffin was already inside the aircraft ready for the flight home to Queensland.

'It's not just that young man's life that has been ended,' Thomson said as the ceremony broke up. In spite of completing seventeen operational tours, for once the tell-it-like-it-is Scot was reflective. 'There's a family back in Australia for whom a large part of their lives has ended. It makes you think of your own children.

'But it should not weaken our resolve,' the Warrant added quickly, walking briskly back to his truck. 'That young man did not give his life for us to throw in the towel and walk away from this.'

23

THE INNER SANCTUM

If you really wanted to touch the pulse of the aircrew it was in the briefing room. The crewroom was for coffee, banter, magazines and planning weddings if you were Caroline and Poppy. It was for yet more coffee, snacking from the fridge, catching up on email, opening the post, watching DVDs and trying to find a school for your children in Bristol if you were Griff.

But the inner sanctum, the confessional, the place to tell it like it was, to listen and to learn was the briefing room. Pre-sortie briefings, conducted by the pilot leading a pair of aircraft (known as pairs-lead), were detailed but rapidly delivered bullet points: a list of grid references, timings, flight profiles, refuelling data, tankers and towlines, weather and mission goals, condensed from the prep work, the 'domestics', that the two crews had done beforehand.

The debriefing took place as soon as the jet had been signed back in and mission reports and 541s were filed.

'It is vital to catch any issues while they are still fresh,' Keith Taylor said. Most debriefs lasted at least an hour and two hours was not unusual. It was where younger members of the squadron would learn by discussing the objectives and goals of a completed mission against the outcomes. However, unlike the army, RAF sortie briefs and debriefs were not led by rank. Whoever was leading the mission led the brief and also the debrief; even if the Boss had flown the sortie but was the wingman.

'Leading a debrief is an art that has to be learned just as much as gaining confidence in the cockpit,' Rocksy Sharrocks said.

The Boss concurred. 'If I could have done something better, I need to be told.'

However there were moments when it paid to listen and learn from the experience of others, as Flight Lieutenant Ollie Moncrieff was about to find out. Now well into 617's deployment, Ollie, like many of the younger aircrew, had replaced initial nerves with confidence and lucidity. However, that confidence was also verging on a swagger that did not always recognise when it was time to shut up and listen.

Moncrieff had just led a sortie to the east of Herat with Squadron Leader Griffiths in the back seat and Joe Hourston and Lucy Williams in the other jet. They had worked with an Italian JTAC searching for rocketing sites.

'Communication is going to be a problem today,' Lucy had said in the pre-brief. 'We've talked to this JTAC before and his English is not that good.'

A convoy was on its way to a FOB along Route 1, notorious for narcotics trafficking. Insurgents had recently attacked another convoy killing eight security guards. This time the convoy made it safely. The two Tornados had provided armed over-watch until the Italian JTAC released them with a cheery 'God Save Your Queen'.

On the way back to Kandahar they flew by the site where a French Mirage had crashed the previous week. Lucy had noted that the crew had been rescued by helicopter inside an hour. Her Dambuster predecessors were not so lucky. In the Second World War Lancasters had the poorest record for bale-outs. The bomb-aimer, flight engineer, pilot and navigator had to escape through a forward hatch just 22 inches (56 cm) wide. The mid-upper and rear gunner had to escape through the rear hatch. While 50 per cent of American bomber crews bailed out successfully only 10.9 per cent of Lancaster crews made it – a statistic that contributed to the appalling total of 55,573 Bomber Command aircrew deaths. It was a loss – greater than any other individual service – that had finally been recognised on 4 May 2011, a few weeks after 617 Squadron's detachment to Kandahar, with the laying of a foundation stone for an impressive memorial to be built in Green Park after a campaign in which Dambuster Tony Iveson had played a leading role.

Williams, Moncrieff, Griffiths and Hourston filed into the airless, windowless briefing room and closed the heavy door behind them. They all stood at the waist-high work-bench in the middle of the floor. Ollie took up position at one end of it, Griff at the other with Joe and Lucy standing either side facing one another.

Ollie opened his debrief with a short résumé of the sortie, ticking off the bullet points from the pre-brief. Everything had gone to plan. He asked for comments.

'Nothing dramatic happened and we kept the Italians happy,' Lucy chipped in.

'Thank you! God Save the Queen,' Joe smiled.

'A very average sortie,' Griff agreed. 'We did what we were tasked to do; nobody got hurt and we all came back safe. Job done.'

Well, not quite. The Warlord had an issue with the way that Moncrieff had handled a refuelling during the sortie. Griff said that Ollie had relied too much on air traffic control to guide him into and from the tanker.

'If you keep asking air traffic they feel duty bound to reply to you,' he explained. 'But that way you block up all the air waves and are taking their attention away from keeping the airspace from getting blocked and aircraft coming into confliction. If they are trying to get somebody to a TIC the last thing they need is some guy hogging the airwaves for a route to a tanker.'

To Griffiths it was like calling 999 for travel directions when you had a perfectly good SatNav.

'I've been doing the refuelling with another navigator for the last six weeks and we had this way of doing it,' Moncrieff said.

'Agreed,' Griff said.

It was usual for an aircraft to approach from 1000 feet below and only when a pilot had visual contact would he be cleared to come up to the same height as the tanker and fill up. Once refuelled the majority of aircraft would leave by climbing away higher, to 1000 feet or more above the tanker and then depart, because other aircraft would be joining the tanker from below.

'I thought it was safer to use air traffic to make sure we had no aircraft directly below us who were coming up to fuel,' Moncrieff said. 'The airspace was incredibly busy.'

'Exactly. It was incredibly busy,' Griffiths agreed. 'But we have got lots of different ways of finding and leaving that tanker without interfering with air traffic. So give them a break, use your equipment in the aircraft.'

Griff said that Moncrieff could have used the tactical air navigation (TACAN) beacon, which would have given him the range to the tanker. He could also have talked to his wingman for added situational awareness and used his radar to establish the position of other aircraft coming up to tank.

Moncrieff shrugged and paused. Was he going to admit he was wrong or push back at Griffiths? *If I am asked to run a debrief and I am the captain of an aeroplane I don't feel that I should be treated like this.* It was exactly how a young Guy Gibson, a fellow graduate of the same school as Ollie, might have felt. Moncrieff pushed back at Griffiths.

'Yes, we can use the stuff we have in the cockpit, but given the crowded airspace I still think that I was right to ask for extra help from air traffic, especially when leaving the tanker.'

The atmosphere in the debrief room was verging on claustrophobic. Lucy gazed down at the floor and fiddled with a piece of paper. Joe was staring straight ahead. Moncrieff looked to them both for help. He was on his own on this one.

There was a sudden silence that captured the air. Then a bang which filled the room. The Warlord's flattened palm had come down heavily on the debrief desk. 'Enough!'

Lucy flinched, cheek bones tightening.

Griffiths stared at Moncrieff. His dark eyes glistened. '*You* are not listening to what I am saying.'

Griffiths knew that statistically as people got closer to the end of their first ops tour they thought they knew everything and that was when they were at their most dangerous. Even though they were in a war and not on a training exercise, training never really stopped.

Griffiths saw Ollie bridling.

'This is getting heavy,' Joe muttered.

'Let me put it this way,' Griffiths continued. His gaze was solely on Moncrieff. 'In the UK air traffic gives you lots of help. They give you heights, they give you ranges, directions and put everything on a plate. They spoon-feed you. You cannot expect that kind of service out here. This is a war zone.

You know how many aircraft are in the airspace. Do more for yourselves. That's all I am saying to you guys. Okay?'

The three aircrew mumbled okay.

'Happy days.'

Lucy and Joe breathed more easily. As they filed back out into the ops room the Warlord called after them.

'Ollie?'

'Yes, Sir?'

'A word.'

Ollie Moncrieff returned to the debrief room with shoulders sloped. *Not another word!*

The door clicked shut.

Ten minutes later Moncrieff reappeared, looking like a man who had been given an extra shot by the doctor. But nobody would ever know what had been said. Like confession there was a tradition that anything said in the debrief room stayed there.

He passed through the intelligence room where a big flat screen TV was showing a Test match live from Lord's. Compared to the desert and dust at KAF the wide-striped green turf looked as though it had been painted by David Hockney. Moncrieff asked cricketing-mad intelligence officer Rich Smith the score. England were now giving India a pasting. Moncrieff knew the feeling.

He walked into the adjoining ops room and saw the smiling SEngO striding towards him.

Stu Clarke was never one to miss the remnants of something hanging in the air. 'Turned out nice again,' he said, as the young flight lieutenant exited into the corridor without responding.

'Something I said?' Clarke asked. By the time Ollie Moncrieff reached the crewroom his normal good humour was returning;

especially when he saw how many parcels had just arrived with his name on.

'Not all debriefs are like that,' he said, but he was still insistent: 'I think I have a valid point. It's *very* frustrating.'

Ollie Moncrieff was not alone in stepping over lines. There had been other examples of junior aircrew insisting that they knew best. Griff mulled it over with Keith Taylor.

'What disappointed me was that you had two other youngsters in that room who were coming to the end of their first tour as well,' Griffiths said. 'If I am getting challenged by one in front of two, then what happens if all three start questioning? You find yourself involved in one horrible situation.'

'They need reminding that this is an RAF squadron, not a flying club,' the Boss said.

'We have a tricky balance here,' Tony Griffiths admitted.

Keith Taylor agreed. Drawing the line between enthusiasm and arrogance was never easy. It never had been. Guy Gibson was one of the great airmen and wartime leaders but he was famous for having a vast ego. A martinet, he did not suffer fools or criticism. His way was the only way. Knowing best may have been what killed him.

Surrounded by 2011's young and thrusting, Squadron Leader Tony Griffiths did not look in the mood for a sherry party. The Warlord was pale and looked exhausted. Sixteen-hour days were catching up on him. If he had been promised thirty years' sleep it would not have been enough.

'I accept that most aircrew are selected because they are intelligent people,' he said. 'Forty per cent have been to university and those who haven't are just as bright. So we have a bunch that are bred at Cranwell to have officer qualities and to make decisions. And now we are asking them to sometimes be led and do as they are told. This is why we are getting these tensions and people like Ollie going why, why, why?

'Sometimes you have to say: "Shut up, do as you are told. We are in the military and the situation we are in dictates that we cannot discuss every single point and decision in minute detail."'

'It's time for us to put a collective foot down,' the Boss said. 'Put a brake on the belligerence. We'll do it at shareholders.'

'Shareholders' was the weekly aircrew meeting usually held on a Sunday evening at KAF. It was also attended by the SEngO and a JEngO. From the Boss downwards it was an informal chance to report progress, raise issues, take stock of where the Squadron was and set the tone and agenda for the following week.

As they arrived at the meeting in a lecture theatre in Cambridge Lines that Sunday 5 June, none of the junior aircrew had any idea of what was to come.

Shareholders was usually chaired by the Squadron second-in-command. Now Ballsy had gone back to the UK, Squadron Leader Sharrocks took the mantle as the new 2iC. Just like Chris Ball, Rocksy liked to keep the business brisk.

It came to Tony Griffiths' turn. 'We have noticed this trend and we are going in hard-nosed over it,' he began, looking around the room. 'Some of the guys have now done six weeks of a first ops tour. For most of the Execs this is their eighth, ninth, tenth and eleventh tour. It's not a case of we know better than you, it is more a case of us having learned something through the pain of experience. We've made those mistakes; don't go making them again. Listen to us. Some of you are not quite listening to us or being as responsive as you should be. To question is fine; it's experience that tells you when you do it and when not.'

One of the other squadron leaders put it more succinctly. 'This,' he said, 'has got to stop.'

Nobody answered back. The point had been made and taken.

24

PULL UP! PULL UP!

It was not long into 617's deployment that Keith Taylor had decided that he and Tony Griffiths should only work days because that was when most bureaucratic and other problems seemed to crop up, which is why the Warlord was now navigator to Ollie Moncrieff and the Boss was flying with one of the other navigators. The realignment of crews meant that Timmy Colebrooke and Gary Montgomery were now flying together.

Both had impressed with their skill and commitment whatever the deployment had thrown at them. They had already developed a close bond.

'There's no front seat snobbery in this jet,' Colebrooke grinned down at Montgomery, as he walked along the fuselage mimicking a tightrope walker, to inspect the rudder. 'Flexibility is the key to air power; write that down!'

Monty, the quieter of the two, referred to Timmy as 'the mouthpiece'. There was an air about them, not just of confidence, that said they had escaped the head boy and the house captain and could not wait to prove themselves in their own right.

They had done RAPTOR work and provided over-watch for convoys and patrols and surveillance support for raids on insurgent compounds: on more than one occasion they had been called to TICs only to find that the situation had been resolved by the time they had got there or that the insurgents had vanished. Monty particularly craved the chance for some dynamic flying.

As he gave the final confirmation that he was ready to take the jet out he said to the liney: 'See you later. Enjoy your lunch.'

Monty was the lead jet and Al Spence his wingman in the other Tornado with Conan Mullineux. Their destination was way up near the Turkmenistan border, where an ISAF patrol had been taking small-arms fire.

An hour or so later Gary Montgomery zipped in over a high ridge that was dotted with houses. Beneath it was a small town and a long winding valley. Timmy Colebrooke made contact with an American JTAC, who told him that the patrol had just neutralised an IED when they had a warning from a friendly Afghan villager that an ambush was being set at the narrowest point of the valley they were trying to travel down.

Spence and Mullineux peeled off to check out buildings and compounds. Montgomery and Colebrooke flew down over the valley to the pinch-point. While Monty got acquainted with the terrain, Colebrooke slewed the LITENING pod up and down the valley. In its floor was a river and running alongside it a narrow road one vehicle wide. At its narrowest point the valley could not have been more than 90 metres wide and there it twisted around a sharp tree-lined bend so it was impossible to see what lay beyond. It was an ideal ambush site but there was no positive sighting of insurgents. All Colebrooke could see were a couple of men, probably farmers, who were using a rope ferry to pull themselves across the river, ordinary rural life going on and a great many farm animals grazing.

By now the JTAC was convinced that he and his colleagues were going to get ambushed up ahead. He called for a bomb.

Colebrooke told him, 'If you get into contact we can help.'

There was a pause. Colebrooke couldn't hear any gunfire or urgency in the JTAC's voice. Normally the two went together.

'We want to take another look,' Colebrooke told the JTAC, hoping to defuse the situation. He did not want to see Americans getting hurt and they would do all they could to stop that happening; equally he wanted them to work a bit harder to achieve a 9-Line before Monty fired in a Brimstone.

They made another sweep down the valley but still they could not find any visual evidence of insurgents lying in wait.

'Not even a hint,' he told the JTAC.

'Can you lay down some noise in the valley?' the JTAC asked.

Monty felt the adrenaline kicking in as he began clearing the airspace for a show of force. Spence took his jet higher and vertically overhead and Mullineux put his camera in super-wide to monitor what they called the ingress into a show of force and then the egress out of it again.

From his wheel at 14,000 feet Montgomery took a look out of his window and assessed the best way of getting into the valley and the hard-jink turns he'd need to make to arrive 100 feet off the ground through its narrowest part – where the insurgents were thought to be hunkered down waiting for the mechanised patrol to come by. The valley did not look any tighter than some of those he flew daily in Scotland. That terrain-hugging flying was the best, with the jet doing what it was meant to do. But there was a difference. As a junior pilot he had never been qualified to fly lower than 250 feet. Now he was, but he had not flown at low level recently. Two thirds of the way through 617's deployment he had done nothing but medium altitude flying, apart from one show of force during the Squadron's first two weeks in theatre when Tony Griffiths had been in the back seat. But that was straight out over flat desert to break up a massing crowd that posed a threat to a patrol of Italians. That was fast away from the traffic lights stuff. Compared to what he was about to attempt that had been easy.

As Monty was fond of saying, 'It's only on operations that you find out if you can really do it or not.'

The difference between flying at 250 feet and 100 feet was like the difference between the relative safety of the slow lane and a fast lane full of chicanes. He could play safe and lay down his noise at 500 feet. That would reduce the risk of crashing into the valley sides but it would lessen the effect. He took one long look at it. He was confident he could crack it. He would have to go into the mouth of the valley like a downhill skier, dropping down and down, picking up speed, but finessing the jet around the easier bends and then streak through the narrow gap before rolling back out and up again.

He dropped the jet down.

'5100 feet,' he said, checking with Colebrooke, 'you've got the fixed point [the target], you have the route?' It came up on his HUD.

'Five miles to go.' Colebrooke's voice was fighting through the buzzing and bleeping on the cockpit comms.

At around 2500 feet Montgomery turned left for his final approach down the valley.

'Three miles to go,' Colebrooke said. Sitting in the back seat he began to feel that he could have reached out and touched the sides of the valley and it was still getting narrower. The G was kicking in. The eager power from the jet's engines was forcing itself into his back. It was like being on the inside of a computer game.

'Pull up! Pull up! Pull up!' Bitching Betty said firmly.

Montgomery made adjustments to his flight path to shut her up.

'Flares ready to go,' Colebrooke said. He would not usually be allowed to fire flares at this height for fear of causing fires but they were coming in over water.

They were now at 250 feet and travelling at 520 knots, nudging 600 mph. Monty looked either side of his HUD display so he could get a better view of the narrowing valley. It felt like it was about to snap shut on them.

'Pull up! Pull up! Pull up!' Betty sounded like she was ready to eject. 'Pull up! Pull up! Pull up!' she insisted.

Monty had a good view from the HUD but it was about five degrees to the right of where he wanted to be. A few touches on the stick. The jet felt good, freed at last to fly fast and low.

Pilot and navigator were in total synchronisation. At 100 feet Gary Montgomery sped his Tornado through the narrowest gap in the valley as Timmy Colebrooke fired off three flares, unleashing a monsoon of bangs and lights. To those on the ground it must have looked like a terrifying firework display. The troops on the ground could not believe it.

'Jesus fuck!' the JTAC screamed. 'Amaaazin' man!'

'Some jets you can hear,' Colebrooke said, 'but you can *feel* a Tornado.'

As the JTAC kept Jesus fucking Monty laughed and turned the jet right and pulled it up hard out of the valley. He felt a mixture of relief at job done and on hearing from the JTAC that the American ground commander was 'very, very happy'.

For Monty the ride back to KAF was the best ever. After weeks of over-watch, 'extremely important but very dull' RAPTOR work or prepping jets for GCAS launches that never happened, he felt that at last he was on the game board, that he had done something useful. He had proved that like his predecessors in the Gulf War who had inspired him to fly as a boy, he could fly low in theatre for real. For a Dambuster of any age it was something in the blood.

For Timmy Colebrooke too it was a coming of age. He was no longer an F3 pumper. 'Monty's a great pilot,' he said. 'To be able to fly at 100 feet on demand having done weeks and weeks of medium level flying and have to go through a very narrow valley with danger at every turn is just incredible.'

Monty and Timmy were now switched to night flying for the rest of the detachment. One early evening in June they were due to fly in a two-ship formation down the south of Afghanistan. After their briefing they went to get kitted up and then walked to their jet.

Even though jets were taking off, crews were sitting on GCAS and the engineers were working flat out under flood-lights to get Tornados fixed up for the next day's flying pro-gramme, the atmosphere at night was much quieter than during the day shift. Sounds were muffled, doors didn't bang. It was almost other-worldly. The 904 and TIW offices were empty. The real-time comms screen had no TICs on it. There was little chance of a GCAS launch. Even insurgents went to bed.

This June night seemed even quieter than usual. The phones were silent, the temperature had dropped into the twenties and the only noise was of a table tennis ball being batted back and forth in the engineers' recreation room.

In the half-light of early morning Flight Sergeant Paul Peden of A Shift left the Squadron building as he always did when he was on nights and walked over to the flight line to assess how many more 'husbandry jobs' needed doing on the Tornados before the day shift came in two hours later.

A usual scene greeted him as he walked down the line of aircraft shelters. The armourers were busy putting weapons on to a jet. Two others which had just returned from the uneventful sortie on which Montgomery and Colebrooke had flown were being serviced. One of them had developed a temperature fault on a turbine bearing.

Peden stopped to talk to two lineys when a large thud shook the ground.

'Shit! What was that?'

'I reckon it was one of those "controlled explosions",' Peden said. The bang sounded as though it had gone off only about 200 metres away; very close for a controlled explosion and they were usually pre-announced by a Tannoy warning in all buildings. Peden did not remember hearing a warning.

For a second Peden wondered: should he yell to everyone to hit the deck face down, as they had been taught in their rocket attack drills? He decided against it. There had been no distinctively piercing rocket attack alarm.

The flight sergeant continued his inspection RES by RES, making sure that everything was in good order and clean and presentable for the day shift, a process that was known as the 'daily reset'. Shifts clearing up after themselves was something that Warrant Officer Thomson was ferociously passionate about. If he came round later that morning and found anything amiss Peden and his JEngO, Flight Lieutenant Al Whitehead, would be in for a 'get-a-grip' conversation when A Shift clocked on again at 7 p.m.

Peden was also on the look-out for foreign object debris (FOD) which could get sucked into jet engines, so he could alert the 'FOD Plod' or sweep up, which happened daily at 6 a.m. He had just reached the rear of RES 5 when the ramp was shaken by a massive explosion just 15 metres away on the other side of the Hesco-bastion wall.

'Get down!' Peden yelled at the top of his voice as he hit the deck. Everybody looked as though they were diving in slow motion. Prone on the concrete Peden was aware of a shock-wave, a blast of air coming across the top of the high Hesco barrier. The thick gauge waterproof canvas of the RES rippled as if it was being shaken hard by an invisible hand. A massive plume of dust and dirt rose rapidly into the air just beyond the barrier. Peden saw four of his engineers in RES 5 pressed flat to the ground, their hands tucked under their bodies and their heads well down, exactly as they had been taught. Then he heard a rattling sound. Something was falling from the sky. Pieces of shrapnel began to shower the Tornado ramp. A lump of metal glanced off Peden's head and bounced away. It was only then that he realised that this was a rocket attack.

The bastion walls had diffused the worst of the blast impact, but Peden knew that rockets usually came in salvos of four to six and because they were supersonic, unlike mortar shells, you could not hear them coming. They could not be guided but they obviously had the range of the Tornado ramp. He could not understand why the siren had not gone off. All Paul Peden's drills kicked in. He had to get his guys into one of the hardened concrete shelters before any more missiles landed, but the nearest was in the direction from which the latest rocket had come. If they stayed where they were they stood a good chance of being killed, either by a direct hit or by a rocket hitting an aircraft and exploding it. There was also fuel nearby, as well as oil drums and missiles.

All was quiet. After staying prone for two minutes Peden yelled to the guys in RES 5: 'Run to the shelter and take cover. Now!'

At 52 years old Flight Sergeant Peden was neither the most svelte nor the fittest man on 617 Squadron and he had trouble with his knees, but he found himself sprinting for the shelter. Powered by adrenaline he leapt over a drainage ditch and overtook one of the younger engineers on the way. Right down the flight line he could see engineers hurtling for other shelters on what was now a beautifully sunny morning.

He was too intent on the engineers getting to safety to be scared. As he made the shelter he was annoyed with himself for not having had everybody adopt their rocket attack drills after the first explosion.

Inside the gloom of the shelter Peden looked about to see who was in there with him. Younger engineers, all in their twenties, were huddling together. Peden's heart was thumping inside his chest. He studied the shelter, a box made of concrete slabs, and wondered how sturdy it would be if it took a direct hit. Nobody said much. They all looked at each other in disbelief. The war had come to them. And then the rocket attack alarm went off.

'A lot of fucking use now!' Peden said. They all cracked up as a sense of relief that they were safe spread through the shelter.

Peden lay with his head on the sand. He sniffed. 'Smells like piss in here,' he said. The guys stifled a laugh. One of them admitted that this was where some of the lads relieved themselves if they got caught short while working out on the ramp. 'Can't wait to tell me mum that I pissed on the flight sergeant,' one of them grinned.

Three minutes after the explosion Peden told his lads to make their way to the Squadron building and put on their helmets and body armour. Back inside a roll-call was taken to make sure that nobody was missing or injured. Then the realisation he had experienced going into the shelter began to come down heavily on the flight sergeant. If he had taken greater notice of the first explosion and got his guys to safety they would never have been so exposed to the dangers of the second closer rocket. He chided himself for allowing complacency to momentarily get the better of him.

There were no more rockets that day and, forty action-packed minutes since he had left the Squadron building, the all-clear sounded and a Tannoy announcement advised that post-attack recovery should begin. Flight Sergeant Peden sent out three teams to inspect the damage and check for any unexploded ordnance. Similar teams were also out scouring all other sectors of Kandahar Airfield.

No Dambusters aircraft had been hit but the engineers did bring back pieces of shrapnel and put them on the line controllers' desk. It was the first time that most of them had seen it close up. Jagged and razor sharp to the touch and blackened by extreme temperature, the pieces were ugly and small but surprisingly heavy. This was all that remained of the missile. The insurgents launched them from four to five miles away, from sand ramps or metal racks, using a simple battery and timer to delay the firing until they were safely out of the way.

Paul Peden could not stop himself looking repeatedly at the shrapnel and thinking about the death and destruction it represented and that the unseen hands that had last touched it had belonged to somebody intent on killing him or his colleagues. He made a promise to himself: next time he would do just what he had done in all the pre-deployment training sessions. Siren or no siren he would order the engineers to hit the ground as soon as an explosion happened and then after no more attacks get them to a secure shelter as fast as possible.

25

HOMING INSTINCTS

On Monday 27 June, 617 Squadron took the Tornado through a historic milestone when a two-ship sortie clocked up the aircraft's one millionth flying hour. Newspapers helpfully pointed out that one million flying hours was the equivalent of flying to the sun and back or 16,000 times around the globe. Since the First Gulf War the Tornado had been on daily operational service for twenty years. Defence Secretary Liam Fox, along with Chief of the Air Staff Sir Stephen Dalton, came out to lavish praise on the jet and they also commended the 'skill [and] professionalism of the aircrew, engineers and support staff who have supported it in service for more than 30 years'.

The entire Dambuster squadron in Kandahar – most of whom had not been born when the Tornado had joined the RAF – assembled nine rows deep forming an arrowhead in front of the two jets on the ramp. Seven had been chosen to hold up the magic 1,000,000 in big red numerals for a commemorative photograph. Keith Taylor stood smiling at the head of his squadron with his Execs and SEngO Stuart Clarke in a row behind him, the Warrant Officer and the JEngOs and flight sergeants behind them.

It had been a long and distinguished journey from 30 October 1974 when Prototype Tornado PO2 was first wheeled out of a hangar at BAE Systems' military research and development facility at Warton Aerodrome in Lancashire to make its maiden flight. The fact that it was 617 that had flown the millionth hour on an operational sortie was extra special to Keith Taylor. It maintained a tradition of the Dambusters getting there first. Although he had to admit that he had had no idea that it was his squadron which had achieved that landmark until he received a message from the UK telling him.

Perhaps the Dambuster most pleased was Flight Lieutenant Jane Pickersgill, who had flown that millionth hour. 'Fantastic; absolutely fantastic,' she grinned. Her name would for ever be included in a significant footnote of Tornado history.

As the ageing swing-wing flew on towards the end of its operational life there was also a historic poignancy for navigators like Jane. Once the Tornado had gone, to be replaced by single-seat aircraft like the upgraded Eurofighter Typhoon or the F-35 Joint Strike Fighter, there would be no more fast jet navigators although she looked forward to a long-term career in the RAF beyond Tornado's projected end of service date in 2020–25.

As a Tornado with special livery marking the millionth hour and carrying the insignia of all the squadrons who had flown it took off from RAF Lossiemouth on a commemorative flight, there were many Dambusters in Kandahar whose thoughts began to turn towards home. In just over two weeks 31 Squadron's advance party would arrive at KAF to begin the handover and the first of 617's aircrew would leave theatre.

The Squadron would have a night's stop-over in Cyprus for what was called decompression training. Decompression was mandatory. This was the chance to relax with a swim in the Med and time on the beach and a cabaret evening with a few beers to help those returning from Afghanistan to get their heads around coming home. Some of 617 just wanted to get straight home but most realised that the Cyprus stop-over was also the chance to begin putting their time in Kandahar into some kind of perspective before they flew on back to normality.

Some members of the Squadron were already mentally on the plane out. Large green metal packing cases in which the engineering managers packed their books and equipment began to appear. This was not what SEngO Stuart Clarke wanted to see. He vented his anger on his JEngOs and flight sergeants.

'If I see one of those in any office, even in the last week before we are due to leave, I'm going to throw it out of the door,' he told them. 'The lads don't have them but if they think we are packing they are going to realise it is the end; which it isn't. Just like them you need to keep the concentration going right until the last day of the detachment.'

The packing cases disappeared.

On 28 June Keith Taylor wrote to the Squadron's families via the Airspace message board about 617's homecoming and also its future plans. The aircrew advance party would be back on 9 July, followed by the engineering advance party four days later and the bulk of the squadron on Tuesday 19 July. The aircraft bringing them home would fly directly from Cyprus to RAF Lossiemouth.

Then he turned to the future. It was time to talk to them about Libya.

'You will have hopefully already heard from your partner/loved one that 617 Squadron is due to pick up responsibility for the Libya campaign, known by the UK as Operation Ellamy, as of 1 January 2012. Our tour of duty is planned to be four and a half months and we will be operating the Tornados from Gioia del Colle in Italy.'

For the families of the engineers, eighteen weeks away had to be balanced by the fact that they were going to be in Italy, out of harm's way. Keith Taylor then slipped in the bad news.

'The plan as it stands is for the Squadron to return to Afghanistan in November 2012 for a four-month tour of duty – which I'm sure you can work out, will include Christmas. We are all looking forward to coming home and being reunited with you.'

However, the Boss was hedging his bets. 'If I hear any news that changes these dates,' he added, 'then please be reassured I will let you know as soon as possible. The older hands among you know that this means that I will be writing to you again!'

26

ALL CHANGE

On 7 July the Dambusters got the two newly-serviced jets they had been promised at the start of their detachment, flown out by crews from 12 and 15 Squadron. While the engineers changed another engine – it was now 13 in 13 weeks – on the aircrew side the endless rotation of Tornado squadrons was beginning once more. On 9 July the first 617 aircrew party landed back in Lossiemouth. The advance aircrew from 31 Squadron had arrived at KAF and were now flying missions with the remaining Dambuster crews to acquaint themselves with the airspace.

One of those who introduced 31's pilots to the idiosyncrasies, vagaries and challenges of Afghan airspace was Lucy Williams.

'It's strange seeing them go through those fears of the unknown because it has made me remember how I felt on my first flight.'

She smiled at those first tentative steps of three months before – the nervousness that she and Joe had felt as they climbed up and were strapped into the jet, the mission data loaded, the bullets in her pocket – replaced now by a honed situational awareness and an intimate knowledge of the airspace.

'Before we flew with 31, we chatted about what we had found difficult or been worried about and tried to get rid of that for them, but you can't get rid of it completely, they have to experience it for themselves. To really understand the airspace you have to fly in it.'

As she neared the end of her deployment, flicking between radio frequencies and knowing who to talk to and when was now second nature to Lucy and all the junior navigators.

'You must make sure that you are robust in your briefing and procedures,' she advised the new arrivals, 'and because the radios on a GR4 are not great out here you always have to have a back-up on where to meet up if you get lost.'

She had one warning for the new arrivals.

'The moment you are airborne and think you have everything covered is the moment you are going to make a mistake. Every sortie is the same, but different.'

That was the way the flying game worked.

The advance party of engineers – replaced in Kandahar by those from the Goldstars – may have been on its way home but right to the end of 617 Squadron's deployment there was no let-up for the remaining aircrew or engineers. In some ways the final days seemed even busier than the first, with everybody focused on achieving the best handover possible to 31 Squadron; no ifs, no buts and hopefully no more engine changes.

Tony Griffiths could see people beginning to wind down and their thoughts stray. Focused to the end, the Warlord reminded the aircrew:

'It is important to run through the finishing line not wind down before you get there.'

There was still work to do.

'The guy on the ground doesn't care if it is your first day in theatre or your last. He wants you there doing the job and not making mistakes. The standard must be maintained continuously.'

*

Stew Campbell's last two weeks were typical of the cat and mouse that insurgents were still playing with ISAF forces, with aircraft 'being pulled all over the place as the demands changed'. Campbell had done three shows of force at night, more than anybody else – 'scary and much nicer when you can see the ground, but a huge adrenaline buzz' – and had been called to many a TIC only to find it downgraded. If there was one acronym that summed up his last two weeks and the entire deployment it was PID: positive identification.

On 30 June Campbell had taken off from KAF to stand in for an American sortie north of Bagram. Once airborne he – and Keith Taylor in the other Tornado – was yanked over to Gereshk district (aka Nahr-e Saraj), Helmand, 75 miles north west of Kandahar where 3 Commando Brigade troops were being fired at from a compound. The marines were mortaring the compound and the JTAC already had the 9-Line complete for a strafe and a Brimstone. He asked the Tornados if they could pinpoint them in the compound so they could better direct their fire. Campbell and his navigator could see muzzle flashes but they were intermittent and not always in the same place. Beyond fleeting shadows on a roof there were no clear signs of people. An observation balloon close to the compound could not spot them either. The compound was surrounded by trees. Somehow the insurgents managed to escape and had now slipped into a tree line. They vanished before they could be positively identified by ground or air.

The next day Campbell was 30 miles west of KAF, called in by the Canadian ISAF troops to investigate a man with a shovel standing by the edge of a road, who was talking to three motorbike riders – who were racing up and down looking for soldiers, and reporting back to him. They were obviously dickers. But they were unable to positively identify him as an IED emplacer. For more than two hours Campbell and Al Spence in the other jet yo-yo fuelled from the tanker as suspicious activity increased on the ground. There was now a posse of eight motorbikes. It looked like something big was about to happen. A predator had now joined the over-watch. But the 9-Line remained incomplete; Campbell's bomb was not delivered.

'PID is crucial,' he said. 'Unless you are 100 per cent you cannot strike; the guy might have been about to dig a hole and take a crap. And then some civilians came by and that was us RTB.'

The 617 Dam outside 904 EAW was now finished. Mitch Mitchell was proud of his work but happy not to be seeing a jigsaw for some time. After much discussion with the engineers and Stu Clarke, Keith Taylor had decided that while the waves of the deluge should be painted in shades of grey the hand-crafted legend, 'DAMBUSTERS 617 SQN', and the lightning bolts should be painted in gold. He felt that something less dramatic was more in keeping with the front of the building than the traditional red and black squadron insignia that the engineers had painted on the flight line blast wall. It was here that the Boss and his aircrew posed for an end-of-tour picture in two rows of smiles radiating out of tired faces.

The engineers were keen to get home because they had been living in a bubble for three months from which there had been no escape. Living, working and sleeping just feet apart, it was no surprise that some relationships had become strained. Messrs Clarke, Thomson and Sharp had their eyes and ears tuned to nip any tension in the bud.

'There are some very short fuses around here now,' Ross Bowman said. 'People's habits can begin to get you down a bit.'

Ziggy Zweig was looking forward to being back in her own place in Elgin and 'getting my personal life and private life back. It sounds a cliché and blonde but it is very hard to be a girl out here. You don't want to play the girl; it doesn't go down well. You've got guys who miss their wives and their girlfriends and you just want to blend in and be one of the guys and not expect anything special. But sometimes I feel it would be nice to throw on a pretty dress and be thoroughly girly'.

She looked forward to the days when she was duty driver. Getting away from the Squadron to run errands or be a taxi was the chance to burst the bubble and get some head space.

The Dambusters might have been on the verge of going home but the Taliban were still active. The assassination of high-profile politicians and security commanders continued. On 11 July Ahmad Wali Karzai, half-brother of President Hamid Karzai, was shot dead at his home in Kandahar City, having survived several other assassination attempts. As head of the Kandahar Provincial Council and a staunch US and ISAF ally he had kept the lid on things in Kandahar.

The Taliban claimed his killing as one of its greatest achievements in ten years.

15 July was the very last day of 617's deployment and Squadron Leader Tony Griffiths kitted up for his final flight as a Dambuster. The Warlord was a tired man. He had huge shadows under his eyes, his skin was parchment pale and he was going to leave Afghanistan with less hair than he had arrived with. But he still walked purposefully to his jet to fly a sortie up to Kajaki Dam, one of two major hydroelectric dams in northern Helmand. Keith Taylor was piloting the other jet with Jon Overton in the back seat.

Nestled in the mountains on the Helmand River, Kajaki's two turbines supply power to several hundred thousand people, primarily in Helmand. Kajaki was a name already etched into British military history. In 2008 an epic British-led operation, known as 'Eagles Summit', after the bird of prey featured in 16 Air Assault Brigade's insignia, had transported a third turbine weighing 220 tonnes on 100 vehicles 115 miles from Kandahar across the desert, bypassing Sangin, and then up to Kajaki. They had fought a famous battle at Kajaki Sofla, a village just south of the dam, which claimed hundreds of lives.

Near Kajaki Griff contacted a JTAC in a valley who immediately asked for a show of force as they withdrew with 3 Commando Brigade from an operation to flush out insurgents who were attacking the convoys. Griff was at 14,000 feet and between him and the marines was a dust-storm. The visibility was down to just over a mile, which was as good as nothing to a jet travelling at around nine miles a minute. It was the worst weather Griffiths had encountered during the whole deployment, like flying into a brick wall. They would have to use terrain following radar (TFR), normally used at night, whereby the aircraft flew itself, to get down low and then hope the visibility would improve enough to do the show of force manually. Griffiths had flown sorties on TFR before in low-level training in the Scottish valleys and in the simulator, but nothing as challenging as this.

A thousand feet above, Keith Taylor and Jon Overton were having atrocious communications problems. The radios crackled and spat and kept cutting out. Whichever frequency Overton tried he could not make contact with the troops on the ground. They flew some route-watches looking for enemy forces but the visibility was so poor it was hopeless.

Griffiths had cleared his airspace. His pilot looped the

aircraft around, put the jet in TFR mode and they were on their way down. They may as well have been in a tunnel or sprinting downstairs in the dark so dense was the dust as they descended. It was like those falling nightmares; the kind of dream where they say that if you hit the bottom you are dead.

When they hit 200 feet they shot out from the dust clouds and suddenly all was clear. Back in manual in blue sky, they rolled out a show of force that would have made statues turn and run.

'Exciting, or what?' Griff called out to his pilot.

Keith Taylor was refuelling when his jet was called to a TIC elsewhere in Helmand, where British soldiers were under fire. Some American A-10s were already overhead and were dropping bombs but they had to go to the tanker. Taylor's Tornado was to replace them, take up over-watch, and be ready to strike again if necessary. Again his radio stopped working in various frequency spectrums. It didn't work in FM either. Overton could not establish contact with the ground. It could have been the atmospheric conditions or faulty aerials or kit on the jet. Whatever the reason, the Boss was becoming increasingly frustrated. This was not how he wanted his last trip to be.

Tony Griffiths' jet arrived from the tanker and flew into the same stack of aircraft now overhead. Above him he had a pair of American F-18s. Unlike Keith Taylor the Warlord was able to talk to the troops on the ground, who were now driving insurgents away from friendly compounds down drainage ditches and along hedgerows. Griffiths followed the retreating insurgents on his pod, reporting their position and numbers to the JTAC, and was ready to warn of ambushes or intervene kinetically. However, this time the enemy had had enough. They had fired their rounds and were now scooting away as fast as they could from a better-armed, better-organised adversary.

When the two Tornados approached the Kandahar runway the weather had worsened once more. The visibility was appalling as they neared the ground and they had to come in to land using the instrument landing system and on a straight-in approach. They did not see the runway lights until they were just 200 feet above the ground.

Keith Taylor had found his final sortie frustrating. There was nothing more aggravating than being able to hear stuff going on down on the ground but not being able to talk to anybody.

Griff could sense the Boss was not in the best of moods. He, however, had enjoyed a fantastic final sortie. It had been exhausting. It had been the busiest of his deployment. He had used every bit of navigational kit in the aircraft.

Job done. Now he felt ready to go home.

During its deployment to Kandahar, 617 Squadron had flown 452 air tasking order sorties and ten GCAS sorties and had clocked up over 1400 flying hours. To put that in context, a whole year's flying out of Lossiemouth would only amount to 2400 hours. During their three-month deployment the Dambusters flew in a week the same hours they would normally fly in a month back home and only missed two sorties in spite of engine changes, problems on the environmental control systems, a host of other snags big and small, and scheduled major servicing to aircraft. It was a remarkable result for the aircrew and the engineers. Thirty-three rockets had been fired into Kandahar Airfield during the deployment, without inflicting a single casualty.

'The engineers have achieved 99.6 per cent success rate in launching aeroplanes,' Squadron Leader Clarke said. 'I couldn't ask for any more. My guys have just kept on delivering.'

As did the aircrew.

'I am seriously proud of them and what they did and the high level they worked at,' Squadron Leader Griffiths said. 'We had some wobbles at the start, and then a growing confidence, and then full-on focus to the end. I may not always have been everybody's favourite person but if you have never been on ops before you have to do a lot of serious growing up really quickly. There's a lot of grown-up people going to be boarding that plane home.'

Group Captain David Bentley, Officer Commanding 904 Expeditionary Air Wing at Kandahar, was sad to see the Dambusters go. He chose his words diplomatically. His new 'lodgers' from 31 Squadron were already arriving and it would not be prudent for him to be favouring one squadron over another.

'The Tornado is extremely valued here in theatre for the kinetic and non-kinetic options it offers and all the squadrons have superbly trained crews and engineers, but,' he added, '617 have been the most gregarious, outgoing squadron through here and have all gone about their business with a real zip.' He paused and then did single out somebody who had left a lasting impression. 'Stu Clarke is immensely professional but he has that very ready quick wit which lifts any room, and diffuses tension,' Bentley said. Throughout the detachment the SEngO had been the bridge between 617 and 904, especially over issues like spares and engine replacement. 'It is characters like that who will make a squadron,' Bentley added. 'It is often the senior NCOs who really mould a squadron.'

After his final sortie Keith Taylor posed over a cockpit shaking hands with Wing Commander Jim Mulholland, Officer Commanding 31 Squadron, and passed over the Kandahar Tornado detachment to him. Now, as the aircraft's wheels left Afghan soil for Cyprus and the decompression stop-over, Taylor could at last begin to relax, probably for the first time since he had taken command of the Dambusters.

'As a squadron boss what you want to do more than anything else is to take your squadron on ops; but I am mightily relieved that everybody is going home safe, that nobody has dropped weapons when they shouldn't have or on to the wrong targets. It is a nice feeling when you know you have been there and done the business and performed very well.'

To the roll of honour that included Normandy, Tirpitz, the Dams and the Gulf Wars this generation of Dambusters could now add Afghanistan.

27

HOME AND AWAY

RAF Lossiemouth, 19 July 2011

The 617 Squadron feeder (canteen) was bursting with wives and children. A raffle in aid of Operation Halfway was in full swing. The station commander, Group Captain Andrew Hine, had come to draw the winning numbers for the five top prizes. In just seven weeks since Emma Sharp and her friends had launched Halfway the wives, husbands, partners and children had run, swum, cycled and baked cakes to raise £2,384, slightly more than their partners had managed in the gym at Kandahar. The bulk would go to RAFA but they would also make a contribution towards a new memorial at Woodhall Spa to honour those Dambusters who had died since the Second World War.

There was another piece of good news. The previous day the Ministry of Defence had announced that RAF Lossiemouth would remain as a major base for the Tornado. RAF Leuchars in Fife, which provided crews and aircraft at high states of readiness twenty-four hours a day, 365 days a year, to police UK airspace and to intercept unidentified aircraft, would cease to be an RAF base.

Emma Sharp made a short speech thanking everybody for

their fundraising efforts but like everybody else her mind was on the imminent arrival of a plane from Cyprus. These final minutes passed agonisingly slowly until Group Captain Hine received a message that the Squadron had just touched down. He went to the aircraft to greet them. Everybody else rushed out of the feeder to stand behind the barriers that had been placed to stop children running on to the airfield. Lizee Taylor, Hannah and Lucy were frustrated they could not see the aircraft from the feeder. In earlier days when Keith returned from operations the homecomings were much less formal and more spontaneous. Health and safety rules meant that they would have to wait until the Squadron was brought over to them on buses.

It seemed to take an age, but eventually the first bus came around a HAS and into view. The door opened and the first to step down and walk towards them was a familiar figure: Lizee's husband, the girls' father, the Boss. More buses arrived, the barriers were removed and at last the families were allowed to rush forward. It was like two waves meeting. Andy Mitchell stooped down to pick up his two-year-old daughter and hug his four-year-old son. Rob Perry sniffed the air and said it was great to experience some Scottish summer weather and 'to feel cold again'. At first Emma Sharp could not pick out Al. Caitlin spotted him first and ran towards him. Emma and Calum followed.

'It was just very, very emotional,' Emma said. 'So pleased he's back; just so pleased.'

Group Captain Hine took a few minutes to congratulate the Squadron and address the families. Keith Taylor made a speech but he kept it short. Just like everybody else Boss Lightyear wanted to get away and get home to his family.

*

After two weeks of post-deployment leave 617 returned to work, but already things had changed. A squadron is never a fixed unit. With an aircrew squadron tour being just two to three years the line-up was continually changing. Seven were moving on to new jobs. A few had already gone. When Keith Taylor, relaxed from a family camper-van holiday in Scotland, walked into his first shareholders meeting there was a raft of faces he barely recognised. The new recruits were a mixture of pilots and navigators 617 had inherited from the recently disbanded 14 Squadron and newly qualified aircrew from the OCU.

From now on the focus was on 617's next deployment to Libya in January and then a return to Afghanistan in November 2012, but first they were straight into a hectic programme of low-level flying, two versus one combat and ramping up all those skills that had not been needed in Afghanistan. The first trip back for all was a pilot–pilot check where a senior instructor on the station sat in the back seat to assess how well the front-seater could fly the jet, setting lots of different approaches. Then it was straight to the simulator for emergency handling scenarios.

Packing up his house in readiness to move to his desk job at Abbeywood in Bristol, Tony Griffiths was already missing Lossiemouth.

'Suddenly it's sinking in,' he said, as he updated his last logbook. 'A big chapter has closed in the book. Angela and I got married up here, we bought our first house, had four kids. Professionally I went from the OCU, to my first tour, to then become an instructor on the OCU, then a QWI, then a display season before I joined 617 and became a flight commander. Career-wise and personally, we've done a lot, achieved a lot and made loads of good friends.'

The shadows under his eyes had eventually gone, like the last guests leaving a party. He had colour in his skin and his hair was growing, making him look less severe and the most relaxed he had been in the best part of a year. Being the Warlord had been 'massively rewarding' he said.

'The Squadron has matured and moved on.'

Keith Taylor had no doubts that one day Griff would command a squadron of his own. 'He's proved he has what it takes.' But after eight operational tours Griff now had to do a ground tour before he could realise that ambition.

'I realise I can't be on ops all my life but I know that every time a squadron deploys there will be part of me that wishes I was there with them.'

There were also new faces among the engineers, forty of whom had come from 14, taking their number past 150. There was an enlarged 617 Tornado fleet at Lossiemouth to keep airborne. There were also some imminent engineering departures.

Warrant Officer Thomson tidied up his office for the umpteenth time, knowing that his future was no longer here, knowing that in a couple of weeks the portrait of Guy Gibson, 'Hero', would be staring down at his replacement, the current Warrant Officer of 31 Squadron, who would be sitting in his seat, in his office.

'I have really mixed feelings,' Thomson said. 'I know it is time to move on and let somebody else have a go at this job. Will I miss it massively? Yes! Am I institutionalised? God, hell yes! Of course I am. I came into the Air Force as a stupid 19-year-old full of piss and vinegar with all these ideas of how I was going to change the RAF, and guess what? I was absolutely wrong.'

In Thomson's time the RAF had shrunk from 90,000 to 40,000.

'I've done what every single engineer wants to become when they join up, a squadron warrant officer. Not only that, I believe I am on the best Tornado squadron in the Royal Air Force.'

He said his abiding memory of Kandahar was 'the guys. They were so switched on. We had a little bit of a crump in the middle but everybody was focused. I can walk away with immense pride in what they have done. And then I come back home and see 18- and 19-year-old lads kicking the crap out of people, looting buildings, hanging round on street corners. Compare that to guys of a similar age on this squadron, so focused and exceeding what I expected. They just got hold of it'.

A stranger to self-doubt, Warrant Officer Thomson looked at the future and said, 'To be perfectly honest, I am absolutely bricking it. I have no idea what I am going to do next because this has been my life for so long. I might even miss spending sixteen hours a day with Stu Clarke!'

There was something else that cemented 617 even more firmly in Stew Thomson's DNA; a strange twist of fate that went back far beyond his thirty-six years in the RAF. A clue lay in a painting that hung in Keith Taylor's office at RAF Lossiemouth. It showed Lancasters bombing the German city of Dortmund. Living in the city then was Stew Thomson's mother.

'She'd have been six or seven years old then,' the Warrant said. 'In 1942 she had been evacuated to a hostel run by nuns in a nice safe area.'

That nice safe area was 27 miles to the east of the city on the banks of the River Ruhr. Right by the Möhne Dam.

'Mum was there when it got bombed. She's seventy-six now but she can still vividly remember all the bodies floating by.'

Luckily for Mrs Thomson she had made it to higher ground

and survived. She came to Scotland when she was 18.

'She met my dad, who was a National Service corporal in the Black Watch, part of the international forces of occupation in West Germany.'

In 2010 Stew Thomson had brought his mother to RAF Lossiemouth and showed her the painting of the Dortmund raid in Keith Taylor's office and the other of Gibson flying over the Möhne Dam. She recognised them immediately.

'That's where they tried to bomb me,' she said. 'Twice.'

When Stew had joined 617 he felt strange at first seeing so many pictures of the Dams being bombed and knowing that his mother was right there.

'She certainly doesn't bear any grudges,' he said. 'She now thinks of herself as Scottish and British through and through and she was proud as punch when I joined 617 and then when I got my Gallopers (Warrant Officer rank badge).'

Stew Thomson's father, who died twenty years ago, had always hoped his son would outrank him by making sergeant. He had surpassed that.

At noon on 10 August 2011 a solo piper was playing outside the front doors of the Officers' Mess at RAF Lossiemouth, as the families of 617 Squadron arrived dressed in their best for the medals ceremony. A pair of Tornados flew overhead side by side and then peeled off in a graceful 'V'. Inside the large Mess dining room Squadron Leader Clarke was putting all his management skills to use to guide the families and their over-excited children into their seats. The Squadron waited outside, many of them unrecognisable in their highly polished shoes, ties and pressed best uniforms. When everybody was seated Clarke explained how the programme would unfold over the next two hours.

'This is a formal occasion,' he said, 'but it is first and last a family day. If the children want to call out to their parents, sisters or brothers, that is fine, so long as it's not rude, and please take all the pictures that you want. After the medals have been handed out we hope you will all join us for lunch in the bar.'

He then nodded to Warrant Officer Thomson, who opened the doors and the Dambusters marched in crisply and took up their positions in four long lines, arranged by rank and alphabetical order facing the audience, just as they had been practising all morning. Children did call out, flashes popped, grins broke out on faces on both sides of the room and there was the inevitable cry of 'Can't see dad!' followed by laughter and relief.

Wing Commander Taylor entered the room with the guest speaker who would present the Dambusters with their Operation Herrick 14 medals. He might have been slightly stooped compared to the young wing commander who had lodged at Keith Taylor's parents' house, but there was no doubting the bearing of Air Chief Marshal John Allison. After his distinguished RAF career, retiring as Commander-in-Chief RAF Strike Command, Sir John Allison was now Gentleman Usher to the Sword of State. A member of the Royal Household, it was his job to carry the sword of state before the Queen on ceremonial occasions.

'Back in 1991 he had asked my station commander at RAF Valley if he could come and present my wings, when he was AOC of 11 Group,' Keith Taylor said. 'In 2011 it means a lot to me that he has agreed to come to Lossiemouth to present the medals to my Squadron.'

As John Allison walked down the line presenting medals and shaking hands one of the masters of ceremony reading out the names was Rob Perry – 'volunteered' by Stuart Clarke as part of his 'Putting Perry on the Map' campaign. The JEngO had taken on the task with more than a degree of trepidation.

After the medals there were some special commendations awarded by Group Captain Dave Bentley, OC of 904 Expeditionary Air Wing in Kandahar, recognising the incredible achievement of the engineers who had ensured that the Squadron had lost only two sorties during its deployment. Perry read the citations as though he had been doing awards ceremonies for years.

He called out the final name: 'Warrant Officer Stewart Charles Christian Thomson.' Last, but rarely least, Mr T marched slowly down the entire length of the room to collect his Royal Warrant from Air Chief Marshal Allison. Many of the younger members of the squadron, who had only seen what Perry described with elegant restraint in the citation as 'a prickly and hardened persona', might have been surprised when they heard that Thomson had been player and then club president of the RAF Lossiemouth volleyball team. Or that he had organised the fête and built an adventure playground at his wife Irene's primary school. Or that he had devoted much of his spare time in his early career studying for an Open University degree in Engineering Science. Irene Thomson and their youngest son Kris, also a teacher, were there to applaud him every step of the way.

There was one Dambuster who did not get a medal pinned on his uniform that day, but he was much in demand. Looking as though he had just stepped out of a Clarke Gable movie, Lieutenant Josh Thompson stood with the families and friends, resplendent in his US Navy Dress White uniform of high-collared tunic with gold buttons and shoulder braid and gleaming white boots. As the ceremony came to an end several of the wives and mothers asked if they could have their pictures taken standing next to the dashing lieutenant.

'Why of course, ma'am,' he smiled. 'It would be my pleasure.'

Ceremony over, the beer flowed in the bar and the Dambusters and their partners and children spilled out into the garden clutching plates of food. Wing Commander Taylor, who joined his parents and family, could relax at last. The ceremony had gone well. He had kept his speech typically short. His squadron had come of age and their achievements had been recognised in front of their families.

Even though corporals queued for food with wing commanders there was still something slightly formal about the informality. The RAF has a traditional messing system based on rank. So among the sergeants and the junior ranks there was an air of being on best behaviour in a place where young male and female officers traditionally misbehaved but were expected to pay for any breakages by cheque the next morning.

For the first time in the last six months Squadron Leader Ian Sharrocks – who now had his surname rather than his nickname sewn to his flying suit to reflect his elevated position as 2iC – was being seriously wrong-footed; not by aircrew but by his sons Harry, aged four, and Bertie, two. They were doing what all small children like to do at adult parties: run full pelt in and out of people's legs. Their father was doing a pretty poor job of restraining them. It was their mother Jennie, who had once worked in publishing, who did the trick. She had had more practice. Ringleader Harry had been christened Harry Max Spencer Sharrocks, abbreviated to HMS Sharrocks.

'Harking back to my naval days,' Rocksy grinned. 'I managed to slip that one past my wife, but I still get some grief for it.'

*

As responsibility for the city of Lashkar Gah was handed over to the Afghan National Army and the Afghan Police on 20 July, all 617's thoughts turned to Operation Ellamy. NATO aircraft had so far flown thousands of sorties taking out tanks and military infrastructure and the Libyan rebels were winning the initiative against Gaddafi's forces, who were beginning to desert to the other side in increasing numbers. Even so, territory hard won was still being retaken by government forces.

In early September Group Captain 'Rocky' Rochelle called 617 reinforcements to Marham. Six air crews were trained ready for flying Libyan air space and a party of twenty engineers were put on standby to go to NATO's air base at Gioia del Colle, just above the heel of Italy.

The first Dambusters to fly out of Norfolk on 14 September were Rocksy Sharrocks and Conan Mullineux in a mixed-squadron four-ship formation of Tornados armed with Storm Shadow missiles. Even though 617 was the lead squadron for Storm Shadow it would be the first time that Rocksy had fired the bunker buster. Four hours and two air-to-air refuelling stops later they were heading into Libya. Mission accomplished, Rocksy and Conan then flew back to Gioia del Colle in Italy to overnight. It had been a five-and-a-half-hour sortie for three intense and intensely satisfying minutes.

The rest of 617's standby aircrew then moved to Marham. Like Rocksy they would fly out of Norfolk for Libya. The party included Keith Taylor, Ollie Moncrieff, Timmy Colebrooke and Gary Montgomery. Monty was the most excited at the prospect.

They spent the day planning the mission, but the evening before they were due to fly it they were all together when Keith Taylor took a call. His face dropped.

'That was Rocky,' he said. 'The sortie has been scrapped.'

Rocksy looked at Gary Montgomery. To say that Monty looked disappointed would have taken understatement into the surreal. The destination that night was the bar of the Officers' Mess.

The Dambusters returned to Lossiemouth. The conflict had entered a final phase. The rebels were advancing on Tripoli. Gaddafi had not been seen but was still issuing defiant messages via radio stations. Were Gary Montgomery's words uttered back in Kandahar, that Gaddafi would fall before 617 deployed, returning to haunt him?

On Thursday 6 October Keith Taylor pulled up outside a new £3.5 million honey stone building at the Cotswold Conference Centre just outside the Worcestershire village of Broadway. He was one of the guests of honour at the opening of Maudslay Court, a new 32-bedroom wing built by local craftsmen in Cotswold stone. A brass band played the *Dam Busters* theme and the RAF March Past. Taylor had been invited to unveil a plaque outside one special deluxe room. Close to a hundred people gathered as he declared 'Room 617' open. The walls inside were covered in prints telling the story of the Dambusters, including a picture of Lancaster bomber AJ-Z 'Zebra' in action on the Dams Raids. This was the bomber of Squadron Leader Henry Maudslay DFC, a pilot who had been shot down and killed with his crew on his way back from the attack on the Eder Dam. He was twenty-one. During the Second World War the Maudslay family had lived on the Farncombe Estate where the Cotswold Conference Centre now stood.

Keith Taylor told them the story of 617 after the raids, from D-Day decoy missions to fool the Germans about where the invasion of France would begin, to service in Malaya, the Cold War, the Gulf War and now Afghanistan. He talked about the aircraft they had flown – Lancasters, Lincolns, Canberras, Vulcans and now Tornados – and weapons they had carried from Upkeep, Tallboy and Blue Steel to the laser-guided bombs and cruise missiles of today.

'I was lucky enough to command this Squadron on its first deployment to Afghanistan,' he said.

But winning wars was no longer just about winning battles. In Afghanistan fire-power was no longer the crucial factor in protecting troops on the ground. Intelligence, knowledge and analysis were what saved lives and much of that now came from the air.

'A mark of the way things have improved in Helmand is that in our three-month detachment we were not called upon to drop any munitions,' he said. 'Also a first for 617!'

When Colonel Gaddafi was captured and killed on 24 October it was only a matter of time before Operation Ellamy ceased, so 617's January deployment was duly cancelled. The Dambusters would now return to Afghanistan in March 2012.

A few weeks after that, on Remembrance Sunday 2011, Keith Taylor laid another wreath at the Dambusters memorial at Woodhall Spa. With him were Gary Montgomery and Jane Pickersgill, who had met the dwindling band of Second World War 617 veterans and more recent Dambusters at the annual Tirpitz Dinner at the Petwood Hotel the previous evening. Keith Taylor knew that his Dambusters were no longer untried and untested as they had been a year earlier.

By the middle of November, as the Remembrance wreaths were beginning to wilt and the colour seeped from the paper poppies, the runway at RAF Lossiemouth was alive with Tornados pumping out flame. Overhead the distinctive swing-wing bombers ripped up and crackled the chilling air over the

Moray Firth as 617 Squadron began its work-up for a return to Operation Herrick and the heat and dust of Kandahar Airfield in March 2012. British troops were already beginning to hand over control of Nad-e Ali in Helmand to the Afghan National Army and the Afghan police, but air power would be crucial in making the transition stick.

Ellamy disappointments aside, it was good to be back at work.

Wing Commander Taylor had also just delivered some very good news to one of his pilots. Lieutenant Josh Thompson would be able to go on operations with the Dambusters.

EPILOGUE

MOVING ON

Nothing stays the same for long on a fast jet squadron. In November 2011 Flight Lieutenant Lucy Williams was back at Kandahar Airfield now flying as a navigator with 12 Squadron. Squadron Leader Chris Ball is the FJ JO Pilot Poster at RAF High Wycombe looking after all the RAF's junior officer fast jet pilots. Squadron Leader Tony Griffiths has a senior post at Abbeywood at Filton near Bristol – home to the Defence Equipment and Support (DE&S) agency – working in the Military Aviation Authority which tests and approves all new and modified equipment fitted to fast jets. His wife Angela won her campaign to get their children into a single school of their choice. Flight Lieutenant Alex Hutchison is now an instructor at the Operational Conversion Unit, 15(R) Squadron, RAF Lossiemouth. Flying Officer Alasdair Spence had been promoted to flight lieutenant and remains with 617 Squadron. Flight Lieutenant Rob Perry is working for Air Vice-Marshal Julian Young, RAF Chief Engineer, at Air Command, High Wycombe. Corporal Andrew Mitchell was promoted to sergeant and has moved to RAF Marham. Sergeant Al Sharp is now Acting Chief Technician and still with 617 Squadron. Corporal (Big) Stuart Young was promoted to sergeant and moved to 15(R) Squadron in January 2012; however, 617 managed to arrange for him to remain on the Squadron for its subsequent return to Afghanistan.

The marriage of flight lieutenants Jon Overton and Caroline Day in Nairn in August 2011 was marked with a fly-past from Keith Taylor on his way home from a training sortie. To Jon Overton's great relief Timmy Colebrooke was prevented from burning a piano. A few weeks later Poppy Cormack-Loyd and Flight Lieutenant Richard Leask were married in Oxford. Poppy's husband had now joined 12 Squadron and deployed within months to Kandahar. Conan Mullineux and Joe Hourston also married their respective girlfriends. Joe now has a young son and is an instructor on the Hawk T2 at RAF Valley in Anglesey. Thanks to Al Sharp's tutelage, Stew Campbell played the pipes at Joe's wedding to the satisfaction of all. In 2012 Lucy Williams married Flight Lieutenant Steve Westley.

When the Dambusters touched down once again in Afghanistan in March 2012, Squadron Leader Rocksy Sharrocks stepped off the Hercules at Kandahar to be told that he had so impressed a promotion board that he had been promoted to wing commander and would leave 617 in the autumn of 2012 to attend the Joint Services Command and Staff College (JSCSC) at Shrivenham in Wiltshire.

In May 2012, the sixty-ninth anniversary of the Dams Raids was celebrated by Dambusters past at Woodhall Spa, where Lizee Taylor gave the speech, and by 617 Squadron at Kandahar Airfield with her husband doing the honours. Both hoped that RAF deployment scheduling would allow Dambusters old and new to come together in May 2013 for the seventieth anniversary of Operation Chastise, the Dams Raids.

In October 2012 Wing Commander Keith Taylor bade

farewell to the Dambusters and left his office at RAF Lossiemouth for a new job at the Ministry of Defence in Whitehall, where he is SO1 Air Platform Protection within the Air Capability area of the Ministry.

BIBLIOGRAPHY

Arthur, Max, *Dambusters: A Landmark of Oral History*, Virgin, 2008.

Brickhill, Paul, *The Dambusters*, Evans Brothers, 1951.

Cooper, Alan W., *Beyond the Dams to the Tirpitz*, William Kimber, 1983.

Cowper-Coles, Sherard, *Cables from Kabul: The Inside Story of the West's Afghanistan campaign*, Harper, 2011.

Hopkirk, Peter, *The Great Game: The Struggle for Empire in Central Asia*, Kondasha Globe, 1994.

Hunter, Jamie, *Fighting Force: The 90th Anniversary of the Royal Air Force*, Touchstone, 2008.

Iveson, Tony and Milton, Brian, *Lancaster: The Biography*, André Deutsch, 2009.

Knowles, David, *Meeting the Jet Man*, Two Ravens, 2008.

Peters, John and Nichol, John, *Team Tornado: Life on a Front-Line Squadron*, Michael Joseph, 1994.

Ward, Chris, Lee, Andy and Watchel, Andreas, *Dambusters: The Definitive Story of 617 Squadron at War 1943–1945*, Red Kite, 2008.

Wilcox, Robert K., *Black Aces High: The Story of a Modern Fighter Squadron at War*, St Martin's, 2002.

ACKNOWLEDGEMENTS

A book like this could not happen without the support and dedication of all those who took part in the events described. First and foremost I am indebted to Group Captain Keith Taylor for his unflagging enthusiasm and insight – and patience – during my many visits to RAF Lossiemouth and while I was with 617 Squadron at Kandahar Airfield in June 2011. Not only did he open up his squadron to me, he did so having only recently taken command of it. That level of openness and confidence probably says all you need to know about the Dambuster spirit. During the writing of this book he has helped with checking accuracy and piloting the text through the scrutiny process with thoroughness and energy.

Those at all levels of the squadron were incredibly helpful and happy to have me witnessing and probing into their lives. It was a privilege and an honour to spend time with you. I would particularly like to thank Squadron Leaders Chris Ball, Tony Griffiths, Ian Sharrocks and Stuart Clarke, who both during and after my time with the Squadron helped explain the technical and the strategic and guided me through the bewildering maze of RAF acronyms, terminology and traditions. Without them this would have been so much more difficult and nowhere near as vivid a story. Thank you too Flight Lieutenant Lucy Williams and Junior Engineering Officer Flight Lieutenant Rob Perry for being early friendly faces.

The other important contributors to Squadron life are the wives, husbands and partners. Thanks to Emma Sharp and Lizee Taylor for their insight into what it is like to be left behind at home, waiting for news from a warzone.

Former Dambusters were just as helpful in placing 617 Squadron in historical context from the Second World War to Afghanistan via the Cold War, the Balkan conflict and Iraq. Thanks to Tony Iveson DFC, who flew with 617 on the *Tirpitz* raid and many others and who has been so instrumental in ensuring that RAF Bomber Command has a deserving monument in London's Green Park to its sacrifice and huge loss of life during the Second World War. Sadly, Tony Iveson died on 5 November 2013, aged 94.

Group Captain David Robertson, who was Officer Commanding 617 from 2000 to 2003, and recently retired Air Commodore Al Monkman DFC, CBE (OC 617 2003–2006) described their experiences with 617 vividly and candidly (not forgetting Al's wife Sandy, who made a delicious supper while we talked). I would also like to thank David, who as Chairman of the 617 Squadron Aircrew Association kindly invited me to attend its annual Dams Reunion Dinner at the Petwood Hotel in Woodhall Spa on 14 May 2011 and the Memorial Service at the Dambusters memorial the following day. It was a great privilege.

Former 617 Squadron Leader David Knowles DFC, and his navigator Wing Commander Andy Turk DFC, now OC of 9 Squadron at RAF Marham, shared their death-defying experience during the first Storm Shadow raid over Baghdad, which is described in these pages. I am also grateful to David, now a crofter and writer, for allowing me to quote from the introduction to his book *Meeting the Jet Man* and to reproduce some lines from one of his poems in that collection, 'Post Modern

Warfare'. Thank you too to two other ex-Dambusters, Wing Commander Jock Cochrane, for bringing to life the famous rivalry between 617 and 9 Squadron over whose bomb finally sank the *Tirpitz* – a tale within the tale – and Jo Salter, who in 1994 was the first woman to become an operational Tornado pilot; with 617 Squadron.

Of all the former Dambusters I pause to offer a very special debt of thanks to Air Commodore S.P. 'Rocky' Rochelle DFC, OBE (OC 617 2006–2008), until recently Station Commander at RAF Marham in Norfolk and who is now Head of Capability Deep Target Attack at the Ministry of Defence. Rocky first came up with the idea of a book about today's Dambusters and saw the end result before anybody else did. Not only did he describe his time with 617 and his career in candid detail over many interviews at Marham but throughout he has also opened doors and kept tabs on the project, always willing to lend support and give advice which has never been less than spot on and reassuring.

Although not of the Squadron, but very much part of it, is 617 Squadron's Official Historian, Robert Owen, who gave me invaluable insight into the Dambusters' early history and the spirit that characterises 617 to this day.

Elsewhere in the RAF I shall never forget the two hours I spent with Squadron Leader Phil Marr from 2 Squadron, RAF Marham, who took me in a Tornado GR4 to Wales (12 minutes) where we flew fast at 250 feet through the valleys to Aberystwyth ('Pull up! Pull up!') and then back to Norfolk and out over the Wash with the afterburners on. His handshake and greeting on landing, 'Welcome to the Tornado Force', was a slight exaggeration, but sitting in the navigator's seat and seeing the world zip by in a new dimension certainly informed the writing of this book. I would also like to thank the then

Officer Commanding 2 Squadron, Wing Commander, now Group Captain, John Turner for allowing it to happen. Also at RAF Marham Squadron Leader John Wilkinson gave me an introduction to the vital work done by the Tactical Imagery-Intelligence Wing (TIW).

Nothing happens without planning. Flying Officer Emma Wilkinson, assistant to Group Captain Rochelle at RAF Marham, and Sergeant Daz Whitta, Corporal Ruth Broadhurst and Linda Dixon in the 617 admin office at RAF Lossiemouth arranged meetings and juggled itineraries end-lessly. Easing me through the daunting paperwork and haz-ardous environment awareness training that took me to Afghanistan was Squadron Leader Michael Bracken (SO2 Media Ops) while Flight Lieutenant Joe Marlow smoothed my way into Kandahar. Many thanks too to Sergeant Ross Tilly and Flight Sergeant Paul Peden for taking the photographs that appear in this book.

I would like to thank all at Orion for publishing this book, but especially my publisher Alan Samson and editorial assis-tant Jillian Young for their constructive help, encouragement and seamless professionalism. Thanks also to Rowland White who brought the project to life very early on. My agent Mark Lucas was as ever invaluable with his guidance in making good things better and with an unshakeable belief that is typical of somebody who went to the same school as Guy Gibson! When he offered me the chance of a 'warm spring break' in Afghanistan I had no idea what a break it would prove to be.

Others who deserve mention here are Marian Stapley who painstakingly transcribed many hours of interviews, my son Milo who read early chapters and pronounced them to be good, and Paul Mansell for his encouragement and sound advice, based on first-hand experience, on all things to do with the Royal Marines.

Lastly I thank my wife, Sarah, for putting up with my frequent absences from home during a year of research and my monastic, and probably monosyllabic, existence while I was writing. As someone from a military family she understood. Her critical input on this as on all other works was invaluable. But most of all I thank her for her love. I could not have done it without you.

ACRONYMS AND ABBREVIATIONS

AIRCM Airborne Infrared Countermeasure
ANA Afghan National Army
ANP Afghan National Police
AO Area of Operation
ATO Air Tasking Order
BDA Boom Drogue Adaptor
CAS Close Air Support
CAOC Combined Air Operations Centre
CI Continuous Improvement
CIVCAS Civilian Casualties
COSOPS Chief of Staff Operations
DF Direction Finding
DFAC Dining Facility
EAG Expeditionary Air Group
ECS Environmental Control System
EKIA Enemy Killed in Action
FAC Forward Air Controller
FLIR Forward-looking Infrared
FOB Forward Operating Base
FOD Foreign Object Debris
GCAS Ground Close Air Support
GLO Ground Liaison Officer
GPWS Ground Proximity Warning System
GPS Global Positioning System

HAS   Hardened Aircraft Shelter
HUD   Head-Up Display
HVT   High Value Target
IDF   Indirect Fire
IED   Improvised Explosive Device
ISAF   International Security Assistance Force
ISTAR   Intelligence, Surveillance, Target Acquisition and Reconnaissance
JEngO   Junior Engineering Officer
JFACHQ   Joint Force Air Component Headquarters
JTAC   Joint Terminal Attack Controller
JTAR   Joint Tactical Air Strike Request
KAF   Kandahar Airfield
MISREP   Mission Report
NVG   Night Vision Goggles
OC   Officer Commanding
OCU   Operational Conversion Unit
OS   On Station
PBF   Pilot Briefing Facility
PID   Positive Identification
POI   Point of Interest
QWI   Qualified Weapons Instructor
RAPTOR   Reconnaissance Airborne Pod TORnado
RES   Rapid Erect Shelter
RIP   Relief in Place
ROE   Rules of Engagement
ROZ   Restricted Operating Zone
RPG   Rocket Propelled Grenade
RSOI   Reception, Staging and Onward Integration Programme
RTB   Return to Base
SAF   Small-Arms Fire

SDSR   Strategic Defence and Security Review

SEngO   Senior Engineering Officer

SINCREP   Significant Report

SOF   Show of Force

TACAN   Tactical Air Navigation

TIC   Troops in Contact

TIW   Tactical Imagery-Intelligence Wing

TFR   Terrain Following Radar

TST   Time Sensitive Target

TTP   Tactics, Techniques, Procedures

UAV   Unmanned Aerial Vehicle

U/S   Unserviceable

WSO   Weapons Systems Operator

PHOTO CREDITS

Photo Section One

'The Boss' © *Crown Copyright 2011/Sergeant Ross Tilly RAF*

After their daily 'Gentlemen's Breakfast' © *Crown Copyright 2011/Tim Bouquet*

A typical honeycomb of high-walled, impenetrable compounds © *Crown Copyright 2011/Flight Lieutenant Al Spence*

A Tornado swoops down © *Crown Copyright 2011/Flight Lieutenant Al Spence*

Flight Lieutenant Al Spence eases his Tornado's refuelling probe © *Crown Copyright 2011/Flight Lieutenant Al Spence*

No place like home © *Crown Copyright 2011/Tim Bouquet*

Tornado take-off from Kandahar © *Crown Copyright 2011/Flight Sergeant Paul Peden*

Flight Lieutenant Joe Hourston flaps behind the AIRCM © *Crown Copyright 2011/Flight Sergeant Paul Peden*

At the end of their detachment, the aircrew pose on the Kandahar flight line © *Crown Copyright 2011/Flight Sergeant Paul Peden*

Relaxed towards the end of the squadron's tour © *Crown Copyright 2011/Flight Sergeant Paul Peden*

Squadron Leader Tony Griffiths and Flight Lieutenant Ollie Moncrieff © *Crown Copyright 2011/Flight Sergeant Paul Peden*

Flight Lieutenant Alex Hutchison focuses in the final minutes before the taxi © *Crown Copyright 2011/Flight Sergeant Paul Peden*

Flight Lieutenant Joe Hourston has a *Top Gun* moment © *Crown Copyright 2011/Flight Sergeant Paul Peden*

Squadron Leader 'Kiwi' Spencer and Squadron Leader Griffiths © *Crown Copyright 2011/Flight Sergeant Paul Peden*

A Canadian Chinook over KAF © *Crown Copyright 2011/Flight Sergeant Paul Peden*

Flight Lieutenant Gary Montgomery and his navigator Flight Lieutenant Timmy Colebrooke © *Crown Copyright 2011/Flight Sergeant Paul Peden*

Flight Lieutenant Poppy Cormack-Loyd © *Crown Copyright 2011/Flight Sergeant Paul Peden*

First-day smiles for navigator Flight Lieutenant Poppy Cormack-Loyd and Flight Lieutenant Ollie Moncrieff © *Crown Copyright 2011/Flight Lieutenant Caroline Day*

In the navigator's back seat © *Crown Copyright 2011/Flight Sergeant Paul Peden*

Never one to shun a photograph, Squadron Leader Stuart Clarke © *Crown Copyright 2011/Flight Sergeant Paul Peden*

Distinctive Bell Boeing V-22 Ospreys © *Crown Copyright 2011/Flight Sergeant Paul Peden*

Flight Lieutenants Lucy Williams and Joe Hourston © *Crown Copyright 2011/Flight Sergeant Paul Peden*

Photo Section Two

Work goes on around the clock, with the engineers working in 12-hour shifts under RES © *Crown Copyright 2011/Flight Sergeant Paul Peden*

617's female navigators © *Crown Copyright 2011/Flight Sergeant Paul Peden*

A Tornado GR4 © *Crown Copyright 2011/Flight Sergeant Paul Peden* (above) and *Sergeant Ross Tilly RAF* (left)

A stickler for order and not a spanner out of place, Warrant Officer Stew Thomson © *Crown Copyright 2011/Flight Sergeant Paul Peden*

617 Squadron's one millionth flying hour © *Crown Copyright 2011/Sergeant Ross Tilly RAF*

An engineer grabs a moment on the Hesko-bastion anti-blast wall © *Crown Copyright 2011/Sergeant Ross Tilly RAF*

The engineers' rec room and welcome respite © *Crown Copyright 2011/Sergeant Ross Tilly RAF*

A pair of Tornados taxi out the runway at Kandahar © *Crown Copyright 2011/Sergeant Ross Tilly RAF*

Lighting the fires © *Crown Copyright 2011/Sergeant Ross Tilly RAF*

SAC Emma Zweig prepares a laser-guided Paveway IV bomb © *Crown Copyright 2011/Sergeant Ross Tilly RAF*

Squadron Leader Chris Ball and Squadron Leader Carl Wilson © *Crown Copyright 2011/Flight Sergeant Paul Peden*

Flight Lieutenant Rob Perry © *Crown Copyright 2011/Sergeant Ross Tilly RAF*

Squadron Leader Ian Sharrocks and Flight Lieutenant Caroline Day © *Crown Copyright 2011/Sergeant Ross Tilly RAF*

A Survival Equipment Fitter © *Crown Copyright 2011/Sergeant Ross Tilly RAF*

Squadron Leader Stuart Clarke © *Crown Copyright 2011/Sergeant Ross Tilly RAF*

Flight Lieutenant Timmy Colebrooke planning a sortie © *Crown Copyright 2011/Sergeant Ross Tilly RAF*

Flight Lieutenant Gary Montgomery shows the strain after a long sortie © *Crown Copyright 2011/Flight Sergeant Paul Peden*
A Tornado returns from a sortie at dawn © *Crown Copyright 2011/Flight Sergeant Paul Peden*